BEIRUT CITY CENTER RECOVERY: THE FOCH-ALLENBY AND ETOILE CONSERVATION AREA

BEIRUT CITY CENTER RECOVERY: THE FOCH-ALLENBY AND ETOILE CONSERVATION AREA

Robert Saliba

SOLIDERE

STEIDL

First published in 2003 in the English language by

STEIDL

ISBN: 3-88243-978-5

Distribution:
Steidl Publishers, Düstere Str. 4, D-37073 Göttingen
phone: +49-551-496060, fax: +49-551-4960649
mail@steidl.de, www.steidl.de

Editor-in-Chief
Nouhad Makdissi

**Photographic documentation, formatting
of plans and elevations**
Hala Hindi, Dina Katmarji, Marina Mattar

Photo archives
Sima Darwish, Dina Katmarji

Electronic photo archives
Dina Katmarji

**Electronic archives, urban and building
plans, permit files**
Khaled Azhari, Zouheir Berjawi, Fadi Jamali,
Souheir Mabsout, Mohamad Mooty

Drafting of chapter 6 plans
Yves Ghosn, Sami Hamawi

Restoration regulations and approval process
Farid Nehme

Research on Aftimus
Abdul Halim Kaissy

Archeology
Hans Curvers

Editors
Shirine Hamadeh, Helen Khal

Follow up, organization and execution
Dorothy Jabbour, Dina Katmarji,
Marina Mattar

Graphic Design, Branding
Nassar Design • Boston, Massachusetts USA
Nélida Nassar and Margarita Encomienda

Typeset in Rotis Sans Serif
The Rotis family was designed in 1989
by Otl Aicher for Agfa, his last type design.
The Rotis family is unique as it combines
esthetic and functional qualities that
makes it highly readable with the versatility
of digital technology.

Production
Bernard Fischer, Gerhard Steidl

Scans and color separations
Steidl's digital darkroom:
Judith Lange, Reiner Motz,
Inès Schumann

Printing
STEIDL, Göttingen, Germany

Binding
Lachenmaier, Reutlingen

Acknowledgements

This publication was made possible by the sponsoring of Solidere who opened their archives and dedicated important human resources to its realization for over three years. As head of publications at Solidere, Nouhad Makdissi helped initiating the book and expanding it from a strictly architectural study of the conservation area to its present coverage. She closely supervised, restructured and edited the successive drafts, and ensured the integrity of the contents. Shirine Hamadeh's detailed comments and perceptive assessment induced substantial improvements to the manuscript.

Together with her in-house team, particularly Dina Katmarji and Marina Mattar, Mrs. Makdissi administered the production of the book, including the architectural drawings, the maps, the illustrations and their copyright releases; coordinated with the graphic design team; and facilitated interviews with key persons both within and outside the company. Based on their experience in the recovery of the conservation area, Hala Hindi located and organized the information on individual buildings from Solidere's archives, and Mona Khechen helped restructure part of the initial draft. Fadi Jamali and his team updated base maps, as well as street elevations from individual permits, and provided the electronic files which served as the basis for graphic editing.

The narrative on the evolution and implementation of the master plan as well as the various projects within the conservation area are based on interviews with a number of professionals at Solidere who accompanied the reconstruction project since its initiation in 1994 and agreed to share their insight: Angus Gavin, Jean-Paul Lebas, Oussama Kabbani, John Nehmeh, and Farid Nehme, as well as Hans Curvers who contributed his extensive knowledge on archeological excavations in the Beirut Central District. Valuable information on quality control and the evolution of stone restoration techniques was provided by Walid Rihane and Nicholas Barnfield who helped in setting quality standards for restoration work at an early stage of the project.

I am also grateful to the architects, engineers and entrepreneurs outside Solidere who discussed at length their projects; in particular Joe Chiha who went to considerable trouble to locate and make available documents on the complex process of reconstructing selected structures from within. Finally, key contributions on the historical evolution of the area were provided by May Davie, Christine Babikian and Carla Eddé.

A special word of thanks to Nélida Nassar and Margarita Encomienda of Nassar Design. Nélida Nassar rose to this book's challenge by providing insights that contributed to the legibility and graphic expression of the text. She devised methods and visual solutions to the many aspects of the design that were seemingly difficult to reconcile.

Finally, the content of this book is by no means exhaustive, it will hopefully inspire others to conduct additional research and new findings as the city continues its rebuilding.

Robert Saliba
December 2003

Contents

Foreword

The idea of a book on Beirut's Foch-Allenby and Etoile area arose in 1999. Solidere had 'delivered the goods'. A new infrastructure with fine finishes had been laid. Splendid buildings stood in well-composed rows at the heart of the Conservation Area, a heritage jewel impeccably restored by a master craftsman. Even the hardest skeptics had to admit defeat. Yet, in real Schadenfreude, some of them argued that it all looked at best as museum pieces, at worst as Hollywood props. For, in the wake of recession, the buildings were still unoccupied; with very few shops and cafés opened, the streets lacked life. By the end of 2001, those who had wagered on Beirut city center scored. Like a precious flower, the area suddenly bloomed, fulfilling our best dreams. It has continued to thrive since, gaining every day in beauty and vibrancy.

We hope that Foch-Allenby and Etoile, offering a showpiece of large-scale, full-fledged restoration in the historic heart of the capital, will serve as a model to stimulate similar endeavors in other parts of the country, along the lines of what has been done to a certain extent in the town of Deir al Qamar. In our case, success has been the fruit of a lot of planning, hard work and organization. Implementation is based on innovative legislation. Regulations and guidelines combining strictness and flexibility govern the conservation and control the townscape. It is imperative to ensure the future preservation of these criteria and achievements. The challenge is to uphold the standards, written and unwritten, that have been observed in the area's buildings and public spaces. Such standards range from quality control and proper maintenance, to esthetic considerations in the design and implementation of all elements including street furniture and signage. That is an integral part of our agenda in 'developing the finest city center in the Middle East'.

The Conservation Area now belongs to the people. Epitomizing an urban phenomenon witnessed in today's cities, entertainment, shopping and window-shopping, or the sheer pleasure of walking among beautiful buildings and landscaped areas, serve as relaxation to an active population and are part of the visitors' sightseeing experience. Whilst it is obvious that people's tastes cannot be identical and that individual creativity should be encouraged, it is important to maintain the visual harmony achieved so far, and to develop a shared sense of esthetics and responsibility towards the community, based on culture and civic pride. This will be even more imperative as Beirut and its city center continue to grow. In the face of functional, demographic, economic, social, esthetic and technological changes, new aspirations and standards may expose Foch-Allenby and Etoile to undesirable transformations.

It is therefore our hope that relevant public agencies, possibly in collaboration with well-informed private committees, will commit to the preservation of this historic townscape. Economic considerations should encourage such a policy here and elsewhere. A high value added is undoubtedly attached to heritage. Preserving and reviving archeological sites, historic cities and city centers is highly instrumental in attracting visitors, and has a powerful spread effect in drawing tourist-related services and even new residents.

Nasser Chammaa
Chairman - General Manager
Solidere

Introduction

As the traditional heart of public, business and tourist activity prior to its extensive devastation during the 1975-1990 Lebanon war, the Beirut Central District (BCD) constituted a prime target for postwar reconstruction. An undertaking of such a scale necessarily called for the articulation of a grand vision which, logically, could only be realized through the establishment of an appropriate legal and institutional framework designed to guide the multidimensional aspects of the project. With this approach in mind, the Government of Lebanon in 1994 entrusted Solidere (The Lebanese Company for the Development and Reconstruction of Beirut Central District) with the redevelopment of the war-damaged city center according to a pre-approved Master Plan. Coping with the complex mechanisms of implementation demanded originality in planning, skilled efficiency in operation and a measured degree of flexibility in dealing with unexpected obstacles along the way.

A measure of the success of this revitalization, the area of Foch-Allenby and Etoile has become the main pole of attraction in Beirut's new city center. Yet, no publication so far has thoroughly examined its history and evolving urban and architectural character. This book is intended to fill that gap, bringing forward the area's unique architectural features, and calling attention to the intensive efforts invested in its restoration. The study is concerned with three main aspects of Foch-Allenby and Etoile: its strategic value, its historical value, and its value as a model of an implemented planning vision.

Strategically, Foch-Allenby and Etoile constitutes an important interface zone between land and sea, and as such reflects the relationship of the city to its port and to its central district. It also epitomizes the dual role of Beirut as a national capital and as a port city. Historically, Foch-Allenby and Etoile is representative of the attempts made in the early decades of the twentieth century at modernizing Beirut's city center, paralleled by the emergence and development of new building types. While this architectural development has yet to be documented, the wealth of reference material generated by Solidere, ranging from photogrammetric surveys to building restoration permits, provides a prime source of research on the subject that can help round up the architectural history of central Beirut. As a role-model, the recovery of Foch-Allenby and Etoile as part of the BCD reconstruction ranks among the most important urban revitalization ventures of the turn of this century. The project built on international experience in urban and architectural conservation and adapted that knowledge to local materials and know-how. Furthermore, it extended the restoration process forward to create modern space for offices and retail activities. This book offers a detailed account of that experience, from policy articulation to implementation, and from the consequent revival of traditional crafts to the adoption of up-to-date techniques in restoring buildings and modernizing their interiors.

Thematic Background: Historicizing Modernity

Foch-Allenby and Etoile epitomizes the two waves of modernization that have shaped the townscape of Beirut. The first wave introduced modernity at the turn of the twentieth century. One century later, the second wave historicized this modernity and moved it forward. With Foch-Allenby and Etoile now recovered, Beirut's 'modern past' has been incorporated in the present and future life of the city as a catalyst, a point of departure for a new modernity as well as a new centrality. As such, Foch-Allenby and Etoile reveals the unique relationship of Beirut to its past and future. It also illustrates the basic dialectics engendered on the urban and architectural level by two sets of modernization strategies: for spatial restructuring in the 1920s and 1930s; and for physical conservation in the 1990s.

During the late nineteenth and early twentieth centuries, under the impact of late Ottoman reforms and of French Mandate urbanism, Beirut was recast from a walled coastal town to a westernized port city. The main legacy of this first wave of modernization was the redevelopment of the old city core into a new district. Created during the 1920s and 1930s over the rubble of the intramural town, the Foch-Allenby and Etoile area was intended to celebrate Beirut as the showcase of France in the Levant and the capital city of the new nation-state of Lebanon. This geographically strategic zone formed the interface between seaport and city and was acknowledged as Beirut's modern district. Landward, it was invested with the symbols of the new republic, clustered around a prime civic space shaped and named after the Place de l'Etoile in Paris. Seaward, two streets, Foch and Allenby, were designed as the maritime gateway that linked the city to its periphery and grouped the highest concentration of business and port-related activities in the city center. There, a new building type emerged: the speculative office building, with a modern frontage and a traditional interior.

During the last decade, Solidere's reconstruction project initiated a second wave of modernization, aimed at reshaping the function and structure of the Beirut Central District and bringing it up to international standards. As one of the few areas in the city center to have escaped severe physical damage, Foch-Allenby and Etoile formed the most important link between the city and its recent past. For this reason, it has come to be valued as Beirut's historic core. Landward, it has recovered its civic space and formal townscape. Seaward, it has been distanced from the port by the creation of a new waterfront. Upgraded and enhanced, the area now incorporates the largest pedestrian zone in the capital. Its architectural restoration, which adopted the latest strategies and techniques, has generated a new 'building type': the renovated office building, with a historical façade and a modern interior. Thus, Foch-Allenby and Etoile now stands as a prime showcase of postwar reconstruction.

The two phases of modernization of the Foch-Allenby and Etoile area revolved around three issues:

* The issue of its integration in its immediate urban context and its symbiotic relationship with the historic core, the new waterfront and the reconstructed city center. As an intermediate zone between the city center and the waterfront, Foch-Allenby and Etoile has been shaped seaward by its relation to the port, landward by its relation to the city, and downward by its relation to the archeological strata.

* The issue of its recovery; that is to say, how to reconcile townscape and architectural conservation with the exigencies of economic revitalization, to mediate between preservation and modernization or, more generally, past and future, when a historic area is subjected to the contemporary demands of economic development. This dialectic was expressed at the public level by reconciling the cultural identity of the place with the modernization of the infrastructure; and at the private level by the adaptive re-use of conserved structures for modern business.

• The issue of mediation, or how to translate an urban design vision into an operational process ensuring its realization. For the second time in Beirut's recent history, Foch-Allenby and Etoile has become a successful example of a modernizing vision translated into reality. In this case, it meant establishing a design and legislative framework that could link planning to implementation.

As in other cases of postwar reconstruction and historic district revitalization, there are no standard formulas for resolving such broad issues. Strategies are site- and area-specific; they are tied to functional and economic contexts, the history of the place and the prevalent private and public sector relationships. Nevertheless, a number of useful ideas drawn from the Foch-Allenby and Etoile experience of integration, mediation and recovery may be adapted to other areas at the city and national level, especially such places as Beirut's pericenter districts where colonial landscapes are quickly disappearing, or in the historical cores of small coastal cities. By proceeding from the particular to the general, much can be learned from the case study of Foch-Allenby and Etoile.

Approach and Outline

This book offers a contemporary perspective on the redevelopment of Foch-Allenby and Etoile as an urban area of symbolic and distinctive importance: first, because it is the locus of the national identity, being at the historic heart of the capital; and second, because it exhibits an integrated and homogeneous townscape, in contrast with much of its surrounding environment. As such, Foch-Allenby and Etoile exemplifies — both in its inception during the late Ottoman and French Mandate periods and in its current revitalization within Solidere's postwar reconstruction of the Beirut Central District — a prime concern for the quality of public domain and architecture, which is notoriously absent in the rest of the capital. In documenting the mechanisms through which harmony between the urban and architectural scale has been achieved twice during Beirut's modern history, our study provides a critical examination of those two experiences and highlights their relationship.

The book also reflects on the changing perception of urban heritage. Foch-Allenby and Etoile is the product of two waves of modernization: the first firmly rooted in early post-industrial development and the second in the more recent historical evolution of Beirut. Previously, the predominant notion of heritage had been mainly confined to archeology and to the preservation of individual monuments and of the city's historic core. In recovering Foch-Allenby and Etoile, Solidere extended this notion to encompass the area's early twentieth-century architectural heritage, giving considerable attention to the early modern office building and incorporating the French Mandate legacy within its patrimony. Thus, Beirut is the first city in the Arab Middle East that has come to terms with its colonial heritage and, by extension, with its 'modern heritage'. The 'will to modernize', which has been the driving force in shaping Beirut's urban form ever since the middle decades of the nineteenth century, seems now to constitute a common denominator for all cities in the region. It is in its specific response to this generic force towards modernization that Beirut's uniqueness resides.

In raising the problematic of interpretation, the book recognizes that no single analytical approach is capable on its own to provide the clues to understand the process of reconstruction and recovery of a capital's central district. Only through a combination of different ways of thinking, from a spatial, economic, political, social, cultural and philosophical perspective, can the underlying complexity of such a project begin to unravel. This work is not intended as a comprehensive review and synthesis of those interpretations. The contents emphasize functional, spatial and esthetic considerations, while acknowledging the importance of economic viability, social equity, or cultural adequacy. Many issues have been in the past decade the subject of lengthy debates, some of which left a marked impact on the reconstruction framework and its process. While they are occasionally mentioned in the text, they do not explicitly condition the basic arguments of this book.

We have tried to transcend the controversial debates that have surrounded the BCD reconstruction, in order to avoid the pitfall of a partisan approach. Instead, we have focused on Foch-Allenby and Etoile as a prime historic site having its own unique character and inner dialectics. By understanding those dialectics and becoming aware of the process of their resolution, we can develop a vision that moves beyond stereotyped heritage values to embrace change with authenticity and permanence, and an approach that combines conservation and modernity.

The book is structured according to the main issues of integration between the historical core, the central district and the waterfront, and recovery of the public and private domain. Sustaining the two processes is the mediation between design vision and implementation. In addition to outlining the legal framework and the urban planning and design principles underlying the recovery of Foch-Allenby and Etoile, the book describes the process devised for its implementation, including the administrative mechanism adopted for coordination between the key stakeholders and for the supervision of building design and execution.

Since the aim of this publication is to address a wide audience encompassing both the specialized reader and the general public, architectural illustrations and photography have been given as much emphasis as explicative text. The main intent of the book is to provide a reference document that will convey, in word and image, the architectural diversity of the area, the quality of its historic townscape and the details of its rehabilitation.

Of special visual interest to the reader is the architectural survey of the Foch-Allenby and Etoile area, which contains drawings of restored buildings and a large-scale reference map that highlights the buildings and their relationship to the street and to the area as a whole.

ALLENBY STREET

WEYGAND STREET

FOCH STREET

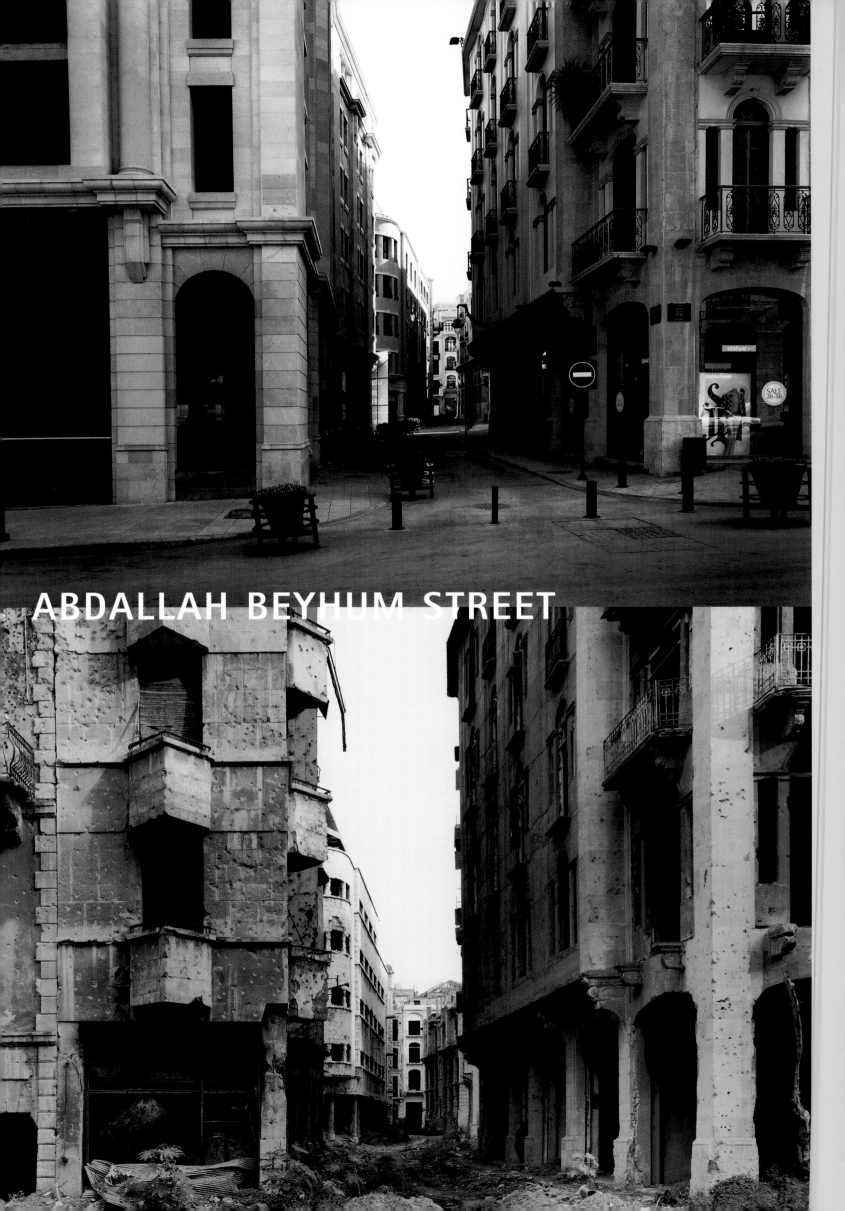

ABDALLAH BEYHUM STREET

MAARAD STREET

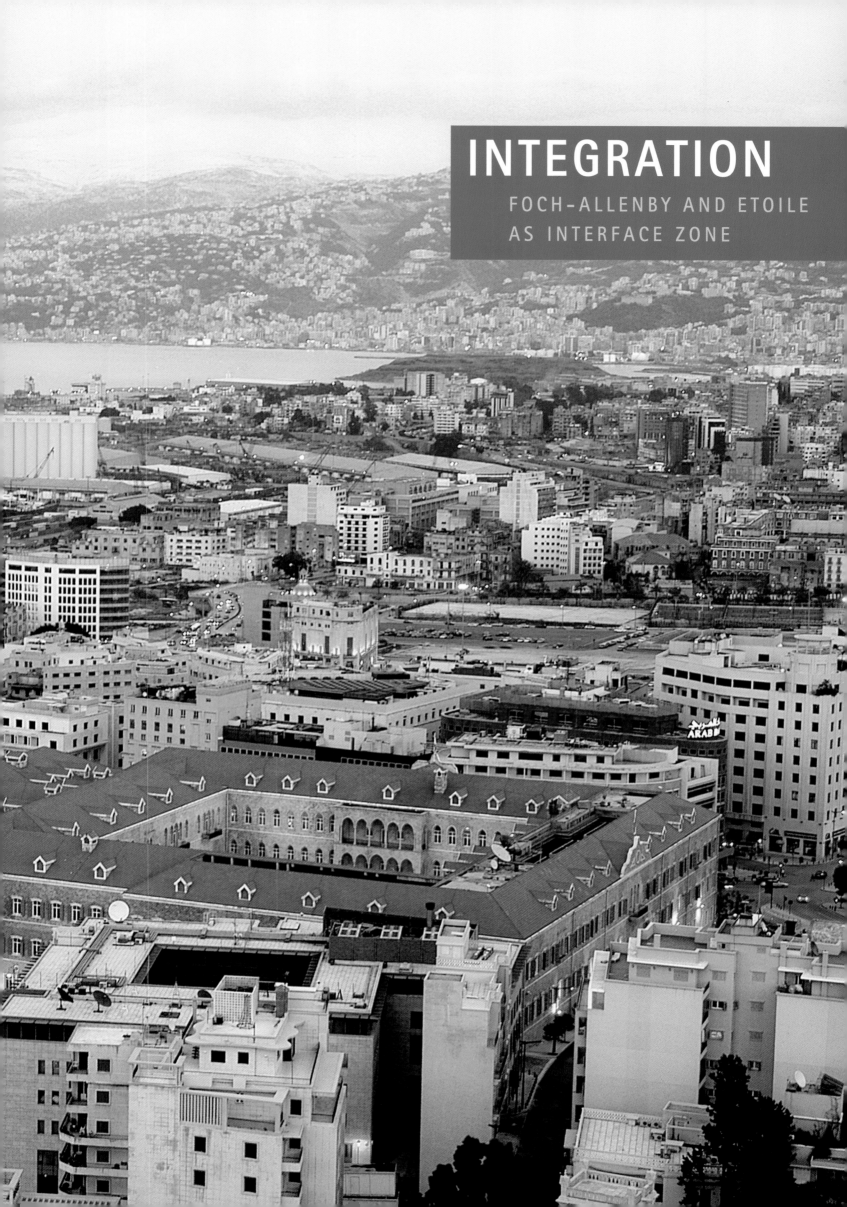

INTEGRATION

FOCH–ALLENBY AND ETOILE
AS INTERFACE ZONE

Aerial view of Beirut city center
showing Foch-Allenby and Maarad,
with the first port basin and the
new waterfront in the background.

Integration   Foch-Allenby and Etoile as Interface Zone

During the past century, the Foch-Allenby and Etoile area of Beirut has evolved from the port district of a small coastal town along the Eastern Mediterranean, to a maritime gateway of the region, to the historic core of a globalizing city center. An exploration of its evolving relationship to the Beirut downtown and waterfront reveals a key underlying process: how the area's internal structure was shaped by this relationship; and how it, in turn, has shaped the internal structure of the new Beirut Central District (BCD). Viewed from a temporal perspective, this two-way process established the 'historicity' of the city core and brought forth patterns of continuity and change.

Foch-Allenby and Etoile has traditionally acted as an interface zone between the port and the city. Historically, it was the domain of interaction between the two, deeply imprinted, landward by the port's accessibility to the hinterland, and seaward by the accessibility of the city to the waterfront. In modern times, as the port expanded east and progressively acquired autonomy, the relationship of this area to the seafront was gradually modified. At present, the creation of a New Waterfront District to the north as part of the BCD reconstruction and development has resulted in further distancing Foch-Allenby and Etoile from the sea. Due to its strategic location, the area thus epitomizes the dialectics of integration between the waterfront and the city center as a whole, both in its making and recovery. Furthermore, the relation of Foch-Allenby and Etoile to its historic urban origins has been recognized and emphasized by the BCD Master Plan. The area's townscape was relatively less impacted by the devastation that the war inflicted on central Beirut from the mid-1970s through the 1980s. By virtue of its location within the confines of the old city, it represented the historic locus of Beirut, a sort of mediator between past and future — between the recovered townscape and the uncovered archeological strata.

In that sense, the Foch-Allenby and Etoile area reveals the historical and geographical logic that has governed change in the city center — a change determined by the dual goal of reaching out to the world market and reaching in to the cultural particularities of its historic origins. By considering the development of the Beirut Central District and Foch-Allenby and Etoile from this wider perspective, the aim of this section is to articulate a reference framework, through which the specificity of Beirut and its interface zone may be viewed within the context of local, regional and global links. Chapter One starts by outlining the main characteristics of interface zones, as shaped by the dialectics of integration between port and city. Then, concentrating on the Mediterranean city as a regional type, it explores the dynamics of change in response to successive waves of modernization, differentiating between coastal and inland cities and between main and secondary coastal cities. Chapter Two introduces Foch-Allenby and Etoile as an interface zone between port and city, with seaward- and landward-oriented sub-areas. This sets a base for investigating within a historical perspective the dialectics of integration between the waterfront and the city center. Chapters Three and Four analyze the planning vision and integration strategies established for the area within the wider city center, as they evolved from the prewar period to the present ongoing recovery.

Chapter 1

Interface Zones Between Port and City: General Issues

The intermediate areas between port and city are usually referred to as port or gateway districts, the former stressing their physical adjacency to the port, the latter their strategic importance as the main access to the city from the sea. In our approach, they are referred to as interface zones — defined as the meeting ground between port and city, the edge where global and local networks meet. Such an interface zone extends landward beyond the waterfront quays to include the port-related district that constitutes the transition between port and city, where both the functions of maritime trade and central business activities are accommodated. Epitomizing the relationship between the city and its port, the interface zone reflects their mutual adjustment to different operative logics pertaining to external relations, spatial expansion, functional and internal structuring. These act in opposite directions — landward and seaward — and it is the degree of integration or segregation between port and city, or the preponderance of one over the other, that shapes the functional and spatial configuration of interface zones. Foch-Allenby and Etoile is a typical example of an interface zone that has been shaped through this kind of interaction.

A consideration of the conceptual bases of interaction between port and city may help provide an understanding of how interface zones work and help identify their general issues. After defining the distinct logics of port and city in general, this chapter proceeds to analyze the way in which the interaction between the two has been accommodated morphologically and culturally through their interface zone since pre-industrial times. Before investigating the case of Beirut in particular, we will examine the Eastern Mediterranean port city as a regional type, and identify the manner in which it responded to the pressures of modernization on one hand, and colonization on the other hand. Using this approach, an attempt will then be made to place Beirut within its general and regional context.

Two Functional and Spatial Logics

Port and city operate at two different levels. The first embodies an international network that depends on a large-scale port infrastructure; the second is made up of an inclusive urban network of local streets and places. As an installation of substantial size, the port is conditioned in its spatial structure by global engineering standards and the evolution of maritime transport technology. Functionally, the port is not only a terminus for passengers and cargo; it is also a transit or break-in-transport site between international maritime trade and local or regional inland trade. The city, on the other hand, is by definition a central entity, which provides goods and services to surrounding areas; its functional and spatial structure is determined by civic design decisions, as well as by the particularities of its local socio-economic and political dynamics. It is this difference between two spatial systems and functional logics that conditions the interrelationship between port and city.

Starting from the middle decades of the nineteenth century, port cities worldwide, irrespective of location and political status, have gone through the same stages of transformation. These are tied to the evolution of maritime transport technology and the changes in international trade, as well as to the phenomenal urban growth that accompanied the spread of industrialization. Han Meyer identifies four stages of port-city development:

- The pre-industrial period up to the mid-nineteenth century is associated with 'the entrepôt port within an enclosed city', where quays and street networks were completely integrated and where the port was the final destination for local distribution and trade.

- The early modern period is associated with 'the transit port alongside an open city'. The divorce between port and city was initiated by the development in port and transportation technology, leading to an unprecedented increase in the scale of port activities. Trade penetrated the hinterland through the territory of the city, and the city expanded into its hinterland.

- The modern period from the mid-twentieth century on is associated with 'the industrial port alongside a functional city'. The port became an autonomous entity where goods in transit could be re-exported after being processed; thus the port became an industrial and transshipment site segregated from the city. Meanwhile, the city underwent an increasing process of specialization and decentralization of functions, with a marked development of communications networks.

- The contemporary, postmodern period is associated with 'the distribution port and network city'. Containerization and telecommunications are re-shaping the port into a domain where "the flow of goods is coordinated and directed" with efficiency and speed, backed by the emergence of a new type of infrastructure, 'the electronic highway'. The city is appropriating old harbor areas as a further link between international and local networks, and attention is given to cruise tourism and waterfront leisure facilities. At the same time, the port is reconsidering the city as "a potential nerve center for logistic organization and telecommunications", encompassing the entire network of business and maritime nodes and including the construction of headquarters or branches of multinational corporations.

These postmodern developments in port-city interface have revived the concern of modern times to recreate the dynamic integration that once prevailed between the traditional town and its port. Throughout the history of port cities, land-sea integration and port-city integration have revolved around two dynamics: morphological integration, which encompasses the physical, and functional and cultural integration, which addresses the encounter between local, regional and international influences.

Morphological Integration

The logics of port and city are mediated through their interface zone, a territory for 'reciprocal cross-overs', to use Stefano Boeri's expression. The port negotiates accessibility for traffic and trade through the city to the hinterland; the city looks to the port for accessibility to the sea for travel and recreation. As Jorge Silvetti explains, "the further inland the city moves, the more the need for efficient access to the waterfront. The more the city extends along the shore, the more permeable the frontal parallel development needs to be." This functional, spatial and visual permeability constitutes the main integrative force between coast and inland. It underlies the morphology (i.e. form and function) of the interface zone as a terrain of their "simultaneous and common history," as Boeri calls it, exhibiting the "analogies and resonance effects that have grown up over generations amidst the sharing of infrastructure."

The historical dimension of the interface zone stems from the fact that most port cities have experienced the passage of many civilizations, each having left its imprint in the archeological layers that lead back to the origins of urban and maritime evolution.

Accordingly, morphological integration is made up of two aspects:
- A horizontal integration between sea and inland, between global and local networks, expressed through design strategies of visual permeability, functional complementariness and accessibility.

- A vertical integration between townscape and archeological layers, expressed through the design strategies of townscape articulation and heritage conservation; that is, the reinforcement of the identity of place.

Cultural Integration

The dynamics of morphological integration, both vertical and horizontal, are subject to the geographic and historic contexts and conditioned by the cultural exposure and exchange specific to each setting. This is particularly relevant in the case of port cities, which by virtue of their coastal location are exposed to extensive foreign influence and act as intermediate territories between the local, the regional and the global. As access poles for foreign trade, culture and tourism, they tend to exhibit cosmopolitan seafronts and gateway districts that 'frame' the access from port to city. This usually means that the port city simultaneously looks to the indigenous and the foreign, the local and the international, modernization and preservation. These dual viewpoints are generators of cross-cultural exchange, the scope of which depends on the degree of cultural permeability of the social and political setting; namely, the extent to which each port city is willing to absorb and assimilate foreign input culturally and socially. At the morphological level, permeability can take different forms, ranging from the superimposition and overlapping to the juxtaposition of traditional and modern urban patterns.

An accelerated and sustained process of morphological mutation constantly redefines, in particular, the regional and local identity of a port city's interface zone. Morphological mutations, or the resulting changes in the functional and physical configuration of urban areas, are substantially shaped by the encounter of the traditional with the modern, i.e. new trends in architecture and advances in infrastructure and construction technology. They are also determined by the interaction between the metropolitan and the provincial, the global and the local, i.e. to what extent port cities are either autonomous or subject to the influence of external political and economic forces.

In order to qualify the phenomenon of interaction referred to above, it may be useful to narrow the scope of the analysis from the global to the regional, before focusing on the local in the next chapter. The Eastern Mediterranean port cities will be taken as an example, since they have a common historical and geographic context, and to a large extent share with Beirut its cultural background.

Figure 1.1
Dual colonial city: Casablanca, 1926.
Separation between the medina and
the 'ville nouvelle'.

Interaction between traditional and modern

Between the mid-1800s and the early 1900s, under the impact of the industrial revolution in Europe and the expansion of colonial trade, Eastern Mediterranean port cities experienced rapid economic development and extensive physical change. Due to their strategic locations and their incorporation within a global network of colonial mercantilism, these cities became gateways for the Western world and the nuclei of modernizing trends. A hierarchy was established between metropolitan ports belonging to colonial powers, like Marseilles, and provincial ports like Beirut. The latter emerged as a satellite port city through which raw materials were exported and manufactured products imported. In addition to being a port city for Western trade, Beirut acquired during that period the status of a provincial capital in the colonial administration of the Ottoman empire.

This double function of Beirut as port and capital city brought forth, on one hand, the expansion and modernization of the old port to accommodate increased freight activity and steam-powered navigation. Thus, the pre-industrial city, with its organic layout, narrow streets and cramped conditions, began to be perceived, not as an interface but as a barrier between the port and its hinterland. At the same time, the city's congested and unsanitary environment itself was deemed inadequate for modern urban living, leading to a thrust to modernize the urban fabric in accordance with contemporary esthetic, functional and hygienic standards. The city core was thus pressured to reshape itself, functionally and visually, into a highly permeable area (see Chapter 5).

The tension between old and new led to the partial or complete overlapping of a modern commercial center over the traditional town. This modernization by superimposition created an additional layer of change over the earlier historical strata. By contrast, inland cities experienced a process of modernization by juxtaposition. Not being linked to a port, the pre-industrial town was spared and a new center grew next to the old core. This followed the dual city colonial model, consisting of the preserved medina on one side and the building of a new city on the other, as in the case of Casablanca (*fig. 1.1*). The same dynamics prevailed in coastal towns in Lebanon, where modest economic growth led to the preservation of the old core and the development of a partially overlapping or completely separate new commercial center adjoining the medieval town (*fig. 1.2*).

As argued in the work of Arnon Soffer and Shimon Stern on the post-industrial Middle Eastern port city, it was the importance of the coastal town and the level of its port activity that determined the type and degree of mutual accommodation between old and modern urban centers. This process of mutual accommodation was affected by another type of exchange: the relations between colonial powers and their provincial capitals.

Interaction between metropolis and province, between global and local

Throughout history, Mediterranean port cities had been organized in a network of city-states or colonies under the hegemony of various empires, notably the Roman, the Arab and the Ottoman. They had to adapt to the tensions prevailing between their own developmental logic and the exigencies imposed by the metropolis or central power, which was often located far from its provinces.

This trend was sustained during the post-industrial period, when port cities underwent parallel processes of modernization imposed by European metropolitan powers. Both the economic destiny and the physiognomy of Mediterranean cities were shaped from outside, by the dynamics of sea trade and colonial interests.

The extent to which the modernization of the urban fabric occurred in each case was largely determined by the scope and type of the 'reciprocal interactions' that existed between center and periphery, between the metropolis and the province (*Note 1.1*).

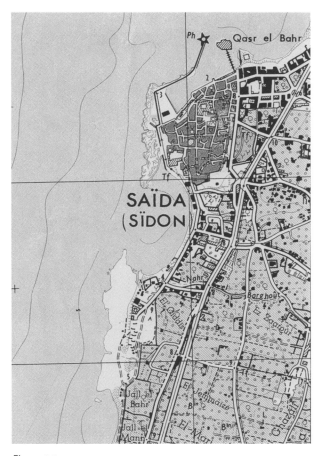

Figure 1.2
Secondary port city: Sidon, with partial overlapping between the old and new fabric.
Etoile square was juxtaposed to the intramural town, while in the case of Beirut it was superimposed over it.

Note 1.1 Irrespective of their colonial hierarchy, both
Marseilles (non-colonial status) and Beirut
(colonial status) were qualified by French
colonial interests of the late nineteenth and
early twentieth centuries as Porte de l'Orient.
The two cities, respectively projected by
Paris as the Mediterranean showcase of Europe
and the Levant, had to 'Haussmannize'
the interface zones between port and city within
four decades of each other: the former
between 1860 and 1880, the latter between
1920 and 1940 (fig.1.3; also see fig.5.35).

In his Paris sur Marseille, René Borruey aptly
qualifies the asymmetrical relationship between
Paris and Marseilles as "an uneven love affair
between this wayward Mediterranean port and
her terribly possessive French lover: the State."
The same remark could apply to Ottoman and
French Mandate Beirut, as well as to other
principal Mediterranean port cities like Haifa
or Alexandria.

In the case of Ottoman Beirut, however, Jens
Hanssen explains that "these dynamics were
by no means marked by a clear-cut imperial
versus local antagonism, but rather they developed in the context of reciprocal interactions
on the imperial, regional, and local levels." A
similar argument is developed by May Davie
about French Mandate Beirut.

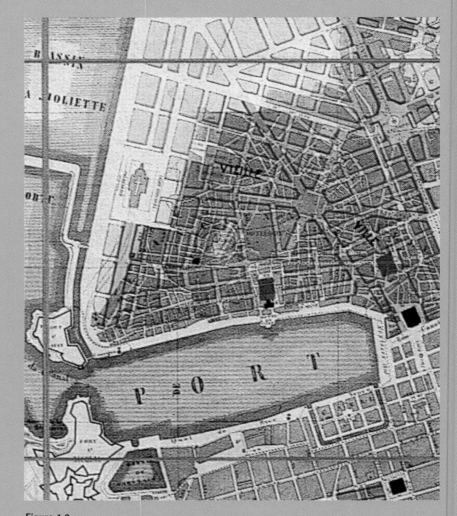

Figure 1.3
Marseilles, municipal project 1858.

With the passing of colonialism, the regional dynamics between center and periphery transmuted gradually into a global-local dynamic. Meanwhile, ports continued to be shaped by technological innovations in maritime transport and the growth in freight activity. With the expansion of transshipment and containerization and the industrialization of port areas for the processing of goods, the port became a fluid, autonomous and ever-growing space, shifting away from the city center and becoming tied to a global transport network. Furthermore, the contemporary development of satellite communications reduced the relevance of physical proximity for the provision of port-related services. Abandoned port basins and warehouses created a sharp edge between urban centers and their shorelines, and the city began searching for a new relation with the waterfront. A new vocation was sought for the interface zone which generally kept moving further inland as the city grew, while more terrain was possibly gained over the sea.

According to Ariane Wilson, attempts at the revitalization of port areas that followed the American model until the 1960s, were based on the creation of scenic drives along the shoreline or on a dedicated redevelopment of old harbor areas for recreation and tourism. This approach was criticized for emphasizing the waterfront in isolation from the city and for ignoring the city's original maritime activities and its surviving structures. More recent attempts at waterfront revitalization have shown a higher concern for the site's identity by following two main approaches:

- The recycling of maritime activities and the provision of 'multifunctional programs', as opposed to 'mono-functional plans'; a clear example is the integration of sea passenger terminals and transit facilities into multiuse development zones.

- The 'conservation of cultural reminders', especially the naval heritage, with projects such as maritime centers and museums.

However, Wilson suggests that, instead, "We must look elsewhere for authentic aspects that might serve in defining guidelines for urban design. Not in the traditional function of the port, nor even in its seafront location, but in the cultural history of the connections between infrastructure zone and city." What she calls for is a solid historical understanding of 'reciprocal crossovers' between port and city.

The following chapter addresses this specific concern through the case study of Beirut. Focusing on the Foch-Allenby and Etoile area and based on Meyer's theory, it examines both port and city center during the first three phases of modern development and reveals how the area has responded morphologically and culturally to local, metropolitan and global forces at once.

Note 2.1 In Beirut, the relationship between port, city and
their interface zone, Foch–Allenby and Etoile,
was shaped by three main dynamics:

- Seaward, the extension of the waterfront and
the modalities of access/egress to/from the hinterland. The modernization of the port proceeded
unobstructed by physical barriers or ownership
issues, with land reclaimed from the sea to
accommodate the new maritime infrastructure,
and engineering schemes implemented as conceived. The port expanded east, progressively
acquiring territorial autonomy and creating an
industrial zone between the city and the sea.
The pre-industrial port district was reshaped into
a modern maritime gateway, expressing
the increasing importance of the port in relation
to the city.

- Landward, the dynamics of centralization and
decentralization of institutional, commercial and
industrial activities. The increasing administrative
and financial importance of Beirut led to the
creation of a specialized central business district
and the decentralization of the residential
functions towards the periphery. Furthermore,
with the inner city densification and the growth
of peripheral areas during the 1950s, 1960s,
and 1970s, commercial and financial activities
began diffusing towards alternative urban centers.

- Within the interface zone, the visual, functional
and physical permeability linking port and city
center. The irregular street pattern of the intramural city was reshaped into a rectilinear layout
that enhanced both visual permeability with
the waterfront and functional communication
between the port and its hinterland. Foch–
Allenby and Etoile became the locus of imported
building types and models that expressed the
increasing cultural permeability to the West. The
redefinition of its urban character was a response
to the needs of the port for office buildings and
storage space, and the needs of the capital city
for major institutional buildings.

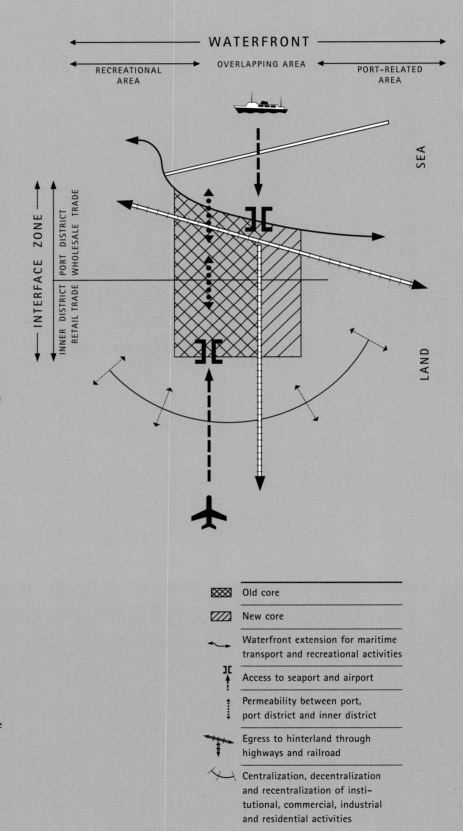

WATERFRONT

RECREATIONAL AREA   OVERLAPPING AREA   PORT-RELATED AREA

SEA

LAND

INTERFACE ZONE

INNER DISTRICT   PORT DISTRICT
RETAIL TRADE   WHOLESALE TRADE

⊠ Old core

⬚ New core

↔ Waterfront extension for maritime
transport and recreational activities

Access to seaport and airport

Permeability between port,
port district and inner district

Egress to hinterland through
highways and railroad

Centralization, decentralization
and recentralization of institutional, commercial, industrial
and residential activities

Chapter 2

From the pre-industrial to the late modern period, the Foch-Allenby and Etoile area retained its vocation as an interface zone between the port and the city (see chapter 5). The area came to reflect Beirut's double status as a regional port and capital city and served as a common ground for their evolution.

In view of its homogenous architectural character, Foch-Allenby and Etoile is generally perceived as a single spatial entity. In fact, its two sub-areas were historically clearly demarcated — to the north, Foch-Allenby, which traditionally constituted the port district; and to the south, Etoile, which lay in the heart of the capital city and epitomized national political life. The area has thus been conditioned by two factors: seaward, the evolution of maritime activity; and landward the forces of the urban centralization or decentralization of administrative, commercial and financial activities.

As in other port cities, the scope and dynamics of those different activities initiated a progressive divorce between port and city, constantly calling for a redefinition of the relationship between Beirut's city core and its expanding waterfront. The purpose of this chapter is to investigate how the evolving interaction between the port and city shaped the physical and functional structure of Foch-Allenby and Etoile. It intends to show how each phase of the development of this area brought forth new strategies of horizontal integration between land and sea and generated different levels of cultural permeability, particularly to Western trends. These strategies are analyzed spatially in terms of three sets of forces that impacted the port, the city and the interface between the two (Note 2.1).

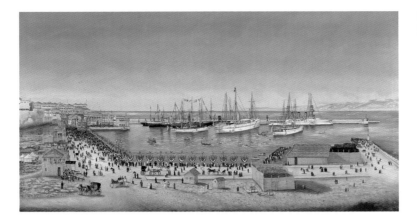

Figure 2.1
Kaiser Wilhelm II's visit to Beirut in 1898.

Figure 2.2
Inauguration of Beirut railroad station
on March 1, 1903.

Figure 2.3
The western docks with the imposing
Imperial Ottoman Bank building.

Figure 2.4
The new jetty as sea promenade.

Chapter 2

Pre-Industrial Port City Integration

Early nineteenth-century Beirut was a pre-industrial town confined within the limits of its defensive walls. A caravan station at the city's eastern gate served as the main access/egress point to regional trade routes. The intramural town consisted of a port-related lower town, the present Foch-Allenby, and a bazaar-related upper town, the present Etoile. Between the two, a main thoroughfare connecting the eastern and western gates occupied approximately the location of the present Weygand Street and corresponded roughly to the Roman Decumanus, formerly believed to be the Decumanus Maximus.

The harbor was strongly anchored within the intramural town, forming both a defensive front and a trading outpost. A network of north-south alleyways connected to the main thoroughfare ensured functional and physical permeability between the port and the lower town, upper town and town gates. A strong port-city integration prevailed in a context of slow maritime activity and limited population growth. Harbor-related activities and services, such as loading and unloading, warehousing and repair yards, generated little demand for additional space; and in the absence of rural to urban migration, the city did not need to expand beyond its defensive walls.

The area adjoining the port already exhibited a cosmopolitan character. As described by Leila Fawaz, travelers "first crossed a relatively new and pleasant part of the town just outside the port area. The only two good streets of Beirut were to be found there, lined with the largest stone houses of the town. Just beyond was the street inhabited by bankers and money changers, and beyond that the Greek quarter, with its coffeehouses and cabarets."

Emerging Segregation

The growth of Beirut is linked with its evolution into a regional port after the development of steamship navigation, and following its promotion to the rank of a provincial capital in 1832. Its role was reinforced by the opening in 1857 of the Beirut-Damascus road, which provided a link to the hinterland. To accommodate the increasing freight activity, the enlargement and modernization of the

traditional harbor became an economic necessity. Financed by the Compagnie Impériale Ottomane du Port des Quais et des Entrepôts de Beyrouth, primarily with European investment capital, the projects undertaken between 1887 and 1893 led to the construction of deeper and wider basins and larger warehouses and the creation of more mechanized loading and unloading facilities (*fig. 2.8*). Further enhancing accessibility to the hinterland, a railroad inaugurated in 1903 had its terminal located in the port area, fronting the old city (*fig. 2.2*). With the upgrading of its port facilities and land communications, Beirut became a major port along the Eastern Mediterranean. In 1888, when Beirut became the capital of a provincial administrative entity (Wilaya) of the Ottoman empire, it also benefited from the extensive urban development work initiated by the Ottoman authorities.

The modernization thus set in motion seaward by the French and landward by the Ottomans, began generating a tension between the port and the city, and the integrated settlement of pre-industrial times gave way to a progressive divorce between the two. As early as 1863, M. Stoecklin, consulting engineer for the port extension, had remarked (as quoted by Laugénie): "It is not enough to build quays; these need to have convenient access to the city center. This is where difficulties begin. Old downtown quarters neighboring the port amount to a blind maze of dead ends, alleyways and covered passages through which it would only be possible to open an avenue at enormous cost... But a more radical solution is possible: the extension of Martyrs' Square over its full length all the way to the waterfront."

This early insight clearly announced the main issue around which the port-city interface was to revolve in the following century and a half; namely, visual and functional permeability, or how to connect port to hinterland through the city, and city to sea through the port. The old town was already perceived by Stoecklin as a barrier against fluid access to regional roads.

The urban area emerging around Bourj, or Place des Canons (today's Martyrs' Square) to the east of the old city core, was considered to be the necessary visual corridor through which modern Beirut could open up towards the Mediterranean.

Figure 2.5
The implemented Foch-Allenby and Etoile plan.

– – – – Conservation Area boundaries

———— **Implemented sections of the urban design scheme**

– – – – **Unimplemented sections of the urban design scheme**

1 Cinema Rivoli

2 Grand Theatre

3 St George Greek-Orthodox Cathedral

4 St Elie Greek-Catholic Church

Delahalle scheme   **Figure 2.6a**   **Figure 2.6b**   **Figure 2.7**
Rendered view   Oblique view of   Plan.
from the sea.   the model.

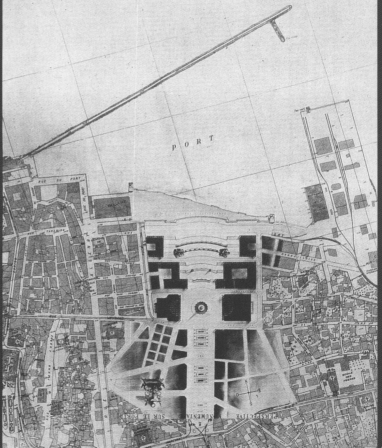

By the turn of the twentieth century, the waterfront had become the nerve center of all transport routes, as well as the heart of merchants' activities. It also portrayed the flamboyant face of the modernizing city and its commercial and banking vocation, with key buildings, such as the Imperial Ottoman Bank, the Orosdi-Back department store and the Customs building, developed over the enlarged western docks fronting the old port district (*fig. 2.3*). The relocation of the Ottoman Bank from Bourj Square to the waterfront highlighted the tension between two areas competing for preeminence as the new heart of the city. The harbor became a showcase of maritime works and architecture, exhibiting imported engineering skills from the Ponts-et-Chaussées and styles from the Beaux-Arts schools. Both the Beirut-Damascus road and railroad, and the port, were managed by the French company Régie Générale des Chemins de Fer et Travaux Publics.

Functional permeability was maintained between port and city. The new jetty became a popular promenade (*fig. 2.4*) and the waterfront's western edge was developed into a hotel and entertainment area, enhanced during the following two decades by the creation of the Avenue des Français. By 1915, modernization had reached the heart of the old town. The port district was redeveloped, and half a century after Stoecklin's recommendation, connectivity between port and city was finally initiated. The migration of residential functions towards the peripheries of the old city accentuated its transformation into a modern business district. This was reinforced by two trends that were to set in during the following decades: the centralization and specialization of inner city functions.

Preponderance of Port over City

The opening of the old city core to the harbor proceeded in two phases: the making of Foch-Allenby as a new port and wholesale trade district in the 1920s; and the making of Etoile as a new administrative, institutional and retail trade district in the 1930s. Hence, in less than twenty years, Beirut's dual identity as port and capital city was imprinted in the morphology of the interface zone between port and city, namely the Foch-Allenby and Etoile area. Although the two sub-areas retained their earlier defining boundaries, their urban fabric was transformed from a medieval organic pattern to a Beaux-Arts geometric pattern.

The east-west thoroughfare, relabeled Weygand Street, separated the Foch-Allenby and Etoile sub-areas; while two north-south arteries ensured horizontal integration between port, city and regional routes. Foch Street linked the port to the Beirut-Damascus road; Allenby and Maarad streets formed one continuous visual corridor linking the port to the new heart of the capital city, the Place de l'Etoile (Nijma Square).

The townscape of Foch-Allenby and Etoile reflected imported European and Oriental revivalist styles, combining the city's westernizing and regionalist outlook. According to Kamal Salibi, "In Lebanon alone, the impact of the modern world arrived with grace, stage by stage, and often upon local invitation; and the accommodation to it also came gradually and with equal grace." However, the modernization process did not come full circle. Design schemes for the Place de l'Etoile and Place des Canons (Martyrs' Square) remained partly unfulfilled, due to the interference of powerful representatives of the Beiruti bourgeoisie and the religious communities' Waqfs (inalienable property trusts), anxious to protect religious landmarks and communal properties (*Note 2.2*). The active role played by local figures in challenging decisions imposed at the metropolitan level (i.e. by the French Mandate power) distinguishes Beirut from other Mediterranean cities, such as Alexandria, where modernization rested mainly in the hands of foreigners and left more leeway for a complete implementation of urban design intentions.

The Incomplete Modernization Scheme

Note 2.2 Three factors prevented the completion of the modernization scheme destined to make Beirut the French Mandate showcase in the Levant (see chapter 5). The initial intention of the 1926 Duraffourd (see fig. 5.33) and 1930 Danger (see fig. 5.34) designs was to prolong the Allenby-Maarad axis to the pine forest on the southern edge of municipal Beirut. This would make Etoile Square the radiating circulation center linking port to city center and to the expanding periphery. The extension of the Allenby-Maarad axis was interrupted by the building of the Grand Theatre, which closed the perspective of Maarad Street. Furthermore, the eastern radial streets intended as a link between Martyrs' Square and Etoile Square, the old and new cores, were truncated owing to the presence of landmark religious buildings and Waqf property. Finally, the connection of Martyrs' Square to the sea failed to materialize (fig. 2.5). The 1934 Delahalle scheme (fig. 2.6 – 2.7) envisioned Martyrs' Square as the formal gateway of the city, articulated around a wide and monumental civic space stepping down towards the sea. This sumptuous design reduced Foch and Allenby, both in scale and function, to two business gateways whose role was to facilitate linkage between port and city.

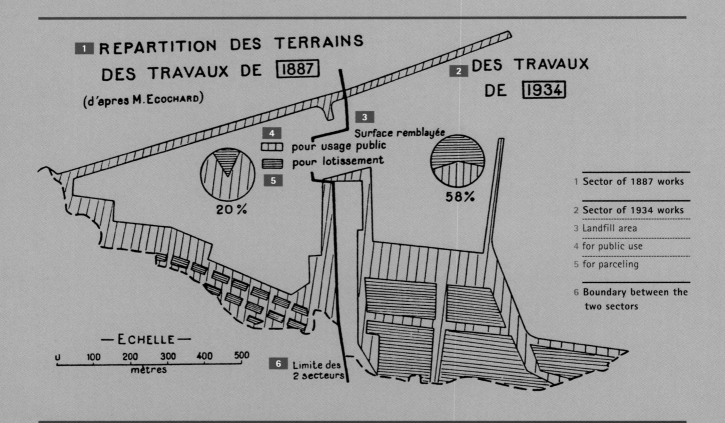

REPARTITION DES TERRAINS DES TRAVAUX DE 1887 (d'apres M.Ecochard)

DES TRAVAUX DE 1934

Surface remblayée
pour usage public
pour lotissement

20 %

58 %

— ECHELLE —
0   100   200   300   400   500
metres

Limite des 2 secteurs

1 Sector of 1887 works

2 Sector of 1934 works

3 Landfill area

4 for public use

5 for parceling

6 Boundary between the two sectors

The Port of Beirut in the 1950s: A shortcut to the Middle Eastern hinterland

Note 2.3 As mentioned by Jean Laugénie: "The port enjoys an exceptional location* despite competition from the Suez Canal. The distance between Beirut and Baghdad by road is roughly equal to that of Paris-Nice, while Beirut-Teheran only slightly exceeds the Paris-Lisbon trail. If, instead of passing through Beirut, goods reach Baghdad via Bassorah or Tehran via Khoramshar, further to paying dues for the right of way through the Suez Canal, they would have to travel an additional 5,000 km to Baghdad and 5,350 km to Tehran. This is about the same as the journey from London to Beirut via Gibraltar or from New York to Gibraltar (5,900 km). The journey would be extended by 12 to 15 days, as well as by some 580 km of railway between Bassorah and Baghdad. Given this, Beirut does seem to have earned some of the flattering designations that are sometimes conferred upon it."

*Road distances:
Beirut-Damascus 150 km, Beirut-Amman 300 km, Beirut-Aleppo 380 km, Beirut-Baghdad 1,000 km, Beirut-Teheran 2,000 km.

Figure 2.8
Two phases of the Beirut port extension: 1887, 1934 *(based on M. Ecochard)*

First phase: 1887-1893
Addition of a 770 m breakwater, a jetty, and 1252 m length of quays. The reclaimed land amounted to 79,000 sq m. Around 20% were allotted for sale.

Second phase: 1934-1938
Addition of a second basin extending the existing breakwater from 770 m to 1200 m, and adding 1790 m of new quays, including 800 m of deepwater quays. Reclaimed land amounted to 167,000 sq m, with 58% allotted for the building of warehousing and a free zone.

Underlying the differences in urban logics between city and port, the port extension was carried out in strict conformity to engineering plans. While the city was constrained by its physical urban fabric, the port had no territorial markers to bypass and could extend over the maritime public domain to reclaim land for infrastructure and allotment. Furthermore, the port extension pertained to a wider regional issue. The French and British mandates were competing for access to the eastern Mediterranean hinterland, the former stressing the Beirut-Damascus-Baghdad axis; the latter, the Haifa-Amman-Baghdad axis. The upgrading of the Haifa port in 1932 gave the impetus to further improve the port of Beirut. A second basin was thus added between 1934 and 1938, and new warehouses and a free zone were built (*fig. 2.8*). This gave Beirut the edge over competing ports, further encouraging transit and trade and creating on-site product transformation industries for re-export purposes. By the second half of the 1930s, Beirut had become a major regional port of the Eastern Mediterranean.

The preponderance of the port over the city was noticed at that time by the geographer Richard Thoumin: "Between 1922 and 1930, business began to grow to hitherto unknown proportions. Agencies of all descriptions mushroomed, particularly commission houses and transport companies. These two types of activities sum up the functioning of Beirut itself..."

Port company offices and warehouses created a clear physical edge, to the east of the central district, between the city and the waterfront. Port-related services, such as import-export agencies, banks and insurance companies moved west, penetrating the adjoining Foch-Allenby to reach up to Etoile. By the late 1930s, the old core had completed its modernization cycle. A composite landscape of medieval and neo-Ottoman souks extended east and west of the formal, Beaux-Arts-style Foch-Allenby and Etoile area. They were bordered to the south by Place des Canons and to the north by the waterfront, two new competing centers of activity marked by a high concentration of key institutional and commercial buildings.

Growth and Centralization, Decentralization and Decay

After Lebanon gained its independence in 1943, the dialectics between port and city continued to follow their course: landward through an increased functional specialization of urban functions; and seaward through additional port expansion.

The port of Beirut flourished as the gateway for transit and re-export trade to Syria, Jordan, Iraq, Iran and the Arabian Peninsula. With the diversion of trade from Haifa to Beirut in 1948 following the creation of the state of Israel, Beirut became the prime port on the Eastern Mediterranean and a highly competitive break-in-transport pole for reaching the Middle Eastern hinterland. Geographer Jean Laugénie emphasized the strategic location of the port of Beirut in 1955 when the port company's concession was coming to an end (*Note 2.3*).

However, Laugénie reiterated the concerns expressed by Stoecklin one century earlier with respect to the port's accessibility to the city: "Towards the city center, the clearings to the port are obstructed by a Waqf (inalienable religious trust) property at the lower end of Martyrs' Square. A modern cinema (the Rivoli) has been built, and behind it lies the wholesale vegetable market, which in fact bars traffic during the day. Nor is there any effective thoroughfare from Martyrs' Square to the rest of the city, since the side clearings east and west provide no convenient roads; indeed, given the layout of the city, the western exit is as good as redundant, making a long detour necessary via the promontory." The opening of Martyrs' Square to the sea and to the regional routes was once more presented as a central issue, the Foch and Allenby streets having been diagnosed as overcrowded arteries (*fig. 2.9*).

The linear development of the buildings occupied by the port company, along with the railway itself, had set up an even stronger built-up edge between the port and the city. In addition, free zone activity encouraged the development of an adjoining wholesale trade area for storing and selling heavy or bulky merchandise (such as steel, wood and sanitary equipment), which was outfitted with auxiliary facilities (such as cafés, bars and accommodations for sailors, port employees and truck drivers). This area further reinforced the visual, functional and spatial barrier between port and city. The increasing pressure of maritime commercial traffic led to the addition of a third basin in 1967, and a fourth was approved before the start of the war in 1975. After 1950, a progressive shift in passenger traffic came as the newly opened Beirut airport created an alternative gateway to the city. However, by the mid-1970s, the successive port extensions had taken over the city's eastern waterfront, stretching out beyond the periphery of the central district towards the river at the eastern confine of municipal Beirut.

Despite the significant expansion in activity during that period, the port was no longer the sole mover of the urban and national economy. From 1943 to 1975, Beirut had developed into the region's financial center, thanks to political stability and a liberal economic system. This growth reinforced specialization in the central business areas. While a number of established banks and insurance companies remained in Foch-Allenby, Riad al Solh Street, at the western edge of the Etoile area, emerged as the prime location for financial headquarters, encouraged by the presence of such facilities as the Post and Telecommunications building. Foch-Allenby, on the other hand, continued to be penetrated by port-related wholesale trade and warehousing activity (*fig. 2.10*).

The growth of Beirut as a whole also resulted in the decentralization of commercial and financial activities, some of which started migrating to the Hamra district in Ras Beirut. In turn, government offices began moving to the periphery of the city, and a new parliament building was planned (and later implemented) outside the city center, facing the National Museum on Damascus Road.

By the mid-1970s, Place de l'Etoile had lost its original formal character and had become a crowded roundabout invaded by cars and pedestrians and the overflow of activities from the neighboring souks.

By contrast to the integrated character of the pre-industrial port city and the flamboyant waterfront profile of the French Mandate period, the waterfront bordering the Beirut city center saw its functional and industrial character emphasized in the post-Independence period. As a result, it started acquiring a negative urban image, especially to the northeast in the direction of the port. Furthermore, the spatial and visual connection from the city to the sea, through the triple axis of Foch, Allenby and Martyrs' Square, remained obstructed by the auxiliary functions of port-related facilities. Meanwhile, the initial function of the waterfront's western section as a hotel and entertainment district, was reinforced.

By 1975, at the outbreak of war, the difficulty of access between the port and the hinterland had severely affected the fate of the interface zone between port and city: commercial port activities had moved further eastward, the bulk of passenger traffic had been diverted to the airport, and many business and administrative activities had relocated towards various peripheral centers.

The hostilities triggered a cycle of destruction that extended over fifteen years. Beirut's central district and port were paralyzed at an early stage of the war and their infrastructure was heavily damaged. The Foch-Allenby and Etoile area and the Riad al Solh Street, which were relatively spared, retained most of their buildings as well as their urban fabric. As a result, those areas became central to the vision that guided the conception of successive wartime and postwar plans, which served as a starting point for the development of the Master Plan governing the ongoing reconstruction by Solidere of the Beirut Central District.

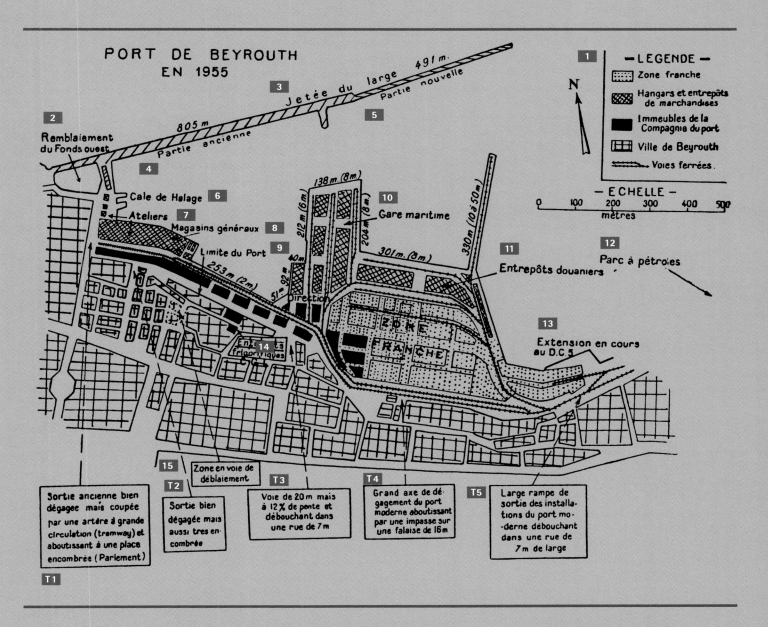

PORT DE BEYROUTH EN 1955

- LEGENDE -
Zone franche
Hangars et entrepôts de marchandises
Immeubles de la Compagnie du port
Ville de Beyrouth
Voies ferrées

- ECHELLE -
0 100 200 300 400 500
métres

Jetée du large 491 m.
Partie nouvelle
Partie ancienne
805 m

Remblaiement du Fonds ouest
Cale de Halage
Ateliers
Magasins généraux
Limite du Port
Direction
138 m. (8 m)
212 m (6 m)
204 m (8 m)
301 m. (8 m)
330 m (10 à 50 m)
Gare maritime
Entrepôts douaniers
Parc à pétroles
Extension en cours au D.C.5
253 m (2 m)
51 m 92 m
40 m
ZONE FRANCHE
Entrepôts frigorifiques

Zone en voie de déblaiement

T1 Sortie ancienne bien dégagée mais coupée par une artère à grande circulation (tramway) et aboutissant à une place encombrée (Parlement)

T2 Sortie bien dégagée mais aussi très encombrée

T3 Voie de 20 m mais à 12% de pente et débouchant dans une rue de 7 m

T4 Grand axe de dégagement du port moderne aboutissant par une impasse sur une falaise de 16 m

T5 Large rampe de sortie des installations du port moderne débouchant dans une rue de 7 m de large

---

Figure 2.9
Beirut port and vicinity: critical assessment of accessibility to and from the port, 1955.

1	Legend	
	Duty-free zone	
	Warehouses and entrepôts	
	Beirut Port Company buildings	
	Beirut city	
	Rail tracks	
2	Western seabed landfill	
3	Offshore jetty — 491 m	
4	Old section	
5	New section	

6	Towing dock
7	Workshops
8	General stores
9	Port boundary
10	Naval station
11	Customs warehouses
12	Oil storage
13	Extension in progress
14	Refrigerated depots
15	Area being cleared

T1 Old exit, unencumbered, but intersected by a main circulation artery (tramway) and leading to a congested square (Parliament)

T2 Exit with good accessibility, but also very crowded

T3 20 m artery, but with 12% slope and ending on a 7 m wide street

T4 Main exit from the new port, leading to a dead-end on a 16 m sea cliff

T5 Wide exit ramp from the modern port facilities, leading to a 7 m wide street

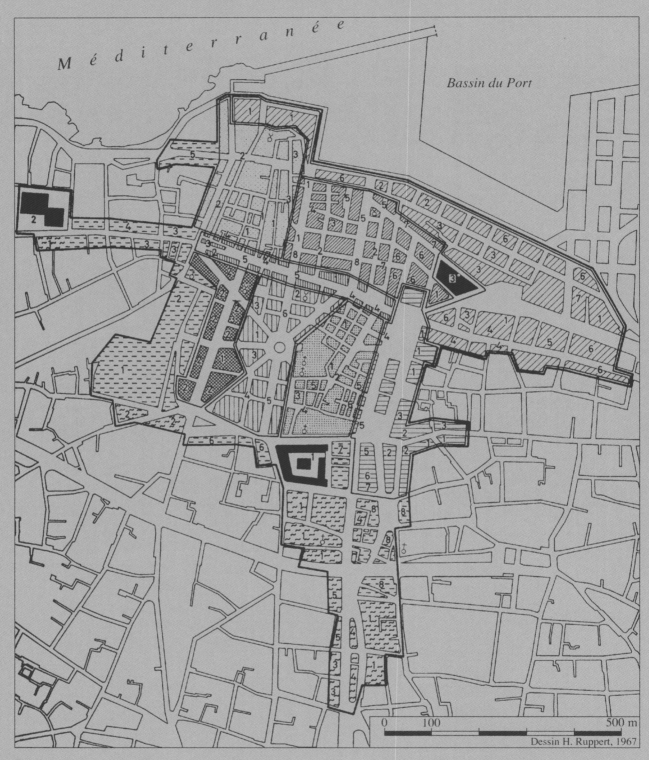

Figure 2.10
Beirut in the late 1960s: commercial
quarters and distribution of main activities.

"OLD SOUK" SURROUNDING SOUK SURSOCK
1 fabrics
2 fruits and vegetables
3 meat
4 fish
5 shoes
6 gold

 UPMARKET SHOPPING AREA SURROUNDING SOUK TAWILA
1 women's apparel
2 upmarket retail
3 fabrics and tailors
4 flowers and bibelots

 WHOLESALE SOUK
1 import-export
2 ladies fabrics
3 household goods
4 carpets
5 food products
6 fruits and vegetables
7 crates and bags manufacturing
8 retail trade

 MODERN WHOLESALE SECTOR
1 lumber
2 marine/sailing hardware
3 iron
4 sanitary ware
5 tools
6 import–export
7 bars, restaurant and money changers (facing the port)

 ETOILE AREA
1 Parliament
2 Great Mosque
3 banks, airlines and travel agencies
4 women's fabrics, clothing and tailors
5 groceries
6 leather and shoes

 WEYGAND STREET, TRADITIONAL COMMERCIAL ARTERY
1 Municipality
2 tailors
3 gold and jewelry
4 money changers
5 various retail outlets

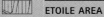 RIAD AL SOLH STREET
1 main Post Office
2 banks, insurance companies
3 Orosdi-Back department store

 ENTERTAINMENT AREA AROUND MARTYRS' SQUARE
1 cheap hotels
2 cinemas
3 night-clubs
4 money changers
5 inexpensive restaurants and cafés
6 wholesale electric ware and appliances
7 roasted chicken outlets

 COMMERCIAL CENTERS
1 Lazariya
2 Starco
3 Byblos

 FORMER EXTENSIONS OF THE CITY CENTER
1 Grand Serail
2 Courts of Justice
3 electric ware and musical instruments shops
4 spirits
5 electric ware and souvenir shops
6 small hotels, cafés
7 food wholesale
8 miscellaneous retail

 RECENT BUSINESS DISTRICT EXPANSION
1 brokers and import-export businesses
2 banks and travel agencies
3 specialist shops; medical, clinics and laboratories
4 electric ware, wholesale and retail
5 car showrooms and spare parts

Satellite picture of Beirut and the
city center, March 2002.

Chapter 3

Evolving Planning Vision

The 1975-1990 Lebanon war seriously compromised the role of Foch-Allenby and Etoile as an interface zone between the port and the city. For a while, the port was held by militias that ransacked the free zone, and illegal ports developed on several points along the coastline. Violence and devastation paralyzed all activity in the city center and even denied access to it. The city itself saw the flight of its inhabitants and of economic activities, and new commercial nodes began springing up in the suburbs. To the north, the visual relation of Foch-Allenby and Etoile to the sea was compromised by a wartime waste-dumping site on the shoreline facing the former Normandy Hotel.

Apart from the effects of war, the growth of the port towards the east, along with its progressive autonomy through containerization and transshipment, shifted the locus of auxiliary port facilities away from the city center. The first basin, built in 1887, lost its original depot function, divesting Foch-Allenby from its traditional role as the commercial port district. Thus, the port-city relationship had to be redefined in full consideration of those functional and physical changes.

This chapter investigates continuity and change in the planning vision, focusing on how the successive master plans of the war and postwar period approached the integration of Foch-Allenby and Etoile with the capital's port and city center.

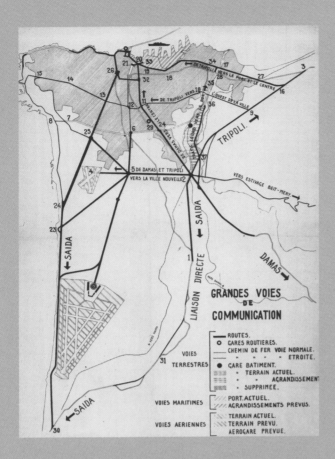

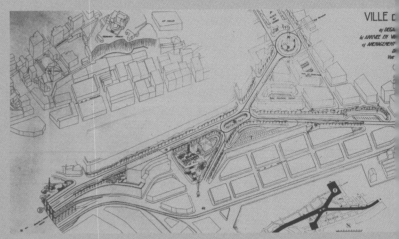

Figure 3.1
Ecochard plan: main circulation
network, 1943.

Figure 3.2
Ecochard proposed scheme for
Martyrs' Square, 1943.

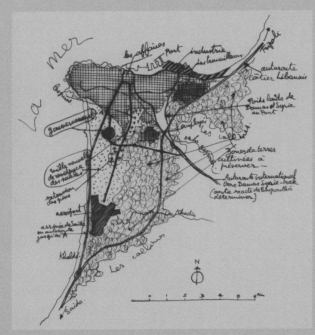

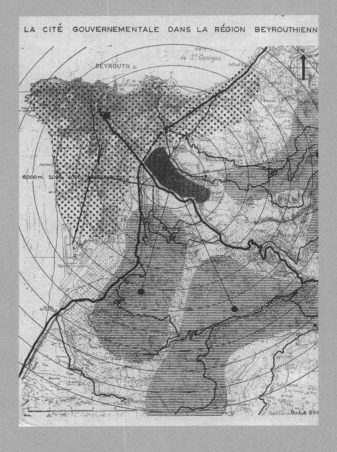

Figure 3.3
Ecochard plan for metropolitan Beirut:
land use strategy, 1963.

Figure 3.4
Doxiadis' Cité Gouvernementale plan, 1959.

Prewar Plans

As far back as 1943 and 1963, Michel Ecochard, the French planning consultant who was twice commissioned to produce a master plan for Beirut, considered the city center as a saturated entity in need of being relieved by a 'healthy' city in the outskirts. Following a functionalist-rational approach, he articulated his master plan around the three 'communication' systems (*fig. 3.1*) of sea, land and air traffic, stressing the primary role of infrastructure in directing greater Beirut's suburban growth, decongesting the center of the capital, and linking seaport and airport to the national highway system. On the level of the city center, the heavy road network clearly segregated between port and city. Martyrs' Square, envisioned by Danger and Delahalle as a formal maritime gateway and a social arena open to the sea, was approached by Ecochard from a functional perspective. Its northern side had to be linked to the port diagonally by a multilevel artery, in an effort to relieve the heart of the city from traffic congestion (*fig. 3.2*). Along the same line of functionalist planning, Ecochard proposed moving government facilities outside the dense commercial center (*fig. 3.3*). In 1959, the same ideas were advanced by the Greek urbanist Doxiadis in his 'La Cité Gouvernementale dans la Région Beyrouthienne' (*fig. 3.4*).

In brief, a functional city was envisioned alongside an industrial port, along Meyer's description of the modern stage of port-city development. Decongestion, decentralization and functional specialization superseded the formal concern for visual and functional permeability between port and city that had led to the inception of Foch-Allenby and Etoile in the 1920s and 1930s.

Wartime Plans

The Beirut Central District Plan of 1977, commissioned by the Beirut Municipality and undertaken by the Atelier Parisien d'Urbanisme (APUR) shortly after the outbreak of war, placed the same emphasis as Ecochard on rationalizing traffic flows and modernizing the infrastructure. The ring road around the BCD was to be reinforced and completed with new links to existing highways and major arteries and the addition of a tunnel connecting to a coastal expressway. This section of the ring road, passing along the northern seafront, clearly outlined the separation between port and city. However, the APUR plan recognized the implications of the port's eastward shift. Accordingly, it extended Foch and Allenby streets over the first port basin through a decked development, the 'Dalle du Port', in order to create a new quarter, with parking underneath and a high-density zone above that would include a shopping plaza. Visual and functional permeability towards the waterfront were thus ensured, at least along the building alignment of Foch and Allenby streets, which constituted the old maritime front. On the other hand, Martyrs' Square would keep its configuration but gain a large underground parking structure; and the Foch-Allenby and Etoile area was to be partly pedestrianized in order to enhance its character and connectivity with the adjoining souks (*fig. 3.5*).

Like the prewar modernist plans, the 1977 master plan relied heavily on the restructuring of the transportation system and espoused the policy of land use specialization, i.e. the decline in residential use in favor of commercial and especially office use. However, the plan brought forward three major changes that were to have a definitive impact on subsequent master plans with regard to the relationship between the port and the city including their interface zone, Foch-Allenby and Etoile:

- The shift in strategy from decentralization to recentralization, with downtown Beirut assuming a central role in the city and the nation.

- The creation of a new international façade along the waterfront, in continuity with Foch-Allenby over the Dalle du Port.

- Recognition of the heritage value of the late Ottoman and French Mandate legacy with emphasis on its rehabilitation, hence on the historical conservation of the Foch-Allenby and Etoile area.

During a truce period in 1983, the contracting firm Oger Liban initiated the first rehabilitation attempt. It conducted an architectural survey of surviving buildings in the Etoile area and began repairing its elevations. However, this process was interrupted by the resurgence of hostilities.

The APUR plan, which was not adopted until 1983, had to be updated to accommodate later war damage incurred by Beirut's central district. The plan was followed in 1986 by the Master Plan for Greater Beirut, prepared by the Institut d'Aménagement et d'Urbanisme de la Région d'Ile de France (IAURIF). In this master plan, the central district was conceived within the wider context of Greater Beirut. A hierarchy of secondary metropolitan sub-centers was created around the central district, which stood as the focal point for wholesale business and trade. The plan aimed at consolidating the position of Beirut as the nation's capital and as a regional and international center, in which government, administrative, commercial, financial, cultural and recreational activities would be located.

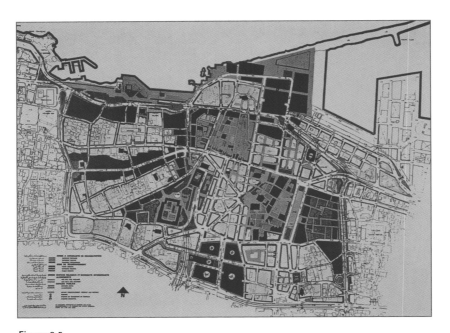

Figure 3.5
APUR wartime plan, 1987.

Figures 3.7, 3.8, 3.9
Rendered views, initial postwar plan.

Figure 3.6
Initial postwar plan, 1992.

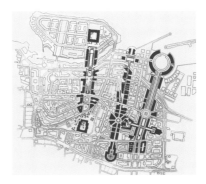

Figure 3.10
Proposed view corridors, initial postwar plan.

Initial Postwar Plan

Following the end of the war in 1990, a Beirut Central District (BCD) reconstruction plan was prepared by Dar Al-Handasah, an international firm based in Beirut. It was amended following an extensive public debate and approved in 1992 (*fig. 3.6*). In line with the APUR infrastructure scheme, the new plan further emphasized the network of urban highways around and through the BCD, and the conservation of Foch-Allenby and Etoile as a historic district. However, as explained below, it modified in a bold and drastic way the sea-land interface zone. The proposed northern through-traffic road, grade-separated below ground level, formed a strong barrier between the historic city core and the waterfront. Foch-Allenby was to be bridged over the expressway to join the new reclaimed land on the seaside. The first basin was to be transformed into a wide circular deck terminating the Martyrs' Square axis. Spatially defined by a megastructure with parking below and high-rise development above (*fig. 3.7*), the new plan looked like an overblown interpretation of the Dalle du Port in the APUR plan. Westward, the landfill was to be reshaped into an island separated by a canal from the St George's Bay. The international façade of the BCD was to extend across the whole waterfront, with a bold imagery of twin towers (*fig. 3.8*). The most distinctive and daring feature of the plan with respect to the integration of the city to the waterfront were the three open-view corridors leading seaward respectively from Martyrs' Square, Allenby Street and the Serail hill (*fig. 3.10*).

In brief, the 1992 plan was a hybrid of three different planning visions: first, the Haussmannian grand design tradition of the turn of the twentieth century underlying the inception of Foch-Allenby and Etoile; second, the modern functionalist tradition of the 1960s with its emphasis on infrastructure and towered development; and third, the romantic neo-regionalist image of a Mediterranean-Levantine city with red tile roofing (*fig. 3.9*). This mixed vision, rendered as a finished product in eye-catching perspectives, seemed overpowering and artificial to city residents and overdesigned and too definitive to professionals.

Although the plan was somewhat amended, by increasing the density to reach the level allowed under prewar regulations and by readjusting the design of the landfill, the heavy road network with its interchanges, overpass and bridges remained overpowering elements.

There were three main features to the plan with regard to the interface zone between the port and the city. The first was the daring design of the Dalle du Port as a strong statement of appropriating a transitional area, the first basin of the port, for tourist and commercial uses, thereby acknowledging the shift of the operating port eastward. The second was the extension of the Martyrs' Square axis to the sea; this brought to resolution a long-term controversy going back to the second half of the nineteenth century, from Stoecklin, to Laugénie, to Duraffourd and Danger. Third, the plan strongly established the identity of Foch-Allenby and Etoile as the new historic core, and an evolving interface zone between the successive extensions of the waterfront northward and the periodic mutation of the inner city southward.

The final BCD Master Plan, developed in consultation with the French firm Sato et Associés and adopted in 1994, addressed critical issues of the 1992 plan. The Master Plan reduced the amount of infrastructure conflicting with the historic urban fabric; maintained the original width of Martyr's Square; enhanced some historic features like the remains of the Ottoman seashore line and jetty; increased the number of preserved buildings from 110 to 300; and stressed the mixed-use approach by raising the ratio of residential to office space. Furthermore, it maximized visual permeability towards the sea and confined high-rise buildings to the edges of the BCD as landmarks and gateways. Without promoting a clear break with the previous plan, the 1994 Master Plan introduced a main shift in the planning and design ideology, inspired by current practices worldwide.

The following chapter discusses how the strategies of integration proposed by the BCD Master Plan have impacted the overall design of the city center and its link to the waterfront, and looks in detail at the Master Plan as currently implemented by Solidere.

The New Waterfront

Note 4.1 The New Waterfront is the best illustration of
the BCD Master Plan approach in transforming
war-related liabilities into assets for the
city of Beirut and its central district. Fronting the
Hotel District, between the St George's bay and
the first basin of the Beirut port, a site near
the former Normandy Hotel used for rubble and
waste dumping during the war had grown into a
major environmental hazard (fig. 4.1). Substantial
clean-up of the site and additional land reclamation, together with a completed sea defense
structure, are preparing for the development
of a 60-hectare extension to the BCD. The New
Waterfront District will accommodate a modern,
mixed-use district, with a 74,000-square-meter
waterside public park. The sea defense system
consists of a submerged reef, followed by a
caisson line supporting a stepped public promenade, which will form an extension to the existing Beirut Corniche (fig. 4.2). In addition to
the Beirut Marina built to the west of the new
waterfront, another marina is planned to the
east, next to the first basin of the port of
Beirut (fig. 4.3-4.4).

Figure 4.1

Figure 4.2

Figure 4.3

Chapter 4

Present Strategies of Integration

The ongoing postwar reconstruction of the Beirut Central District (BCD) brought about new territorial dynamics in the Foch-Allenby and Etoile area. The extension of the waterfront and the physical and functional autonomy of the port altered the relationship of Foch-Allenby and Etoile to its urban context. The area was now conceived as the capital's historic core, and the idea was to anchor the BCD in its recent past, while at the same time turning it into a modern business and financial center.

The recovery of Foch-Allenby and Etoile was implemented by Solidere according to the Master Plan (*fig. 4.4*) for the BCD reconstruction and development (see Chapter 13). The ten BCD sectors defined by the Master Plan included a new waterfront district (sector D), which was to be developed on reclaimed land around the initial landfill facing the Normandy Hotel. With this extension of the BCD, the Foch-Allenby and Etoile area was further distanced from the sea to the north (*Note 4.1*). Landward, the functional and spatial relationship of Foch-Allenby and Etoile to some of its surroundings was redefined, taking into account the fact that several adjoining areas — especially to the east and southeast — had been destroyed or severely damaged as a result of the war. At the same time, the area's relationship with the underlying urban strata was emphasized through the highly significant archeological zone at its eastern edge, bordering Martyrs' Square.

The Master Plan thus addressed two concerns vis-à-vis the Foch-Allenby and Etoile area: on one hand, it ensured the area's horizontal integration to the city center as a whole; on the other hand, it stressed and capitalized on its vertical integration to the subterranean urban past. A review of the strategies adopted in that regard, at both the district and sector levels, will help to offer insights into those modalities of integration and show how Foch-Allenby and Etoile and the city center mutually shaped each other's spatial structure.

Figure 4.4
The BCD Master Plan including
proposed modifications to Sectors A
and D (see page 188).

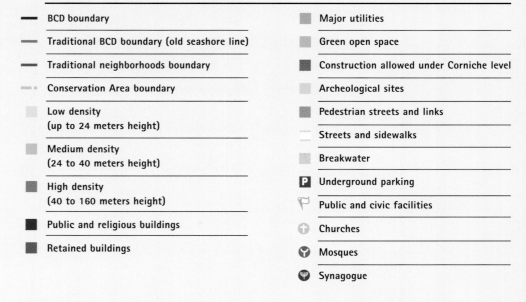

▬ BCD boundary	▮ Major utilities
▬ Traditional BCD boundary (old seashore line)	▮ Green open space
▬ Traditional neighborhoods boundary	▮ Construction allowed under Corniche level
▬ Conservation Area boundary	▮ Archeological sites
▮ Low density (up to 24 meters height)	▮ Pedestrian streets and links
▮ Medium density (24 to 40 meters height)	▬ Streets and sidewalks
▮ High density (40 to 160 meters height)	▮ Breakwater
▮ Public and religious buildings	🅿 Underground parking
▮ Retained buildings	⚑ Public and civic facilities
	✝ Churches
	☾ Mosques
	✡ Synagogue

Figure 4.5
BCD pedestrian network and open spaces,
visual corridors and urban markers.

— BCD boundary

— Traditional BCD boundary (old seashore line)

∙∙∙∙∙ Pedestrian streets and links

▨ Archeological sites

▨ Green open spaces

■ High density (40 to 160 meters height)

▨ View corridor

Horizontal Integration

Foch-Allenby and Etoile and the nearby Riad al Solh Street were the areas least impacted by the war. Forming a cohesive whole, they exhibited a distinct urban character as the financial, governmental and religious nucleus of the BCD. Together with the westward Serail hill, they were designated as the Conservation Area. They also constituted the anchor around which were articulated the remaining sectors of the BCD and its network of streets and open spaces. The new urban structure devised by the Master Plan, and originating from the Conservation Area, revolved around the creation of a visual, physical and functional permeability between the historic core, the city center and the waterfront. This was achieved through complementary design strategies.

Extending visual corridors

All BCD sectors were initially articulated around four visual corridors, which emanated from the Conservation Area and integrated old and new street patterns (*fig. 4.5*):

- The Serail corridor (sector C) opens up the view from the Serail hill to the waterside park through a red-tiled pitched roofscape subject to strict building height controls, thus enhancing both the natural and historic contexts.

- The Martyrs' Square axis (sector H) extends visually from the ring road, which delimits the southern edge of the BCD, through the square towards the sea. Considered as the most important formal open space of the BCD, its urban design is to be the subject of an international competition that aims at highlighting its new spatial identity and establishing land use guidelines.

- The Maarad-Allenby and Foch axes, complementing the Serail corridor and Martyrs' Square axis, extend north to the waterfront, linking the historic core to the new waterfront district through uninterrupted sea views. Here, planning emphasis was placed on visual continuity, with a set of streetwall controls guaranteeing a cohesive public frontage. The existing street alignment was retained in the Conservation Area, and the reclaimed land was planned following a grid pattern with the same concern for a cohesive frontage that defines street character and scale.

- A fifth axis/visual corridor was introduced in a 2001 amendment to the BCD Master Plan. It linked the Hotel District (sector B) to the Beirut Marina.

- Of equal importance are the four view corridors toward the east, which celebrate the visual axes from the city center toward the mountains. Those on the New Waterfront District, on the alignment of the Ottoman Wall, focus on the norhern peak of Mount Sannine, across St George's Bay. Those along Zeitouneh Avenue and across the Etoile area provide general views toward Beirut's mountain backdrop.

This theme of 'grand axes', manifested in a dramatic and formal way during the French Mandate period through the creation of the Foch and Maarad-Allenby avenues, constitutes an integrating feature of the new Beirut Central District, from its southernmost extremity to its new northernmost waterfront. Accordingly, the same street alignment and perimeter block development has been kept between the existing and extended sections of Foch and Allenby.

Differentiating development densities and creating urban markers

In addressing density distribution, the Master Plan took into consideration the natural landform and unique attributes of the BCD site. High structures were to be positioned away from the visual corridor linking the Serail ridge to sea and mountain views. They were distributed as urban markers framing the new extensions of Foch and Allenby and the main gates to the BCD. A complementary measure was to differentiate development densities in relation to the particular character of each sector. Low densities were reserved for residential neighborhoods and medium densities suggested for the Conservation Area and its vicinity.

Building a non-intrusive circulation network

In addition to the linear open spaces that enhanced visual permeability, the Master Plan devised an efficient circulation network to ensure fluidity of movement and easy accessibility at sector and district levels. In order to avoid the disruptive impact of a bold and extensive road network on the city fabric, features like grade-separated interchanges, overpasses and bridges were avoided in favor of landscaped avenues. A flexible grid in newly developed areas aimed at minimizing any barrier effect between major BCD sectors. The road network consisted of the ring road, which defined the city center and its western, southern and eastern edges; an internal network of at-grade streets, with primary roads looping around the Conservation Area; and a network of pedestrian streets linking squares, parks and activity nodes (*fig. 4.5*).

In Foch-Allenby and Etoile, the segregation between pedestrian and vehicular movement followed the prewar physical fabric of the area. Weygand Street became the only through traffic artery crossing the area from east to west, separating it into two sub-areas: Foch-Allenby to the north and Etoile-Maarad to the south. Foch and Allenby, treated as major north-south axes, were extended to cut through the waterfront district and lead to the new corniche. The remaining network was given a distinct pedestrian priority, with access limited to service and emergency vehicles.

Promoting functional complementarity

Foch-Allenby and Etoile played an important role in shaping the physical and spatial structure of the BCD. In reverse, the planned land distribution in the area was shaped by that of the central district as a whole, and by the new waterfront configuration. Now distanced from sea and port, the Foch-Allenby and Etoile area was assigned an alternative function destined to complement the range of land uses in surrounding sectors and to address current market trends. The high prevalence of key government and religious buildings in the BCD established a strong communal and national identity. The public domain, utilities and buildings had to be renovated to accommodate state-of-the-art office and retail requirements.

Vertical Integration

The Foch-Allenby and Etoile area included the most important landmark buildings and distinctive streetscapes in the city center. Its rich historic strata and unearthed finds gave it added dimension as an archeological site of prime significance. Within this culturally and historically rich urban setting, the task of reconstituting and rehabilitating the public domain was evidently complex; one had to be at once responsive to the exigencies and pressures of contemporary life and faithful to the district's historic character and unique sense of place.

The dialectical relationship between heritage and the features of a modern townscape raised two major challenging design concerns:
- How to integrate archeology into the emerging functional and symbolic structure of the city (*fig. 4.6*).
- How to respond to parking requirements without compromising the urban fabric of the historic core (*fig. 4.7a*).

Before the war, archeological excavations had already revealed the existence of important Hellenistic and Roman remains in the Etoile area, as well as an acropolis of the Canaanite and Phoenician periods northeast of Foch Street. Extensive postwar excavations confirmed that Persian, Hellenistic and Roman urban grids had left their imprints on the city layout of the Ottoman, French Mandate and Independence periods (*fig. 4.7b*).

Archeological evidence for instance revealed that Souk al Tawila, which once ran parallel to Allenby Street, followed the north-south orientation of an urban grid originating from the Phoenico-Persian period. Other recent discoveries of major importance led to the decision to integrate into the urban landscape four main archeological sites, all confined to the immediate periphery of the Conservation Area and associated with the main periods of the city's evolution. These are: the ancient Tell, the Cardo Maximus, the Roman Baths and the Souks/ancient harbor site. With the conservation of representative vestiges in situ, the four sites will become archeological theme parks, forming with Foch-Allenby an integrated itinerary covering 5,000 years of history (*fig. 4.7c*). As planned, a heritage trail designed to provide a rich pedestrian experience will link the four sites together and lead to other historical sites or landmarks in the Conservation Area: the old (prewar) seashore walk, the Ottoman wall, the pedestrian Maarad arcade, the Etoile area, the Foch-Allenby area, and the site for the proposed Beirut museum.

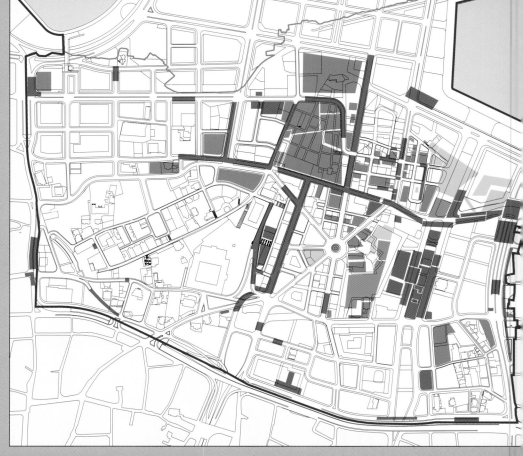

Figure 4.6
BCD postwar archeological
excavation sites.

	Sites excavated for infrastructure construction
	Sites with no direct interference with development
	Sites interfering with public development
	Sites interfering with private development
	Sites with archeological potential

Postwar Archeological Excavations

Note 4.2 Between 1993 and 2000, archeological excavations in 138 different locations in the BCD unraveled the various stages of Beirut's historic growth since the Bronze and Iron Ages.

The ancient Tell of Beirut, located north of Martyrs' Square at the edge of the Conservation Area, constituted the fortified center of the city during the Canaanite, Phoenician, Persian and Hellenistic periods. Starting in the sixth century B.C., urban growth took place outside the fortified center (Acropolis), extending as far west as the modern Hotel District and as far south as today's Amir Bachir Street.

During the Roman period under Augustus, Beirut acquired the status of a Roman colony (Colonia Julia Augusta Felix Berytus) and its center moved from the ancient Tell to the location currently known as the Etoile area. The site of the Roman Forum and related public buildings was delimited by prewar archeological work and confirmed by recent excavations.

Byzantine Beirut followed the Roman urban topography, as indicated by remains of residential and commercial quarters. However, the celebrated law school founded in the early third century A.D. has not yet been unequivocally located in the Etoile area.

From the period of Crusader and Mamluk Beirut, a ditch of medieval fortification walls was found parallel to Patriarch Hoyek Street, as well as watch towers, the Bourj, southeast of Martyrs' Square. The ancient Tell revealed part of a Crusader castle.

From the Ottoman period, excavations unearthed a series of harbor walls to the north of the Souks, between Khan Antoun Bey and the Majidiya Mosque.

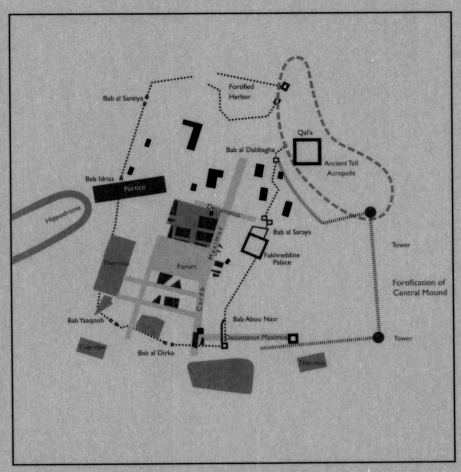

Figure 4.7b
Archeological strata.

⅏⅏⅏⅏⅏	Hellenistic city wall
– – –	Canaanite period
■	Extension of urban area, circa 600–100 B.C (Persian Hellenistic remains)
▨	Roman grid
▩	Known Roman remains
▦	Possible site of ancient building
···▫	Medieval city wall and gates

Labels within the figure:

Bab al Santiya
Fortified Harbor
Qal'a
Ancient Tell
Acropolis
Bab al Dabbagha
Bab Idriss
Portico
Decumanus
Hippodrome
Cardo Maximus
Bab al Saraya
Tower
Fakhreddine Palace
Thermae
Forum
Fortification of Central Mound
Bab Yaaqoub
Bab Abou Nasr
Decumanus Maximus
Tower
Thermae
Bab al Dirka
Thermae

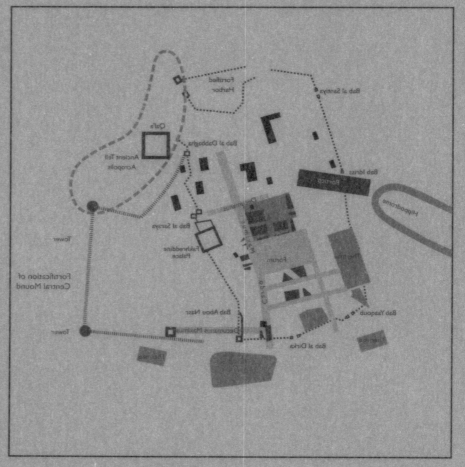

Figure 4.7b
Archeological strata.

⬚⬚⬚⬚	Hellenistic city wall
– ▪ – ▪	Canaanite period
◼	Extension of urban area, circa 600–100 B.C. (Persian Hellenistic remains)
▦	Roman grid
◼	Known Roman remains
◼	Possible site of ancient building
▫··	Medieval city wall and gates

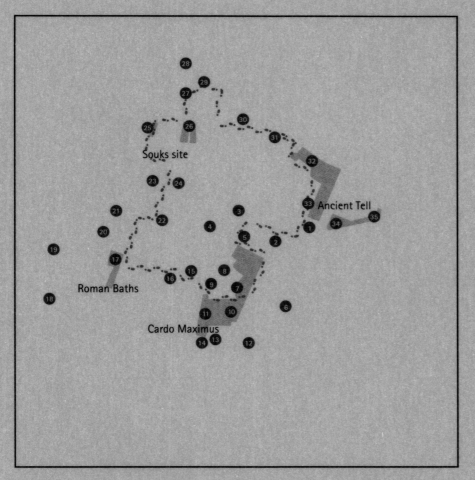

Figure 4.7c
Heritage trail with main heritage sites.

▓	**Archeological sites**
⋯	**Heritage trail**

① **Proposed Beirut Museum**

② **Site of Fakhreddine's palace**

③ **Municipality**

④ **Al Omari Mosque/Crusader Church of St. John**

⑤ **Amir Assaf Mosque**

⑥ **Martyrs' monument**

⑦ **Nouriya shrine**

⑧ **St Elie Greek-Catholic Church**

⑨ **St George Greek-Orthodox Cathedral built over Byzantine Church**

⑩ **Garden of Forgiveness**

⑪ **Cardo Maximus**

⑫ **Decumanus Maximus**

⑬ **St George Maronite Cathedral**

⑭ **Roman columns/"Steps of the 40 Martyrs"**

⑮ **Etoile Square**

⑯ **Site of Roman Forum**

⑰ **Roman Baths**

⑱ **Ottoman Serail**

⑲ **Viewpoint**

⑳ **Ottoman Military Hospital**

㉑ **St Louis Capuchin Church**

㉒ **Amir Munzer Mosque**

㉓ **Site of Byzantine shops and mosaics**

㉔ **Ibn Iraq Mamluk shrine**

㉕ **City wall and archeology garden**

㉖ **Phoenico-Persian settlement**

㉗ **Majidiya Mosque**

㉘ **Khan Antoun Bey Square**

㉙ **Ottoman quayside**

㉚ **Site of ancient harbor**

㉛ **Abou Bakr (al Dabbagha) Mosque**

㉜ **Crusader fort and belvedere**

㉝ **Canaanite city wall**

㉞ **Phoenician city wall**

㉟ **Hellenistic tower**

■ Archeological sites

⸳⸳⸳ Heritage trail

① Proposed Beirut Museum
② Site of Fakhreddine's palace
③ Municipality
④ Al Omari Mosque/Crusader Church of St. John
⑤ Amir Assaf Mosque
⑥ Martyrs' monument
⑦ Nouriya shrine
⑧ St Elie Greek-Catholic Church
⑨ St George Greek-Orthodox Cathedral built over Byzantine Church
⑩ Garden of Forgiveness
⑪ Cardo Maximus
⑫ Decumanus Maximus
⑬ St George Maronite Cathedral
⑭ Roman columns/"Steps of the 40 Martyrs"
⑮ Etoile Square
⑯ Site of Roman Forum
⑰ Roman Baths
⑱ Ottoman Serail
⑲ Viewpoint
⑳ Ottoman Military Hospital
㉑ St Louis Capuchin Church
㉒ Amir Munzer Mosque
㉓ Site of Byzantine shops and mosaics
㉔ Ibn Iraq Mamluk shrine
㉕ City wall and archeology garden
㉖ Phoenico-Persian settlement
㉙ Ottoman quayside
㉚ Site of ancient harbor
㉛ Abou Bakr (al Dabbagha) Mosque
㉜ Crusader fort and belvedere
㉝ Canaanite city wall
㉞ Phoenician city wall
㉟ Hellenistic tower

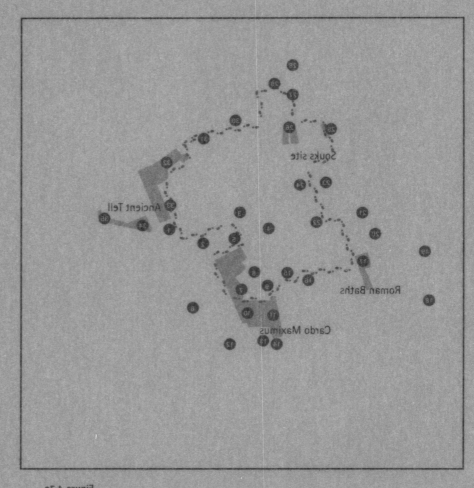

Figure 4.2c
Heritage trail with
main heritage sites.

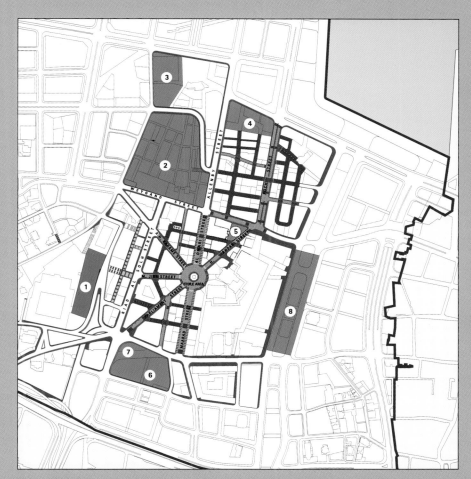

Figure 4.7a
Circulation and parking plan.

— **BCD boundary**

▪ **Sidewalks (granite)**

▫ **Paved vehicular traffic (new basalt)**

▪ **Paved pedestrian street (old basalt)**

▦ **Granite strip**

▪ **Underground parking**

① Serail hill (1200 spaces)

② ③ Souks of Beirut (2500 spaces)

④ Block 93

⑤ Municipality (108 spaces)

⑥ Block 133 (1200 spaces)

⑦ Riad al Solh Square (1200 spaces)

⑧ Martyrs' Square (2500 spaces)

Figures 4.8a to 4.8d
Conceptual drawings of archeological strata;
historic fabric; boundaries; character precints.

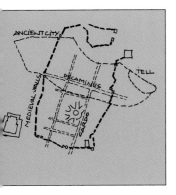

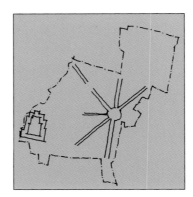
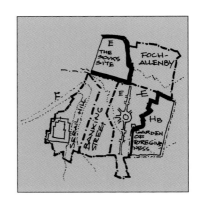

The concept of an archeological trail as a public space feature is an innovation in Beirut. Whereas monumental finds are usually displayed in prime city locations and neighborhood parks outside their original context, the practice adopted in Foch-Allenby and Etoile favored a more contextual approach, while providing at the same time a new form of recreational cultural space (*Note 4.3*).

Among other main concerns addressed by the Master Plan in the Conservation Area was the provision of an adequate infrastructure and parking space (*fig. 4.7a*) with minimal disruption to the historic fabric or damage to the archeological riches. In the absence of multilevel basements beneath retained buildings, the parking requirements of the Conservation Area were mainly accommodated on its immediate periphery. Strategically located, the new Souks of Beirut were equipped with an underground car park providing space for 2,500 vehicles. Three other underground parking structures were planned under Martyrs' Square to the east, the Serail hill to the west and Riad al Solh Square to the south. The only public parking structure within the Conservation Area is located underneath the small square facing the Municipality building.

Defining the Conservation Area

Vertical and horizontal integration strategies helped define the boundaries of the Conservation Area, while emphasizing its character precincts and integrating it within its immediate and wider city context (*fig. 4.8-4.12*). The underlying archeological layers and the preserved historic fabric indicate that the Conservation Area is defined by the boundaries of the fortified medieval town and the adjoining hill, site of the Ottoman Grand Serail. From within, it may be subdivided into four character precincts, each constituting a unique sense of place:

- The Serail hill housing the Grand Serail or Prime Minister's offices and the Council for Development and Reconstruction occupies the highest point in Beirut's central district and presents a coherent architectural character pertaining to the late Ottoman period.

- Riad al Solh, considered as the prewar financial hub of the region, is a linear space strongly defined by early modern buildings displaying their formal identity as headquarters for financial institutions.

- The Etoile area is strongly identified as the political and religious focus of the city center, owing to the presence of the Lebanese Parliament, the clock tower and a number of key religious buildings.

- The Foch-Allenby area, with its eclectic stone elevations, constitutes the first office building sector in Beirut, dating back to the 1920s and 1930s.

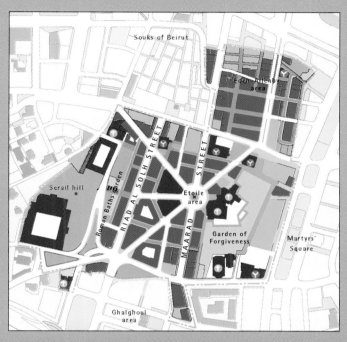

Figure 4.9
Conservation Area and its vicinity.

	Conservation Area boundary
	Private development lots
	Public and religious buildings
	Retained buildings
	Green open space
	Archeological sites
	Pedestrian streets and links

Note 4.3

Roman Baths Garden
At the base of the Serail hill, the Roman baths site has been restored and landscaped with a terraced garden surrounded by an open area for cultural activities (fig. 4.12).

Souks of Beirut
West of the Foch-Allenby area, the late Ottoman souk district is being redeveloped as a mixed-use contemporary shopping and leisure area. The design recreates the historic open space pattern. Preserved heritage buildings, such as the Majidiya Mosque, are being restored and will be integrated into the new fabric of the area. The famed Khan Antoun Bey will be reconstructed with a modern interpretation and will serve as a department store. Archeological finds, such as the Phoenico-Persian site and recently recovered sections of the medieval city wall, will be preserved and enhanced through landscaping (fig. 4.11).

Hadiqat as Samah (Garden of Forgiveness)
Located between Maarad Street and the Martyrs' Square axis, this archeological park, the object of an international design competition, will be land-scaped around such major features as the Cardo Maximus and the venerated Sayidat al Nouriya (Our Lady of the Light) shrine. Delineated by a number of mosques and churches, this open area will also assume the role of a multi-confessional space (fig. 4.10).

Figure 4.10
Eastern edge of Etoile area:
Garden of Forgiveness.

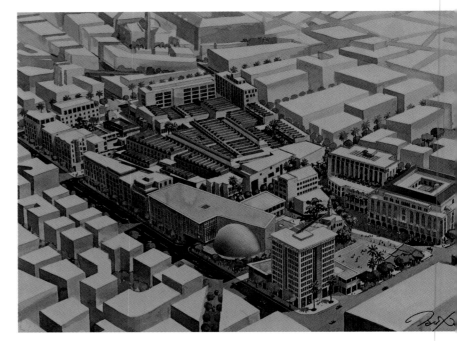

Figure 4.11
Western edge of Foch-Allenby area:
Souks of Beirut.

Figure 4.12
Western edge of Etoile and Riad al Solh
Street area: Roman Baths Garden.

Conclusion: Recapturing a Lost Centrality

The strategies of integration suggested in the BCD Master Plan being implemented by Solidere highlight the complementary natures of Foch-Allenby and Etoile as an interface zone between port and city and as a link between past and future. As such, they reflect Beirut's attempt at integrating its new waterfront and recovering its historic core in its thrust to energize its city center.

At the heart of this quest is Beirut's concern for recapturing a lost centrality. This issue is of particular relevance after the paralysis of the Lebanon war years. Also, in parallel to other cities around the world which were not marked by the exceptional circumstances of a long war, Beirut witnessed business migration towards other metropolitan areas because of more competitive land prices and easier accessibility.

A strategy often adopted in similar cases for reversing this trend, especially in port cities, has been to promote the 'cultural' role of their central districts, by creating an environment conducive to cultural, tourist, recreational and shopping activities targeting the metropolitan elite and middle class. Renewal projects have emphasized the quality of the public domain, with the aim of creating an enhanced 'urban experience' for old port sites and inner district streets, squares and frontages. Such projects have taken a special interest in upgrading the cultural identity of place in an attempt to bring forward the unique character of the city. This strategy was central to the Solidere approach for the conservation and revitalization of Foch-Allenby and Etoile.

The urban renewal movement, qualified by Meyer as "culturalized urbanism", is a free-market approach driven primarily by business concerns. The success of Foch-Allenby and Etoile in revitalizing Beirut is proof of the efficiency of the market-oriented approach to inner-city renewal. While it has been feared by some to favor exclusive businesses and clientele by promoting the corporate image of the BCD, this approach has in fact restored people's confidence and sense of pride about their city center.

At the same time, the renewal of Foch-Allenby and Etoile has set an example of quality conservation and rehabilitation at a regional scale. By actively supporting archeological excavations, the reconstruction project has helped uncover important layers of Beirut's history; it has preserved and displayed the finds within the recovered fabric and has thereby enriched the city center's cultural environment.

The BCD Master Plan and its phasing have transformed Foch-Allenby and Etoile into a catalyst of the city's development and a symbol of its historic identity, as opposed to its prewar role as a predominantly port-related business district. Having been traditionally the seaward gateway of the city, this area has now become the landward gateway to the city center.

Consequently, having been shaped since the 1920s from outside in, as the connection of the port to its hinterland and the city to its waterfront, Foch-Allenby and Etoile is today shaping, from inside out, a new waterfront and city center for Beirut.

This section traces the shaping of Foch-Allenby and Etoile as an interface zone from the mid-nineteenth century to the mid-1970s. Its purpose is to provide the historical background of this area from both the urban and architectural points of view. Chapter 5 provides a descriptive overview of the historical evolution of Foch-Allenby and Etoile into a gateway district, including key dates, photographs and maps, along with a condensed analysis of the parallel development of the Beirut port and city center. Chapter 6 traces the evolution of office buildings from the converted residential type of the pre-1920s, to the transitional type of the French Mandate period and the early modern type of the 1930s and 1940s. The chapter examines the impact of the new parceling on the plan morphology of individual buildings and analyzes the dialectic relationship between the functional and structural order of inner spaces and the visual order of elevations and streetwalls. It also highlights the diversity of styles that constitutes the hallmark of the Conservation Area. Chapter 7 describes the progression of frontage that accompanied the evolution of office buildings in Foch-Allenby and Etoile.

Duraffourd Plan 1928, courtesy Mr. Adib Fares.

VILLE DE BEYROUTH
PLAN GENERAL

Plan établi en 1931 par la Régie des Travaux du cadastre et d'amélioration foncière des États de Syrie, du Liban et des Alaouites à l'aide des plans cadastraux dressés en 1928-1930.

LÉGENDE:
Bâtiments privés
publics
Cotes d'altitude
Courbes de niveau
Murs de soutènement

Left band
Figures 5.1–5.4
Street views of the old town.

Above, top to bottom
Figure 5.5
The waterfront in 1837, by Bartlett.

Figure 5.6
The port in the early nineteenth century.

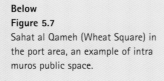

Below
Figure 5.7
Sahat al Qameh (Wheat Square) in
the port area, an example of intra
muros public space.

Chapter 5

Emergence and Rise of a Gateway District

chapter prepared in collaboration with May Davie

The rise of Beirut as a major commercial port goes back to the nineteenth century, when steamship navigation transferred economic activity from inland caravan cities to coastal cities. During the first decades of the nineteenth century, Ottoman Beirut was a secondary trading port, a silk export outlet for Mount Lebanon, and a staging post conveniently located along the coastal Levant axis. The political and economic importance of the city was enhanced under the Egyptian occupation, which started in 1832.

The period between 1840 and 1864 constituted the turning point of Beirut's modern history. The city became the capital of the Wilaya (province) of Sidon. The establishment of the French-controlled Ottoman Bank and the building of the wharf, together with low import duties, attracted foreign entrepreneurs, investors and trading firms. In their wake came a number of consular representatives — French, English, Austrian, Greek, Italian, Belgian, Dutch, Spanish, Swedish, Norwegian and Egyptian — as well as missionary schools. Finally, the construction of the Beirut-Damascus cross-mountain road opened Beirut to the hinterland and made it the principal entrepôt of the region.

The waterfront and the port area

In the 1830s, the waterfront was cleaned and enlarged and the quay and jetty were rebuilt. The western edge of the bay was raised to accommodate the harbormaster, health offices and a new landing wharf for passengers. The imposing caravanserai, Khan al Milaha, together with the customs, the warehouses and a hotel, lined up the southern quay.

The present Foch-Allenby sector corresponds to the lower town in old Beirut, which started at Sahat al Rasif (Slipway Square) in the harbor. This port area functioned as a link to the upper town and to regional trade routes. Merchandise moved from the port to the caravan station at Bab al Dabbagha (Tannery Gate). Khans, warehouses, hostels and coffeehouses, as well as wider streets, differentiated it from the upper town. The area grouped harbor-related activities and catered to bankers, money changers and affluent merchant families who controlled the trade with other Mediterranean ports; according to travelers' accounts, they lived in large stone houses close to the souks and the harbor. Souk al Fashkha, today's Weygand Street, separated upper and lower town. It acted as the main collector for north-south alleyways, and connected Bab al Saraya east, to Souk al Tawila west.

The inner city

The present Etoile sector corresponds to the upper town, which extended to the southern city walls. It grouped local markets and crafts, as well as the city's main administrative and communal activities.

Characterized by narrow and winding alleyways, the upper town was marked by a set of sahat (squares). Some of these squares were equipped with fountains, or bordered with cafés. Some led to such communal facilities as hammams (public baths), bakeries or mills. Others were located around religious buildings, like Sahat al Nouriya and Sahat al Nuffayra, or next to city gates. Sahat al Saraya at the eastern gate between the Serail and al Omari Mosque, was the town's administrative center and its main public square. Finally, some squares stood at the junctions of souks. Among these, Sahat al Khobz was the center of the bazaar. It displayed retail and local produce, including perfumes, musical instruments, clothes, confectionery and food.

Figure 5.8
British Army map, 1841.

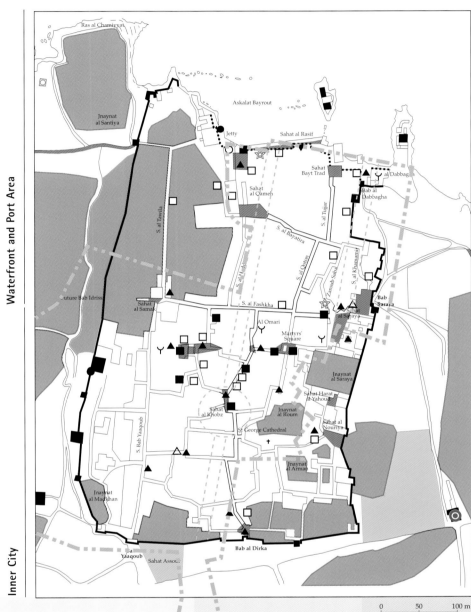

Waterfront and Port Area

Inner City

Figure 5.9
As the 1841 British Army
map is based on different
surveying techniques
from today's cadastral maps,
the Conservation Area
outline is correct within a
few meters difference.

PUBLIC FACILITIES

▲ Fountain

△ Hammam

■ Coffeehouses

□ Khan

▼ Customs

● Harbormaster

○ Sanitary department

☆ Hotel

•••••• Warehouse alignment

▬ ▬ ▬ Conservation Area boundaries

– – – – Foch-Allenby and Etoile area
approximate alignment

OPEN SPACES

▨ Gardens

▨ Existing public space

▨ Emerging public space

═ Main streets

LANDMARKS

◎ Sahat al Bourj tower

■ Tower

⌃⌄ City walls

Υ Mosque

✝ Church

Inner City

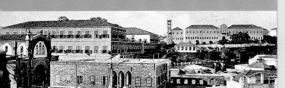

Left band
Top to bottom
Some of the infrastructure and public space improvements introduced during the late Ottoman period.

Figure 5.10
Ottoman infantry barracks (later the Grand Serail), clock tower and military hospital (today's Council for Development and Reconstruction) built on top of the Serail hill.

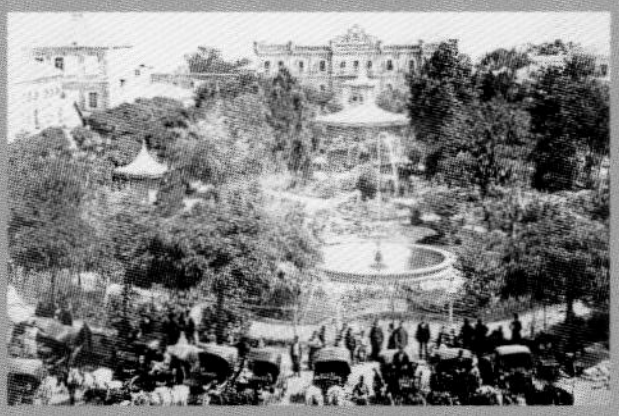

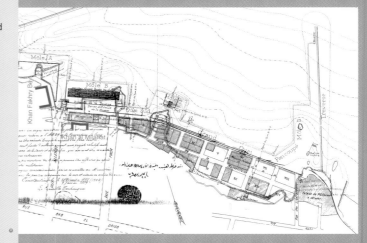

Figure 5.11
Bourj Square.

BEYROUTH

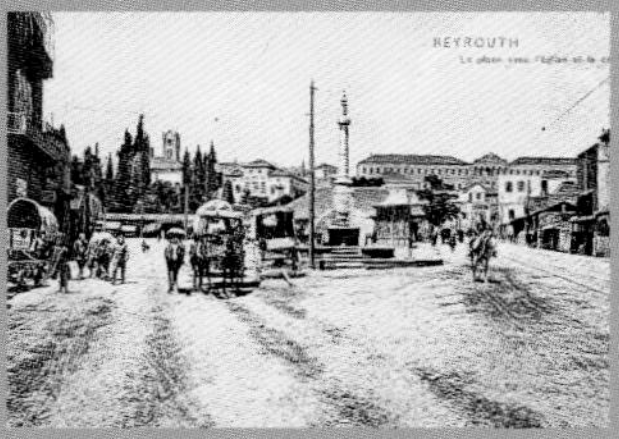

Figure 5.12
Al Sour Square.

Figure 5.13
The tramway.

Beyrouth.
Rue ancienne.

Figure 5.14
Shari' al Jadid.

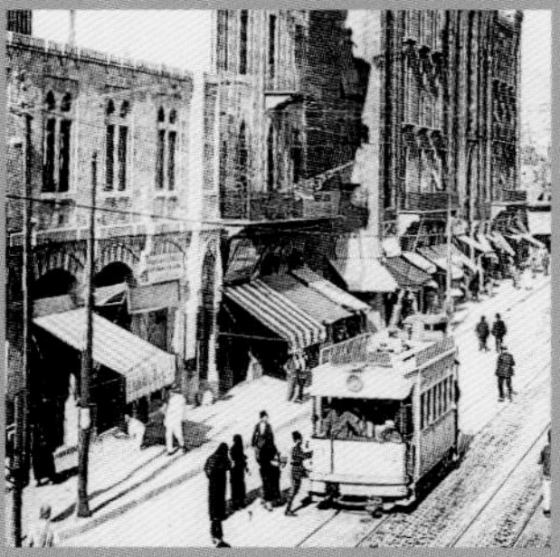

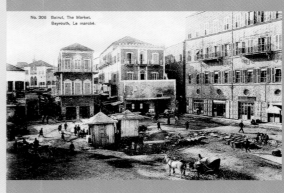

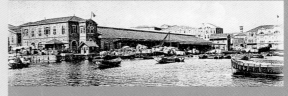

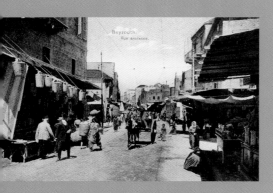

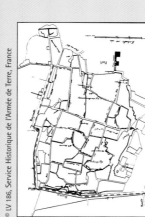

© LV 186, Service Historique de l'Armée de Terre, France

Above
Figure 5.15
1861 map depicting (in red) the proposed western connection of Damascus road with the harbor.

Waterfront

Below
Figure 5.16
The port extension plan dated December 28, 1888 with the location of Foch and Allenby streets (red dotted line); the existing water line (red continuous line); and the footprints of key buildings, such as Khan Antoun Bey, Khan Fakhry Bey and Khan al Milaha (thick red line).

Môle A
Môle B
Khan Fakhry Bey
Khan al Milaha

No. 306 Beirut, The Market.
Beyrouth, Le marché.

Above, top and bottom
Figure 5.17
Views of the new waterfront from a 1905 postcard showing the planned intersection of Allenby street with the port. The two buildings in the center were to be demolished, allowing Allenby street to run along Khan Fakhry Bey.

Figure 5.18
The landing stage and customs warehouses.

In 1888, the Beirut Wilaya became a distinct administrative entity extending approximately from Acre south to Latakia north. Its population rose to 120,000 at the turn of the century. Residential and commercial, as well as administrative activities, expanded towards the city's outskirts, prefiguring the perimeter of current municipal Beirut. An ambitious Ottoman reform program involved regularizing the old town's urban fabric, introducing a modern transportation network and improving public space. Meanwhile, modern souks were built intra muros by prominent merchant families such as the Sursocks. This first phase of early modernization, set in motion by the Ottomans, paved the way for the French Mandate urban initiatives of the 1920s and 1930s. With the growing economic importance of the city, it became vital to build the Beirut-Damascus road in order to open the port to the hinterland. Previously, a caravan track crossing Sahat al Bourj had connected with the port on its east side at Bab al Dabbagha. In 1863, the newly built Beirut-Damascus road shifted access to the west side, bypassing the old town with its narrow alleys and gates. The center of gravity of the port consequently moved from east to west, initiating urban development at the western edge of the old town.

In contrast with the works undertaken to enlarge and modernize the port, the old town was increasingly perceived as a barrier to the flow of people and goods. Hence the idea emerged of cutting through the urban fabric to connect harbor to periphery, using straight arteries to improve linkage to the regional trade routes. In 1878, the Municipality voted a project for modernizing the infrastructure. Its objective was to conform to western principles of hygiene and civic design, as applied by the Sublime Porte in Istanbul and in key provincial capitals. For the first time, modern urbanism was introduced in Beirut. Two perpendicular axes were planned across the old town, respectively linking the port to the Damascus and Sidon roads. The former, the north-south axis (later Allenby Street), started at the port and followed Souk al Haddadin to end at Bab al Dirka. The latter, the east-west axis (later Weygand Street), linked Bab al Saraya to Bab Idriss. Another planned north-south axis (later Foch Street) was to follow Souk al Tujjar and link the port to Hamidiya Square (Sahat al Bourj, today's Martyrs' Square) through Souk al Fashkha (today's Weygand Street). Other provisions involved aligning Souk al Tawila with Souk Bab Yaaqoub (today's Riad al Solh Street); opening a public garden on Hamidiya Square; and extending the north-south (Allenby) artery to the pine forest in the southern outskirts of the city, where a casino was planned.

In 1900, the east-west axis was built. First known as Shari' al Jadid (New Street), it was later renamed Bab Idriss, then Weygand Street. Waqf opposition and lack of funding delayed the other projects until 1915, when the Wali (governor) Bakr Sami Bey obtained the authorization to proceed. Demolition of the old souks began in April of that year, and the new Wali, Azmi Bey, named a commission to settle expropriation payments. Organized by Jamal Pasha, the newly appointed military governor, the operation was funded with donations sent to war victims by local emigrants to the United States. In 1915 and 1916, the two north-south arteries were opened. They remained unfinished until the occupation of the city by the Allied troops in October 1918.

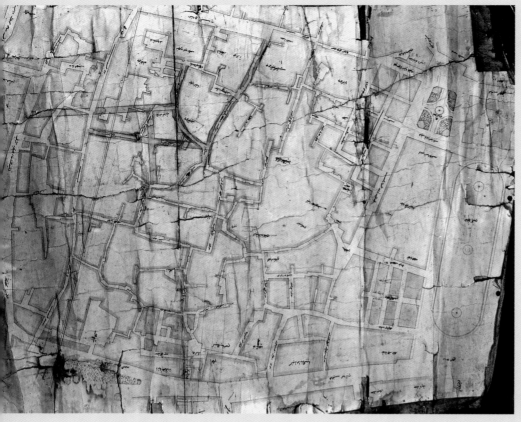

Figure 5.19
Ottoman map, circa 1870–1900.

Figure 5.20
French Army map, 1921.

Figure 5.21
Beirut in 1920
The base map is the first exact survey of Beirut by the French Army, preceding the cadastre undertaken between 1928 and 1930. The overlay reflects the changes generated under the Ottomans between 1840 and 1918, which paved the way for later French urban design interventions.

Waterfront and port area

Inner city

Compared to the 1841 map, three main categories of change are shown in the colored overlay both within the old city and its immediate surroundings.

Creation of squares and public buildings

1 Infantry barracks (today's Grand Serail), 1853

2 Military hospital (today's Council for Development and Reconstruction), 1861

3 Petit Serail, 1884

4 Sahat al Bourj, 1884

5 Clock tower, 1896

6 Sahat al Sour, 1900

- - Conservation Area boundaries

Introduction of modern transportation

Port extension (1893)

▪▪▪▪ Tramway lines (1895)

H+H Railroad (1907)

Regularization of the urban fabric

Main new souks

7 Souk al Jamil (1870s)

8 Souk al Nuzha or Souk Sursock (1880s)

9 Souk Hani wa Raad (1890)

Main streets regularized or cutting through the old fabric

Area demolished in 1915 (later Foch-Allenby and Etoile)

71

REGIE DES TRAVAUX DU CADASTRE ET D'AMELIORATION FONCIERE
DES ETATS DE SYRIE DU LIBAN ET DES ALAOUITES

VILLE DE BEYROUTH
Carte du nivellement direct
(1er, 2me et 3me ordres)

dressée sur le nivellement général
effectué par le Service Géographique de l'Armée

ECHELLE 1/5000

LEGENDE

French Army map 1921, courtesy Mr. Adib Fares.

1920

1925

1928

1937

1938

Left band
Figures 5.22, 5.23, 5.24
Views of the widening of Souk al Haddadin into Allenby Street. The 1925 and 1928 views show a building by Bahjat Abdelnour, one of the period's most prominent architects.

Below
Figure 5.25
The original façade drawing.

Top to bottom
Figure 5.29
1927 aerial view of Beirut, showing the eastern dock and jetty being completed.

Figure 5.30
The new port, inaugurated in 1938.

Figures 5.31, 5.32
The Beirut fair
As described by Fouad Debbas, "The Beirut fair was inaugurated in April 1921. This initiative was conceived and promoted by French authorities. France, as the Mandatory authority, was eager to gain prestige by showing that the Lebanese and Syrian economies were capable of attracting foreign investment capital." The fair took place in Bourj Square (top) and in the southern section of Allenby Street, later to become Maarad (Fair) Street (bottom).

1915

1922

Figures 5.26, 5.27
The 1915 view shows Souk al Tujjar being enlarged to become later Foch Street. The 1922 view shows what is probably the first building constructed by the Municipality on lot 152.

1928

Figure 5.28
Foch Street in 1928.

With the withdrawal of Ottoman troops from the Levant in 1918, Beirut became the capital of the new nation-state and the seat of the French mandate for Syria and Lebanon. The port, enlarged and modernized, assumed the role of gateway to the Orient. The population reached 180,000 by the early 1930s, residential areas doubled in size, and pericenter districts consolidated into urban neighborhoods inhabited by an emerging bourgeoisie of professionals, bureaucrats and merchants.

Infrastructure was highly improved, with the installation of a sewerage network and the addition of a substantial network of asphalted roads. Destined to be the showcase of France in the Levant, the city center was redeveloped along the Beaux-Arts design principles that had already been introduced during the Ottoman period. This second stage of early modernization completed the conversion of Beirut, in less than two decades, from a traditional town to a modern city.

The Waterfront and Foch – Allenby

A major improvement scheme was implemented during the 1930s, transforming Beirut into the largest port of the Eastern Mediterranean. It involved adding a second dock to the east, with a deeper and wider anchorage area; lengthening the main jetty; creating a duty-free zone; and adding refrigerated warehouses, an ice factory, fuel storage and a slipway.

The redevelopment of the city center began in the port-related area. The two arteries perpendicular to the waterfront, opened by the Ottomans during World War One, were named Foch and Allenby as early as 1919. They were cleared in 1921, together with the area behind the Petit Serail, to make room for the Beirut Fair.

A planning committee was assigned for the design of buildings to be erected along the new arteries. The complete demolition of the old souks had created demand for new commercial and storage space, to accommodate international commerce and the transport agencies linked to the port activities. A new building type emerged: the walk-up commercial building, with offices on the upper floors, shops on street level and, for the first time, underground storage space. The Foch-Allenby area was perceived as the entrance gate to the city for foreign investors arriving by sea; hence, it had to show an up-to-date ornamented frontage. This policy was first applied to Foch Street, because of its direct link to the port. The street thus became the architectural showcase for the rest of the city. The Municipality even chose to establish its offices at the intersection of Foch and Weygand.

A façade competition was launched for Foch Street in 1920, while demolitions were still under way to clear the area between Foch and Allenby. Among the candidates who submitted designs were the Khawajas Beshara, Nafelian, Deschamps, Gharghour and Khachou, and Dettray (or Destrée, transliteration of original reference) from Heliopolis (Cairo); and the designs of Deschamps and Dettray were chosen. The Municipality raised a 200,000-pound loan to cover compensating the expropriated owners and building new souks. Hippolite Michel, a Public Works civil engineer, prepared a development plan with advice from a reconstruction committee headed by Omar Daouk, president of the Municipality, and comprising the engineers Youssef Aftimus from Lebanon, Rafler (or Dafler, transliteration of original reference) Afendi from Austria, and the French commanding officer Matthieu.

By 1922, the expropriations were completed and the Municipality auctioned the new parcels. It also financed construction of the first buildings to stimulate the real estate market in the area and thereby reap the fruit of its investment. In 1923, the Municipality built the ground floors of two buildings on Foch, putting up for sale 32 shops, as well as the air rights of the upper floors.

In 1924, plans were laid out for the paving of Foch Street. Souk al Bayatira and the two remaining khans in the area (al Arwam and al Barbir) were demolished. An architectural competition was organized for a third building on the corner of Weygand and Foch. Youssef Aftimus won the competition with an imposing building in the neo-Islamic style, and the 62 shops planned on the ground floor were sold in 1925. The building was to later become the seat of the Municipality. By 1927, Foch Street was completed. It exhibited broad sidewalks and a median with fashionable light poles. An asphalt with a 15-year duration guarantee was used for paving. To enhance the eastern approach from Weygand, a square was laid out on the site of Bab al Saraya. The area ultimately became a prime target for real estate investment.

Figure 5.33
Duraffourd plan, 1928.

Figure 5.34
Danger plan, 1932.

Figure 5.35
The 1932 Danger plan is based on
the first cadastral survey
of the city and the Duraffourd
design scheme of 1928.

Left, top to bottom
Figures 5.36a, 5.36b
Aerial views of Beirut before and after completion of the Etoile area, 1926 and 1943.

Right
Figure 5.37
Aerial view of the Beirut city center, 1928
The Etoile and Foch-Allenby areas were at an early stage of their development. The Maarad Street alignment was already defined by a group of buildings under construction. Two other buildings marked the northern intersection of Etoile Square with Allenby Street. The southern edge of Foch-Allenby was clearly demarcated by the Municipality building. The northern section showed a townscape in transition, comprising new office buildings along with traditional red tile pitched roof structures.

Al Majidiya Mosque

Bab Idriss

Capuchin Church

WEYGAN

LAW COURT

Clock Tower

GRAND SERAIL
French Mandate
Commission Head

1928

Amir Munzer Mosque

Ministry of Finance

Al Omari Mosque

Municipality

Amir Assaf Mosque

Etoile Square

St Elie Greek–Catholic Church

Evangelical Church

Customs Warehouses

St George Greek–Orthodox Cathedral

Stock Exchange

Petit Serail

Covered Souk (Riad al Solh Square)

Martyrs' Square

Police Station

St George Maronite Cathedral

ALLENBY STREET

MAARAD STREET

Observ [De]

The inner city and Etoile

The rebuilding of the inner city in old Beirut (later to become the Etoile area), was planned in 1926 and implemented in the 1940s. The southern section of Allenby Street was renamed Maarad (Fair), in reference to its former role as the site of the Beirut Fair. It became the axis of a major urban design scheme of highly symbolic value. Intended as the political focus of the city center, the new sector was to host the Parliament building and a formal public square. To avoid an oversupply of office and retail space, residential and leisure activities were included in the scheme. However, financial services prevailed, with a cluster of banks and insurance companies that were to slowly spread towards Souk Bab Yaaqoub, renamed as Fakhreddine Street (today's Riad al Solh Street).

A project called 'Beyrouth en cinq ans' was presented in 1926 by Camille Duraffourd and approved by the Council of Ministers in January 1929. The project included a proposal for a new street layout for the southern part of the city center. A star configuration was adopted, with a focal point and radial streets inspired by the Place de l'Etoile in Paris. Orders were issued to immediately start expropriations and works along the Maarad street. The Banque de Syrie and the Banque Immobilière Tuniso-Algérienne agreed on a loan of 1,200,000 pounds to the Municipality to cover the costs of the project. The area was henceforth named Mahallat al Nijma, or Etoile Square.

The price of land more than doubled in three years, rising from 20 to 46.5 pounds per square meter between 1924 and 1927. By 1927, lots totaling 150 meters of frontage had been sold in Maarad. To further stimulate investment, an architectural competition was held in 1927 for the selection of the three best building designs, with awards of 70,000 francs each. In the same year, the Municipality began construction on a fourth building, located on Etoile Square. A café was planned on street level, with offices or luxury apartments on the upper floors.

In 1929, compensations to expropriated land owners on Maarad Street and the eastern side of al Omari Mosque paved the way for the opening of streets branching off from Etoile Square. The sides of al Omari Mosque were cleared to highlight this historical monument that dated back to medieval times. The preservation of the mosque's western elevation dictated limiting Allenby Street to a 10-meter width. A sum of 150,000 pounds was allocated that year for the development of a building destined to house the Parliament and the National Library. A land swap arrangement allowed the acquisition, to this end, of a triangular parcel on Etoile Square. The design was assigned to Mardiros Altounian, a Beaux-Arts architect at the Ministry of Public Works. In 1932, Altounian also won the competition for the Etoile clock tower, offered to the city by the Lebanese émigré, Miguel Abed.

Meanwhile, two firms, Compagnie des Projets Fonciers and Compagnie Suisse de l'Union de Genève, opened offices in the Etoile area, leading the way for others to follow. The Municipality's technical team, headed by engineer Kartikoff, proposed the layout of secondary streets, starting from the eastern side of the square. Compensations were negotiated for the expropriation of Waqf land and the demolition of religious buildings.

In 1930, the office of Danger Frères was hired to draw a comprehensive development plan for the city center, including the unfinished section of the Etoile area. A 83,000-franc project was submitted to the Mohafez (administrator) of Beirut, but was never implemented. Completion of the Parliament building and the clock tower in 1934 was followed by other construction. Several houses were demolished at Bab al Dirka, and Mahallat al Tawba was cleared to make room for the Banco di Roma building. The western section of the Etoile area was thus gradually shaped and organized around financial activities, later leading to the formation of the banking district along the current Riad al Solh Street. The eastern section, on the other hand, was not completed, in order to preserve a number of places of worship. Consequently, two of the planned radial streets were ultimately abandoned in the final Etoile scheme.

Figures 5.38, 5.39
Two designs were sent to the Lebanese government from Mexico by the donator of the Etoile Square clock tower, émigré Miguel Abed. One of them was hailed in the local press as 'the Eiffel tower in Beirut'.

برج ايفل في بيروت

تصميم الساعة الكبرى

Right, top to bottom
Figure 5.40
A 1929 view of the Etoile area being cleared out. The press commented: "Returning after years of emigration during the war, it is difficult to recognize Beirut, the old town, with its narrow streets and souks, having been replaced by a new city, the creation of modern design, a mirror of the government's determination and good management."

Figure 5.41
A 1934 view of the grand Parliament cupola under construction, as reproduced in the press.

1929

1934

Figures 5.43a, 5.43b
Top and bottom, two maps
showing the stages of the
Etoile area development at
the beginning and end of the
1930s. The overlay in red
shows the old town layout.

Figure 5.42
Panorama of the Etoile Square after
completion, 1944.

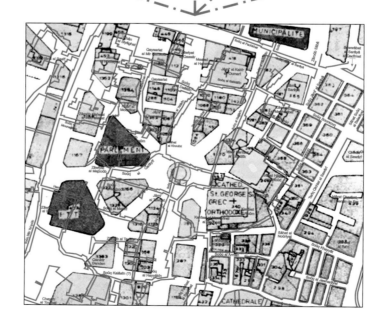

Chapter 6

From Khan to Office Building

In nineteenth-century Beirut, khans were multifunctional structures that housed a wide range of amenities for both local merchants and foreign traders. They included shops, storage space, workshops and lodging; and, in some cases, accommodated financial institutions and consulate offices. Khans were named after a specific trade, like Khan al Musika (music); or a type of merchandise, like Khan al Harir (silk); or according to the vocation of the district, like Khan al Milaha (shipping) (*fig. 6.1*). Those built in the latter part of the century were occasionally named after their owners, like Khan Tabet, Khan Fakhry Bey and Khan Antoun Bey.

Khans were originally 'inward-looking' structures, built around an open courtyard and accessed from the narrow streets of the intramural city. They lacked formal elevations, other than a decorated portal signaling their entrance to the passerby. In the second half of the nineteenth century, as a new pattern of wide streets emerged as a result of the city's modernization, khans began to transform into extroverted structures. Khan Antoun Bey exhibited an imposing symmetrical elevation, with a variety of window shapes and colonnaded upper floor balconies that overlooked the port area (*fig. 6.2-6.4*). The street elevation of Khan Fakhry Bey, at the end of Allenby, included corbelled balconies and wrought iron balustrades and brackets (*fig. 6.5*): the repetition of the same window unit over the full width of the khan's façade prefigured the modular elevation of modern office buildings.

At the turn of the twentieth century, two other types of commercial/office buildings emerged: the exclusive corporate headquarters or branch office; and the rental or speculative building. The former was usually designed as a sophisticated structure aimed at promoting the image of a commercial or financial institution. The Imperial Ottoman Bank belonged to this category (*fig. 6.6*). Speculative buildings, meanwhile, formed the majority of commercial constructions during this period. The earlier ones adopted the prevalent central hall building type, with a red-tile pitched roof, triple arch and corbelled balconies. This building type aimed at accommodating apartments and hotels, as well as commercial units, with shops or storage on the ground floor and offices or workshops on upper floors. Among its best-known examples were the no longer extant cluster of structures at the entrance of Souk Sursock and the buildings lining the Avenue des Français on the waterfront (*fig. 6.7-6.8*). Speculative or rental buildings complemented existing khans. They were small- to medium-size structures that could be developed by a new breed of middle-class landowners and entrepreneurs.

Figure 6.1
The inward-looking Khan al Milaha in the foreground.

Figures 6.2, 6.3
The outward-looking Khan Antoun Bey.

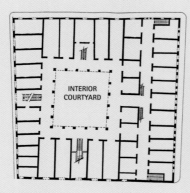

Figure 6.4
Khan Antoun Bey original plan.

Figures 6.5
Khan Fakhry Bey street frontage.

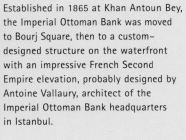

Figure 6.6
Imperial Ottoman Bank
on the waterfront.

Established in 1865 at Khan Antoun Bey,
the Imperial Ottoman Bank was moved
to Bourj Square, then to a custom-
designed structure on the waterfront
with an impressive French Second
Empire elevation, probably designed by
Antoine Vallaury, architect of the
Imperial Ottoman Bank headquarters
in Istanbul.

Figure 6.7
Avenue des Français with
central hall buildings as
hotel structures.

Figure 6.8
Entrance to Souk Sursock
with central hall
buildings as mixed-use
commercial structures.

An Early Avant-Garde Structure: Tanios and Massoud Building

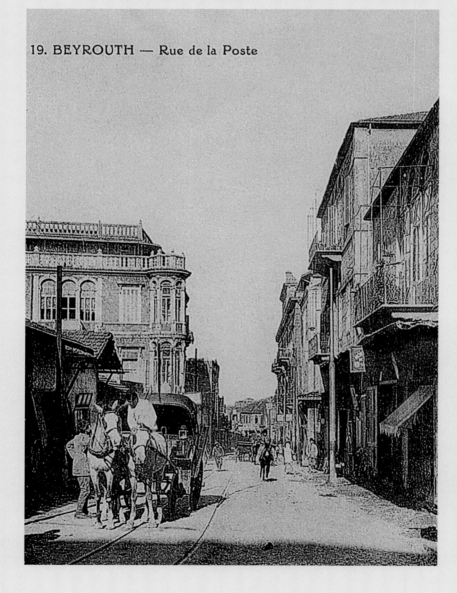

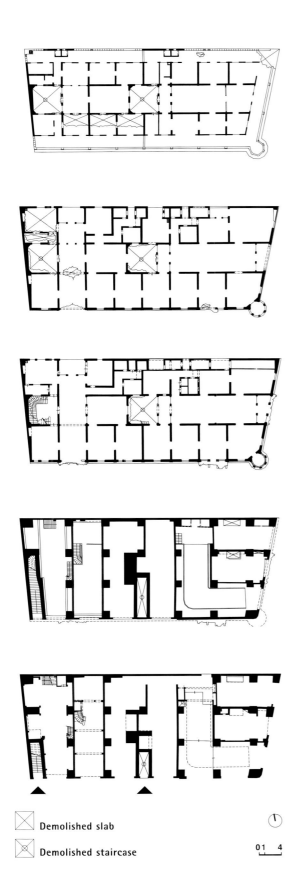

 ⊠ Demolished slab

⊠ Demolished staircase

01 4

Figure 6.11
Tanios and Massoud building, postwar ground,
mezzanine, first, second and third floor plans.

One of the first avant-garde structures that announced the emergence of the distinctive office building as a new commercial type was the Tanios and Massoud building at Bab Idriss. Featured on 1905 postcards (*fig. 6.9 - 6.10*), the building probably dates back to the turn of the century. It has a traditional structure, with vaulting on the ground floor and bearing walls on upper levels. Compared to its surrounding structures, all of which belong to the central hall type and display a cubical mass, red tile roof and triple arches, the Tanios and Massoud building stands out in terms of siting, façade configuration and architectural vocabulary. The building was clearly conceived as a contextual structure. It consists of an elongated mass, adapted to the configuration of its site. A corner tourelle marks the entrance of the street that leads to the port. A semi-circular arch replaces the traditional pointed arch. This neo-classical influence is also present in its elevation, in such details as window surrounds, cornices and balustrades. A recessed attic floor with a clearly defined parapet replaces the traditional red tile pitched roof.

In plan, the building generally conforms to the central hall type, but produces new features (*fig. 6.11*): the central hall extends from the eastern to the western side of each floor and is interrupted in the middle and at the end by a double stairwell that serves the two adjoining apartments on the floor. As shown in the ground level plan, stairwells are reached by narrow corridor entrances to maximize the commercial frontage at street level. Though originally designed for both residential and commercial purposes, the Tanios and Massoud building heralded in its physiognomy the office building type that would permeate the Foch-Allenby and Etoile area a quarter of a century later.

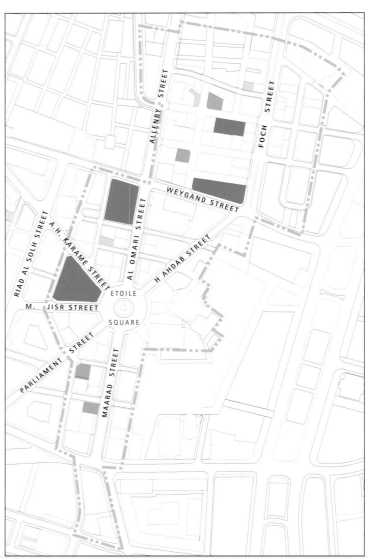

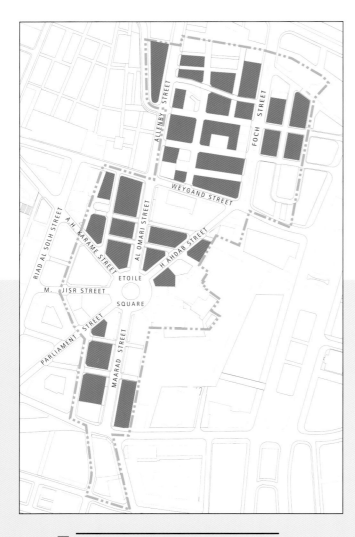

Foch–Allenby and Etoile area boundary

Figure 6.12
Block and parcel plan.

■ Sample of large size lot

■ Sample of medium size lot

□ Sample of small size lot

■ Buildings with original basement

Figure 6.13
Buildings with basement.

Changing Plan Morphology

After the razing of the city's medieval fabric in the early twentieth century, the superimposition of a geometric layout, orthogonal in Foch-Allenby and star-shaped in Etoile, produced a large diversity of block and parcel configurations and sizes (*fig. 6.12*).

East of Foch Street, blocks are narrow and accommodate either block-size parcels with peripheral access or medium-size parcels opening on two parallel streets. Some blocks that had been fragmented into small-size parcels were difficult to plan due to their configuration and reduced area. West of Foch and along Allenby, most parcels are of the medium-size category; they are arranged back-to-back in square and rectangular shapes and form a relatively uniform orthogonal pattern. Finally, the Etoile area exhibits a wide range of irregularly shaped blocks and parcels, resulting from the radial street configuration.

Despite the diversified block and parcel layout, the distinguishing features of the new fabric are its wide and rectilinear streets and the absence of alleys and dead ends. This ensured optimal street accessibility and visibility for each parcel. A small number of parcels occupied entire blocks, accessed from four sides; the remaining parcels were corner and infill lots, accessed from one or two sides.

Along with the modernization of the urban fabric, the buildings themselves underwent an accelerated process of structural, spatial and stylistic change. Commercial, administrative and public structures took the lead over residential structures in terms of technological and stylistic innovation. The use of reinforced concrete liberated the ground floor from stone vaulting and facilitated the creation of a basement (*fig. 6.13*); it also liberated upper floors from bearing walls and allowed more flexibility in internal planning and partitioning. Accordingly, the office buildings of Foch-Allenby and Etoile were conceived as skeleton structures, wrapped by elaborate stone envelopes acting as self-bearing elevations. The stone envelope followed the perimeter of the building parcel, with no setbacks from either street or adjoining lots, and lot coverage and street frontage were consequently optimized.

Various solutions were devised for an efficient articulation of vertical and horizontal circulation, a rational subdivision of the space available for lease, and the provision of natural ventilation and lighting. Upon examination of the original building layouts in Foch-Allenby and Etoile, it becomes evident that the solutions varied primarily according to the lot size, location and shape.

Small-size parcels

A solution prevalent in small, square-shaped corner parcels was the use of a corridor entrance with a straight flight of stairs leading to the first floor (*fig. 6.14-6.15*). The building entrance, located against a lateral party wall, was reduced in width to minimize interference with the commercial street frontage. Beyond the first floor, vertical circulation consists of a single or a double-flight stairwell tucked against rear party walls, liberating the external building periphery for use as additional office space. In narrow and elongated sites with wide frontage (*fig. 6.16-6.18*), the stairwell, occupying the full depth of the parcel, incorporated the building entrance and became part of the external elevation; it read clearly from outside through a differentiated treatment of window shapes and external finish. As for the layout of office spaces, two patterns of organization prevailed. The first (*fig. 6.15, lot 129*), reminiscent of central hall planning, consists of a symmetrical layout punctuated by a central bay window on the main elevation. The second (*fig. 6.15, lot 130*) has a non-symmetrical and non-hierarchical layout, most evident in the uniform treatment of openings on the main and lateral elevations. Although the two adjoining lots 129 and 130 were similarly shaped and positioned as corner sites, the first had a frontal stairwell clearly expressed in street elevation, while the second had an inner stairwell reached through a lateral corridor entrance. In general, the use of inner versus front stairwell predominated, irrespective of lot size and shape.

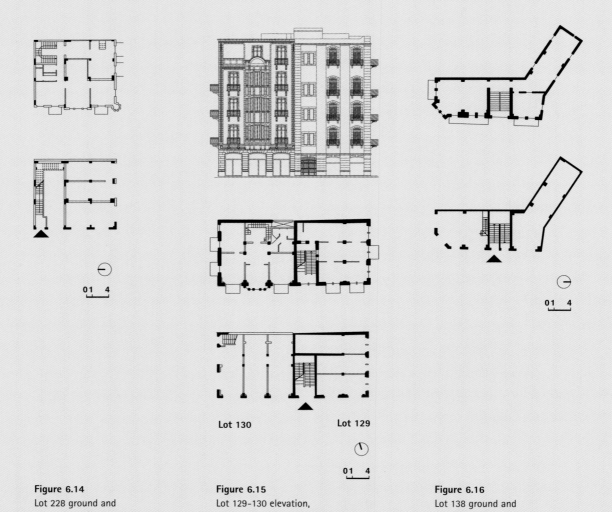

Figure 6.14
Lot 228 ground and
first floor plans.

Figure 6.15
Lot 129-130 elevation,
ground and first floor plans.

Figure 6.16
Lot 138 ground and
first floor plans.

Lot 130   Lot 129

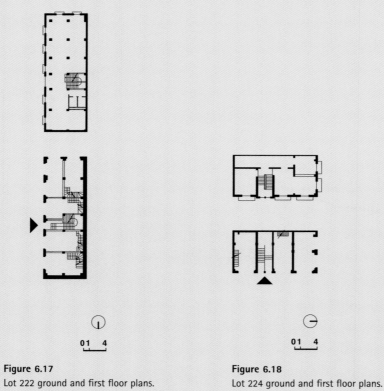

Figure 6.17
Lot 222 ground and first floor plans.

Figure 6.18
Lot 224 ground and first floor plans.

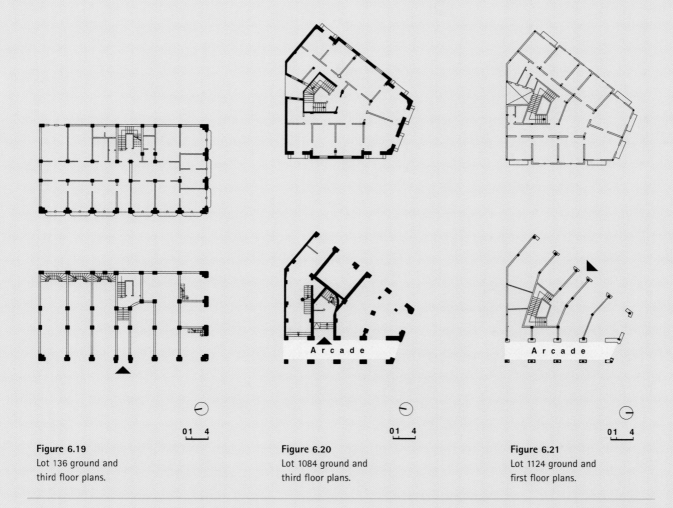

Figure 6.19
Lot 136 ground and
third floor plans.

Figure 6.20
Lot 1084 ground and
third floor plans.

Figure 6.21
Lot 1124 ground and
first floor plans.

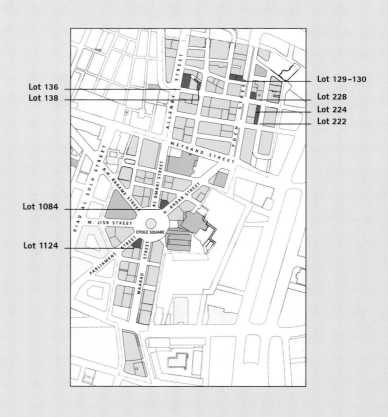

Medium- and large-size parcel

On rectangular, medium-size parcels, despite the wider street frontage, the same solution of linking to a rear stairwell was adopted (*fig. 6.19*). In the polygonal-shaped parcels around Etoile Square, the stairwell was transformed into a central core and a recess into the back party wall formed the lightwell (*fig. 6.20-6.21*).

As for spatial organization, a uniform subdivision dominated the layout. In the case of lots 1084 and 1124, a foyer with two single-loaded corridors were wrapped around the central core for the distribution of peripheral office spaces; while in lot 136, a double-loaded corridor was adopted, further optimizing horizontal circulation. The use of a central core instead of a central hall arrangement is clearly linked to the emergence of modern office buildings and reflects a tendency that was further emphasized with the increase in parcel size. In the block-wide Municipality building, the central core was expanded and planned as a cohesive entity (*fig. 6.22*). Two large semi-circular staircases were positioned on either side of a lightwell extending from the ground floor up, forming a kind of atrium space. The two opposite staircases were backed by a series of storage and sanitary spaces flanked by two single-loaded corridors. The difficulty in reconciling the rectangular central core with the elongated polygonal site resulted in an irregular subdivision of office space and an excessive circulation area.

With time, nevertheless, a higher level of efficiency in internal planning resolved this problem as it arose in similarly configured buildings. There, the design of a regular and clearly defined skeletal structure succeeded in binding the modular core and peripheral office spaces together into an integrated whole (*fig. 6.23*). Such layouts represent the maturation of the first generation of distinctive office buildings, the service core-corridor type, which differed from the central hall type where the central hall itself is used as a distribution device for offices. An alternative layout is exhibited in large-scale parcels with twin structures, separated on the ground level by a walk-through passageway extending to the full depth of the site (*fig. 6.24-6.26*). The passageway allowed for the creation of internal elevations along its length, separating the building in two and eliminating the need for a large-size service core with single-loaded corridors. The result is a central hall layout for each of the twin buildings that is reminiscent of the apartment buildings of the time.

Compared to the single-core building, the layout of the double-core building is indicative of the transitional type between traditional and modern, suited for both residential and office use. At the urban scale, the twin-building arrangement has the merit of increasing permeability at street level by opening up elongated and deep city blocks to cross-pedestrian circulation. This is in contrast with single-core buildings, like the Municipality, where the walk-through passageway on the ground floor is turned into an entrance hall closed on both sides by an imposing portal.

Service Core – Corridor Buildings

Figure 6.22
Lot 179 ground and
first floor plans.

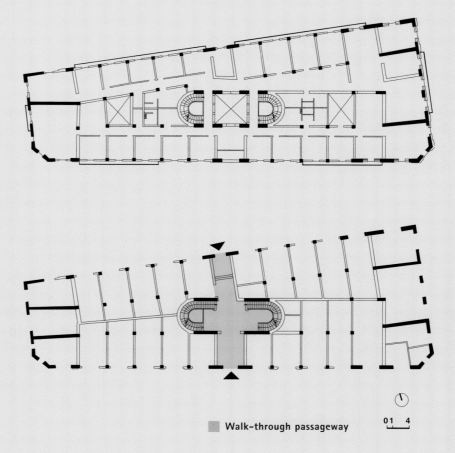

■ Walk-through passageway   01 4

Figure 6.23
Lot 157 ground and
second floor plans.

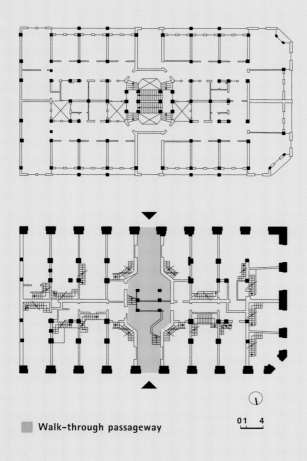

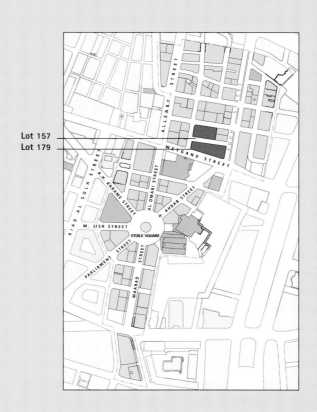

■ Walk-through passageway   01 4

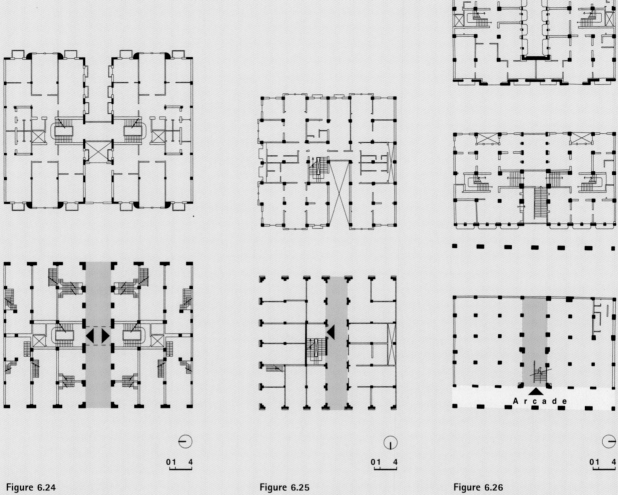

Figure 6.24
Lot 128 ground and third floor plans.

01 4

Figure 6.25
Lot 1144 first and ground floor plans.

01 4

Figure 6.26
Lot 201 ground, mezzanine and first floor plans.

01 4

■ **Walk-through passageway**

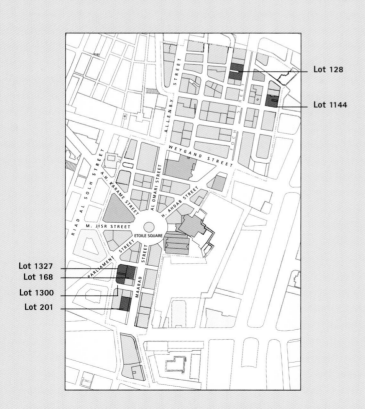

Permeable Urban Arrangement

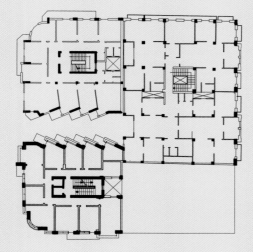

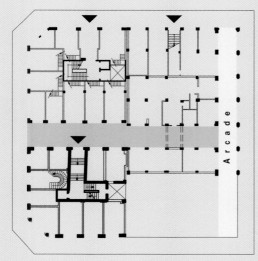

Figure 6.27
Lots 1300, 1327 and 168 ground,
first and third floor plans.

01 4

Figure 6.28
The walk-through passageway.

Typical examples of twin buildings acting as permeable urban fronts in the Foch-Allenby area are the buildings on lot 128 (*fig. 6.24*) linking Foch and Tijara streets, and on lot 1144 (*fig. 6.25*) linking Uruguay and Argentine streets. A more elaborate version can be seen in two rows of buildings in the Etoile area, which sit back-to-back along a walk-through passageway linking the Maarad arcade to Mgsr Toubia Aoun Street (*fig 6.27-6.28*). In summary, the buildings of Foch-Allenby and Etoile illustrate the passage from a multipurpose central hall plan, traditionally used for residential and non-residential structures, to the corridor-type plan and non-hierarchical layout suited specifically for modern office space. Underlying the variations between these two models was an equal concern for optimizing the development of prime urban land for retail and office use. The creation of an envelope that followed the parcel's boundaries aimed at maximizing retail frontage outside and usable office space within by ensuring an efficient floor layout. While small lots provided little leeway in envisaging alternative room arrangements, middle- and large-scale buildings shared a preference for the central hall versus modular-corridor layout. The choice of plan may have been related to the propensity to accommodate both residential and non-residential use, thereby attracting a wider range of tenants, since the Foch-Allenby and Etoile area was originally planned as a mixed-use zone.

This evolution from the central hall to the modern plan is also expressed at another level: the partial dichotomy between the outside and the inside, between the esthetic requirements of public frontage and the functional and structural requirements of internal planning, as illustrated in the Maarad buildings. By examining the ways in which these requirements have been reconciled, we may reach a better understanding of the building types that form a transition between tradition and modernity and of the dynamics of their adaptation to urban sites.

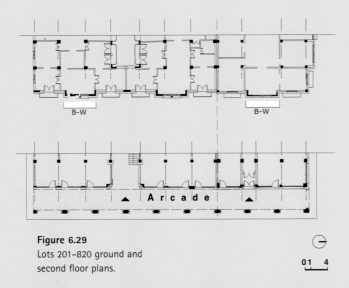

Figure 6.29
Lots 201–820 ground and
second floor plans.

01 4

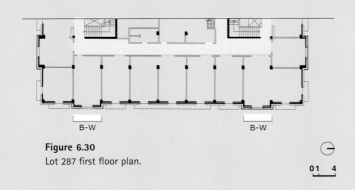

Figure 6.30
Lot 287 first floor plan.

01 4

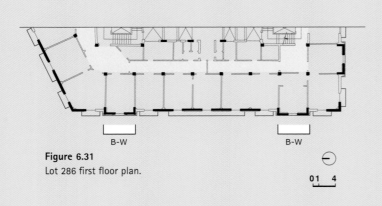

Figure 6.31
Lot 286 first floor plan.

01 4

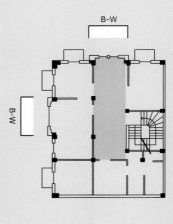

Figure 6.32
Lot 221 first floor plan.

01 4

Corridor

Central hall

Bay window
B-W

Figures 6.33, 6.34, 6.35
Lots 1154, 1142, 201.

Inside-Outside Dichotomy

One might have expected to find behind the uniformity of the Maarad frontage a modular approach to internal space planning, adapted to the rhythm of the repetitive arcade. While this assumption stands for the majority of structures, including irregular corner sites around Etoile Square (*fig. 6.20-6.21*), some cases show a discrepancy between the geometric order of their elevations and their interior division and structure (*fig. 6.33-6.35*). In lot 201, for example, this is reflected in the absence of alignment on street level between the street arcade and its interior elevation (*fig. 6.29*). The former is subdivided into six bays and the latter into seven bays: a walk-through passage in the center and three shop fronts on either side. The upper floors follow the reverse approach: office partitions are not aligned with the interior structure; they follow instead the geometric order of the elevation.

This lack of correspondence between the outside and the inside is prevalent in both central hall and corridor type buildings. In the first case, bay windows are sometimes used on the main and lateral elevations, despite the symmetrical layout of the plan (*fig. 6.30*). In the second case, the bay window becomes an external device aimed at breaking the monotony of a uniform and flat public frontage instead of reflecting the prevalent order within (*fig. 6.31-6.32*).

This autonomous treatment of elevations is indicative of the increasing independence of the outside from the spatial arrangement within, the former giving priority to public frontage, the latter to spatial efficiency. However, both interiors and exteriors were impacted by the modernization process. While the plan morphology was re-shaped by real estate speculation and functional specialization, the building envelope was redefined by structural hybridism and stylistic imports. A study of the changing vocabulary and syntax of elevations can help understand another facet of transitional buildings, namely their external incorporation of modernizing trends.

Development of Multiuse Commercial Centers

In addition to headquarters buildings, exemplified in the imposing structures of Riad al Solh Street, the second generation of office buildings in Foch-Allenby and Etoile included the multiuse commercial center, a major example of which is the Grand Theatre building (*fig 6.36*).

Prior to those developments, the upper floors of the Foch-Allenby and Etoile buildings were sometimes rented out as apartments or hotels, depending on the market demand, and roofs commanding a view were leased to cafés or restaurants. It was this flexibility in the use of a given space that heralded the emergence of the multiuse commercial center, which grouped entertainment, retail and office activities in a single structure. The opening of the Grand Theatre building in 1930 paved the way for the spread of this new building type in different areas of Beirut city center, encouraged by the increasing popularity of movie theaters. The first multiuse commercial centers were to be followed between the 1940s and 1960s by such landmarks as the Lazariya and Starco commercial complexes. Parallel to the emergence of this new building type, a morphological change occurred in some existing buildings, such as religious edifices, under the impact of new parceling and other real estate considerations. For example, al Dabbagha Mosque (designed by Mardiros Altounian in the 1920s as an extroverted perimeter structure) had its prayer hall raised to the first floor in order to accommodate shops on street level (*fig. 6.37*).

To conclude, in less than three decades (1920s to 1940s), the office building underwent an accelerated functional and physiognomic change, from its origin as a converted dwelling space to its eventual transformation as a multiuse commercial center. Its interior was subject to increasing specialization and spatial efficiency, and its exterior evolved from stone-jacketing to curtain walling and from turn-of-the-century eclecticism to early modernism. The current rehabilitation of office buildings in Beirut's Conservation Area, by contrast, aims at preserving the historic envelope while modernizing the interior, thus meeting the double challenge of reinstating the original character of Foch-Allenby and Etoile while bringing its buildings up to contemporary standards of efficiency and comfort.

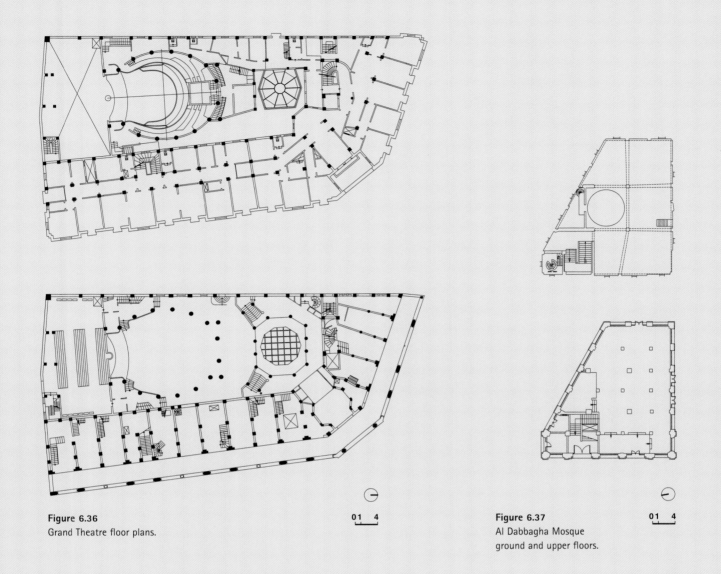

Figure 6.36
Grand Theatre floor plans.

01 4

Figure 6.37
Al Dabbagha Mosque
ground and upper floors.

01 4

Figure 6.38
Grand Theatre prewar picture.

Stone Jackets with Exposed Masonry

Figure 7.1
Lot 141 elevation.

Figures 7.2, 7.3
Lot 1146 elevation and detail.

Stone Jackets with Mixed Finish

Figure 7.4
Lot 173 elevation.

Figures 7.5, 7.6
Lot 152 elevation and detail.

Figure 7.7
Lot 1153 stone jacket
with stone and brick.

Chapter 7

Evolving Frontages

As mentioned earlier, the 1920s and 1940s witnessed the progressive passage from stone-bearing to concrete structures, redefining in the process a new vocabulary and syntax for building enclosure. This passage generated a range of intermediate frontage types revolving around the simultaneous use of stone and concrete that reveals the transformation of building envelopes into simple enclosures and forecasts the curtain walling of the modern period. It also clarifies the transition from the eclecticism of the 1920s to the early modernism of the 1930s, with the resulting change in building materials, techniques and overall composition of building façades.

From Stone-Jacketing to Stone-Cladding

The replacement of stone-bearing walls by a concrete skeleton structure resulted in a new type of building envelope: the 'stone jacket'. From outside, it conveys the impression of being a traditional bearing wall. However, it is structurally autonomous and is able to support protruding elements, such as corbelled balconies and bay windows. At the same time, it forms a highly sculptured surface, especially with its elaborate stone portals that confer a unique identity to each building. Stone jackets with exposed masonry (*fig. 7.1-7.3*) were reserved for high-cost structures, located for the most part in the Etoile and Maarad area. In cost-conscious constructions, stone jackets (*fig 7.4-7.6*) were made with lower quality sandstone finished with stucco; while exposed masonry was preserved for protruding elements, such as bay windows, brackets and balconies, or for frontage highlights, such as rusticated corners, building base, horizontal bands and window surrounds. A unique example of high-cost stone-jacketing with mixed finishing is the building on lot 1153. Its exposed masonry and infill panels in red brick enhance the façade structure and detailing (*fig. 7.7*).

With the increasing use of concrete, stone jackets became composite envelopes, with infill masonry panels fitted between concrete slabs, then plastered. Protruding elements like corbels and balconies were cast in reinforced concrete and formed an integral part of the skeleton structure (*fig. 7.8-7.9*). Ornamental detailing and opening surrounds were either executed in carved stone high-

lighting the main features of the façade, or cast in concrete and painted in darker or lighter shades. The Foch-Allenby area exhibits a wide variety of such composite elevations with mixed frontage construction. In most cases, stone-jacketing was used for the building base, enhancing it at eye level.

Both stone jackets and composite envelopes convey an impression of solidity, owing to the predominance of wall surface over voids. Having been liberated from their structural function, composite envelopes allowed for the first time the creation of repetitive larger-size openings, prefiguring the exteriors of modern office buildings. This is observed in the elevation on lot 229 (*fig. 7.10-7.12*), where the traditional emphasis on the central bay gave way to a uniform treatment of the entire elevation using the same type of opening. A glazed ornamental bay bringing the inner structural order to the foreground replaces the traditional punched window. Composite envelopes may therefore be considered as an intermediate type, contemporaneous to stone-jacketing, that gave rise to a new approach in the design of building exteriors. They allowed a higher degree of inside-outside integration and reversed the ratio between solid and void prevalent in earlier envelope types.

Cast stone elevations emerged at a later stage (*fig 7.13 - 7.15*). Their corbels, window surrounds and ornamental detailing cast in concrete reproduced the rich vocabulary of stone detailing; even plastered exteriors reproduced the elaborate detailing of stone jackets through surface geometric patterns. Cast stone elevations may be considered as the last stage before the outset of early modern buildings with their stone-clad envelopes (*fig 7.16 - 7.18*). Grouped behind the Maarad axis and extending west towards Riad al Solh Street, they exhibit a new visual order and constitute a clear break vis-à-vis previous types. In these buildings, ornamental bays were abandoned in favor of abstract orthogonal openings and stone-jacketing and infilling were replaced by stone-cladding. In many structures, corner bays were introduced, reflecting a complete disengagement of the envelope from the inner structure.

Composite Envelopes

Thus, a different esthetic emerged, strongly anchored in a modernist vision of building exteriors and interiors and opening the way for the progressive abstraction of the building enclosure into a thin membrane of glass and aluminum.

Figures 7.8, 7.9
Lot 146 elevation and detail.

Figure 7.10
Lots 230-231, 229, 228 street elevation.

Figures 7.11, 7.12
Lot 229 elevation and detail.

■ Cast Stone Envelopes

Figure 7.13
Lot 170 elevation.

Figures 7.14, 7.15
Lot 224 elevation and detail.

■ Stone-Clad Envelopes

Figure 7.16
Early modern building in
Mgsr Toubia Aoun Street.

Figures 7.17, 7.18
Corner bays of modern buildings.

Figure 7.19
Lot 130 central bay building.

Figure 7.20
Lot 25 central bay building.

Figure 7.21
Lot 130 French windows.

Figure 7.22
Lot 27 glazed French windows.

Figure 7.23
Lot 136 paired French windows.

Figure 7.24
Lot 170 glazed bay windows.

Figure 7.25
Lot 140 glazed bay windows.

Figure 7.26
Lot 1137 bay windows.

Accordingly, each of the successive generations of envelopes belonging to the 1920s and 1930s produced its own vocabulary of openings, related to the changing use of stone from a structural material to an infill material to a thin cladding material. This changing use was also expressive of the envelope's separation from, reintegration into, then disengagement from the inner structure. Such differing relations constantly redefined both the surface treatment, the building exteriors and their visual relationship to the inner structural organization. How this vocabulary of openings, protrusions and finishes was brought together to produce a coherent and distinctive syntax of building elevations is the subject of the following paragraphs.

Horizontal and Vertical Ordering Systems

An analysis of frontage forms reveals a dual system of façade organization: a horizontal system that regulates the relationship between the building center and edge; and a vertical one that is expressed in the articulation of the building base, body and crown. The general order of the façade is determined by the predominance of either one of the two systems, or by a balance between the two (see Architectural Survey, lots 136 and 128).

The majority of early 1920s' office buildings follows a horizontal hierarchical system (*fig. 7.19-7.26*) that puts the accent on the central bay. The latter is emphasized by its protruding mass, which forms a bay window supported by ornamented corbels above street level. It has wider openings and an elaborate stylistic vocabulary that sets the tone of the whole elevation. Central bays, conveying an impression of formality and monumentality, reinforce the visual distinctiveness of the building and usually appear on the street elevation (*fig. 7.19-7.20*). The non-hierarchical ordering system, on the other hand, consists of a flat street elevation with repetitive openings, in tune with the modular organization of modern office space. It features a wide range of opening types, from French windows (*fig. 7.21-7.23*) to bay windows (*fig. 7.24-7.26*).

The building base (*fig 7.27-7.28*) is clearly differentiated from the rest of the façade by wide openings for storefronts, a massive treatment of stone coursing and rich detailing on portals. The base extends vertically up to the mezzanine floor which, in some cases, accommodates an additional floor. This occurs mainly in buildings along the sloping street of Maarad. There, the difference in height between the lowest and uppermost street arcade allows the inclusion of an independent floor, or entresol.

The transition between base and body (*fig 7.29-7.35*), referred to as the transitional band, constitutes one of the richest and most complex sections of the street elevation in terms of ornaments, details and structural elements. The transition is handled by a continuous row of brackets of various sizes and shapes (*fig. 7.29-7.32*) or by massive corbels springing out from piers at the base (*fig. 7.33*). Clearly visible at street level, the transitional band receives an elaborate ornamental treatment and incorporates a large concentration of architectural features, from corbels and cornices to bases of bay windows and balconies. A system of symmetrical juxtapositions and vertical alignments of the various elements can generate a large variety of solutions. In some cases, the balconies and bay windows extend over the full length of the elevation, setting a clear edge between the building body and base (*fig. 7.34-7.35*).

The transition between body and crown is less complex (*fig 7.36-7.42*). It consists mainly of a cornice with an ornamental parapet, handrail or pediment and, in most cases, an attic floor which is set back (*fig. 7.36*).

The cornice may vary from a simple projecting ornamental molding to a cantilevered slab supported on brackets (*fig. 7.38-7.42*). Likewise, the parapet and handrail section varies from the simple to the highly elaborate. A picturesque treatment of the roof consists of ornamental cresting, a distinctive feature of the neo-Ottoman style (*fig. 7.37*). Most attic floors were added during the Independence period and are consistently set back from the main elevation to minimize their visual impact from the street.

With the emergence of the early modern façade, the tripartite subdivision of elevations into base, body and roof was largely simplified (*fig 7.43-7.52*). Balconies and bay windows, being essentially features of domestic architecture, were gradually abandoned, to be replaced

Building Base

Figure 7.27
Lot 130.

Figure 7.28
Lot 1154.

Transition Between Base and Body

Figure 7.29
Lot 144.

Figures 7.30, 7.31
Lots 1080, 286.

Figures 7.32, 7.33
Lots 131, 157.

Figures 7.34, 7.35
Lots 146, 170.

Figure 7.36
Lots 228, 229, 230 transition between body and crown.

Figure 7.37
Cresting of Municipality building.

Figures 7.38, 7.39, 7.40, 7.41, 7.42
Parapets and handrails from simple to complex.

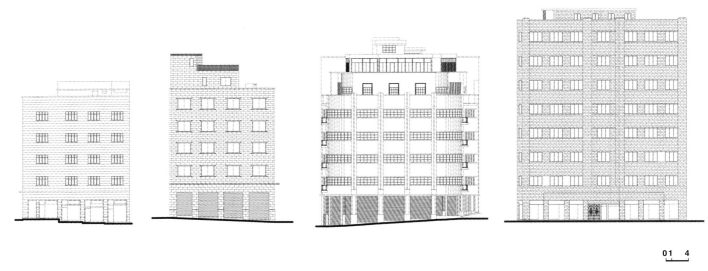

Figures 7.43, 7.44, 7.45, 7.46
Repetitive bay system, lots 1283, 1281, 1354, 202.

Figures 7.47, 7.48, 7.49, 7.50
Non-symmetrical composition, lots 1301, 1315, 1220, 1300.

Figures 7.51, 7.52
Curtain wall for modern structures, lots 1353, 448.

by flat façades with a repetitive bay system (*fig. 7.43-7.46*). This reinforced the distinctiveness of office buildings as a specialized building type. With the disappearance of the central hall plan, non-symmetrical elevations became predominant (*fig. 7.47-7.50*). This development led to a third generation of office buildings, characterized by a complete disappearance of balconies and the adoption of the curtain wall. Only a few of the extant structures on Foch-Allenby and Maarad belong to this category (*fig. 7.51-7.52*).

Stylistic Diversity

Beyond construction materials and façade composition, Foch-Allenby and Etoile owes its architectural identity to the diversity and distinctiveness of its building styles. This diversity mainly stems from the juxtaposition of three types of frontages:

- The eclectic fronts of Foch-Allenby.

- The neo-Ottoman fronts of Maarad.

- The early modern fronts of the area between Etoile and Riad al Solh Street.

These reflect the chronological development of Foch-Allenby and Etoile from the 1920s to the 1940s, as each style expressed the emergence of a new generation of office buildings.

Eclectic gateway fronts

The wide range of architectural styles characteristic of Foch-Allenby is related to the emergence of the area as a gateway to the city from the modernized port (*fig. 7.53-7.76*).

Competitions launched by the Beirut Municipality during the 1920s (see Chapter 5) had brought in Western architects, mainly French, and encouraged the injection of imported styles and their emulation. The nineteenth century fin-de-siècle eclecticism that characterizes Foch-Allenby was originally developed in the West prior to the emergence of early modernism. Architects were free to draw inspiration from different sources; inventiveness and originality were valued above stylistic rigor. Consequently, buildings in this area escape any clear stylistic classification.

Building styles featured in Foch-Allenby are a provincial and late version of this eclecticism. They represent an impressionistic mix-and-match of historical revivalism, Haussmannian eclecticism, Art Nouveau and Art Deco. The predominant influence was the late Haussmannian building, characterized by elaborate ornamentation borrowed freely from the Greek, Renaissance and eighteenth-century (mostly Louis XV) styles, with bay windows extending vertically over the midsection of the building and standing on a massive stone base incised horizontally with deep stripes (*fig. 7.54-7.55*). Rarely could a building be precisely attributed to a single style, except for some unique examples like the building on lot 104, which has a clear Art Deco style (*fig. 7.56*). Instead, a variety of styles were usually applied to a single building, with a predominant style expressed in major façade elements such as bay windows, shapes of openings, handrails, corbels and window surrounds. In some instances, the same element was reinterpreted in different ways, as in the case of the recurring Palladian bay (*fig. 7.57-7.60*). Usually, the base of buildings and the transitional band between base and body received the highest amount of stone carving, owing to their high visibility from the street. This shows in the remarkable stone carving of corbels (*fig. 7.61-7.67*) or in the detailing around portals (*fig. 7.68-7.75*).

For the Municipality, such Western-influenced architectural façades and detailing were a sign of modernity, and their adoption was an attempt to promote an international image of the capital. This approach was criticized at the time by the local press, which called for a national identity in architecture (see page 121) — an identity associated with the kind of 'oriental architecture' featured in two public buildings in Foch-Allenby: the Municipality building and al Dabbagha Mosque. The oriental style was soon to be adopted for the entire Etoile area.

Figure 7.53
Fakhry Bey and Allenby streets
eastern elevations.

Figures 7.54, 7.55
Lots 153, 148 Haussmannian eclectic façades.

Figure 7.56
Lot 104 Art Deco style.

Figures 7.57, 7.58, 7.59, 7.60
Lots 1135, 149, 170, 174, palladian bays.

Figures 7.61, 7.62 7.63 7.64, 7.65 7.66, 7.67
Corbels.

Figures 7.68, 7.69, 7.70, 7.71, 7.72, 7.73, 7.74, 7.75
Portals.

Foch-Allenby Eclectic Gateway Fronts

Figure 7.76
Foch Street eastern elevation.

Figure 7.77
Maarad arcade.

Neo-Ottoman formal fronts

While the eclectic fronts of Foch-Allenby expressed the international vocation of Beirut as a regional port city, the formal fronts of Etoile symbolized the official identity of the city as the capital of a new nation-state. This formalism was represented both by the neo-Ottoman style of the Maarad axis and the Municipality building and by the early national style of the Parliament building and the Etoile Square clock tower. The former epitomized a regional Arab belonging; the latter was a quest for national particularism grounded in heritage. While the arcaded building type adopted on Maarad is reminiscent of the formal streets of baroque Europe, it may also be viewed as a modern interpretation of the traditional riwaq, a protective shield against sun and rain in the humid and hot Mediterranean climate.

Clearly contrasting with the eclectic frontages of Foch-Allenby, the repetitive arcades of Maarad convey an air of formalism, grandeur and homogeneity (*fig. 7.77-7.105*). Beyond its apparent unity, however, lies a variety that shows in the detailing of shop openings (*fig. 7.78-7.80*), portals (*fig. 7.81-7.86*), balconies and windows (*fig. 7.87-7.89*), corbels and capitals (*fig. 7.90-7.104*). On the ground level, this diversity is made explicit by the treatment of the internal elevation of the arcaded passage and in the details of the arcades themselves. The best example of diversity within unity can be seen in the arcaded façade fronting al Omari Mosque. There, the repetitive rhythm of the Maarad arcades is interrupted to accommodate the large ornamented portal marking the entrance to the mosque. The street width was reduced to 10 meters in order to preserve the portal. This formal integration of a historic structure within the general order of the street is one of the most successful urban design gestures in the area.

Early modern business fronts

Besides the eclectic fronts of Foch-Allenby and the formal fronts of Etoile, a new type of street front began developing in the late 1930s between Etoile and what was to become the Riad al Solh Street. It consisted of high-rise elevator buildings, dressed in stone and exhibiting early modern fronts with repetitive openings. Compared to the eclectic architecture of the 1920s and 1930s, these new frontages were imposing, both in their scale and visual austerity (*fig. 7.108-7.127*). They reflected the buildings' main function as banking and financial institutions. As such, they heralded the emergence of the Riad al Solh Street itself as the hub of regional banking headquarters, when by the middle decades of the twentieth century Beirut had become the most important financial center in the Middle East.

Figures 7.78, 7.79, 7.80
Shop openings.

Figures 7.81, 7.82, 7.83
7.84, 7.85, 7.86
Portals.

Figures 7.87, 7.88, 7.89
Balconies and bay
windows.

Figures 7.90, 7.91, 7.92, 7.93, 7.94, 7.95, 7.96, 7.97, 7.98, 7.99
Corbels.

Figures 7.100, 7.101, 7.102, 7.103, 7.104
Capitals.

Figure 7.105
Elevation on Maarad Street.

Designing Our Streets
"I want something national in my homeland"

My thanks go to the Municipality of Beirut for its initiative in equipping our city with streets and proceeding to clean it from the rubble that was a disgrace to the sight and a nuisance to the inhabitants. Consider the buildings being erected on Foch Street; it will not be long before we see the street filled with large shops and spacious apartments.

However, there is one point I often alerted the Municipality and the Government to, last year, in the columns of this newspaper; namely, to build according to Oriental designs adapted to the country's character, that agree with its customs and serve its people. I learnt at the time that the Government had given the matter some concern and placed it in the hands of engineers for consideration; but up to now we have not seen any result.

The main streets belong to the city and its residents. I mean that not in the sense of possessing the land in lieu of its real owners, but in the sense that the Municipality, which represents the people, has the right to set a model for building, and to encourage landowners to follow that model in future construction, with the hope of improving the streetscape in harmony with existing buildings and avoiding any repulsion to good taste or visual esthetics.

This approach was not followed. In the main streets, there is a variety of neighboring designs and ornaments that do not fit together. They diverge in form, structure and source. While one building carries patterns from Paris, we find others adjoining it reflecting New York's commercial buildings and, on the opposite side, buildings that follow the massing of German structures.

Consequently, you hardly find in the city a proportionate, harmonious streetscape that your eye can accept or your heart enjoy, or that could remind you of the Oriental style of architecture, which had a great impact on architecture in general. The importance of this contribution is still evident in Andalusia's Alhambra and Alcazar; Morocco's mosques and schools; Egypt's splendid mosques and magnificent tombs; al Quds' (Jerusalem's) al Aqsa Mosque; Damascus' Umayyad Mosque; and in other countries of the East.

I do not favor such architecture just because it is Oriental, but because it fits the nature of our land, with its clear skies, bright sunshine and the beautiful colors of its mountains, orchards and fields. Such land must have a bright, cheerful style of construction that is adapted to the gifts that nature has endowed it with. Therefore, I cannot find justification for these dark, congested buildings with small narrow windows that remind us of the London gloom and fog. One of these buildings in Beirut is the Bourse, where they are working on darkening the building front and increasing its massiveness through the use of a cement material that offends the eye and saddens the heart.

The Municipality of Beirut is selling plots of land on Allenby Street and in no time we will see buildings rising there. Has the Municipality thought of making a building prototype that should be emulated in order for this street to emerge as a show case of good taste befitting Beirut as the capital of Lebanon, land of science in the East and gateway to the Syrian hinterland? The Municipality could organize a competition among architects; whoever wins the trophy would be given a substantial prize and gain an extensive reputation.

My opinion on how to build this street has been published several times before in this newspaper. There is no harm in reminding the reader about it. Beirut is quite exposed to the heat of strong sun in the summer and to heavy rain in the winter; therefore, the best way to construct is to protect the inhabitants from the heat and rain. One way is to structure arcades over the sidewalks in front of retail outlets. These arcades would be supported by double columns standing between the successive arches. Through such a design, the landlord would gain space to build over the arcades, while the inhabitants would find shelter underneath from heat and rain. The city would thus be enhanced by an Eastern architectural design, that is adapted to its regional character and its people's traditions.

Oriental architecture does not halt here; it is also distinguished by upper floors that include arched windows with the shape of two-thirds of a circle, engraved with Arabic calligraphy, as foreigners call it, and crenated balconies instead of the red bricks that look as if they were covered by the blood of bulls. I am not an architect, but I would like to see something national in my homeland, at least through architecture.

Al Surouji
Lissan al Hal, 21.2.1923

Figure 7.107
Al Omari Mosque elevation on Maarad Street.

Youssef Effendi Aftimus

Pioneer Engineer-Architect and Arab Renaissance Man

Youssef Effendi Aftimus (1866–1952) may be considered as the most famous and prolific local architectural figure of the first half of the twentieth century. His legacy to the Beirut city center is contained in three preserved landmarks: the Serail clock, the Grand Theatre and the Municipality building. The first overlooks the city from the Serail hill, the second ends the perspective of Maarad Street, and the third provides the gateway to the Foch-Allenby area. Over the Municipality portal, Aftimus left an inscription in Arabic verse: "These are our marks that hint at us: look henceforth to our marks."

His professional career spanned the late Ottoman, French Mandate and Independence periods. As a designer, builder and decision-maker, he was an active participant in the early formation of modern Beirut. Besides his work as an architect, engineer, planner and contractor, he occupied key positions in the public sector: as city engineer from 1897 to 1926 and as the first minister of public works in 1926–1927.

Aftimus represents the eclectic tradition of the late nineteenth and early twentieth centuries. He was known for the neo-Ottoman style, which he applied in his early Beirut buildings, such as the Hamidiya fountain and the Serail clock, built in 1900 to celebrate the anniversary of Abdelhamid II. A strong Egyptian influence was conveyed in the neo-Mamluk style he used in later works, such as the Municipality building (1925) and the Grand Theatre (1930). Aftimus referred to both styles as 'oriental' or 'Arab', a general expression often used in the literature of the time to designate various strands of Islamic revivalism, from Mamluk to Moorish to Ottoman. In Beirut, the oriental style was especially used in public buildings to express regional identity. For European architects, it was an exotic and picturesque style with a high decorative potential that could be conveniently applied as surface veneer to traditional and western building types. However, in important regional capitals, like Cairo and Istanbul, the oriental style was often perceived and cultivated by local and foreign-educated architects as a reaction against westernization.

The architecture of Aftimus was not confined to the 'Orientalist' tradition. His Barakat building (1924) is a clear departure from the traditional apartment house and may be considered as the earliest local example of a stone and concrete structure with Western eclectic elevations. At the same time, his engineering work encompassed such infrastructure projects as the Chekka tunnel, the Damour bridge, and the Nabatiya and Tripoli water systems. Culturally, he was a reflection of his epoch, a hybrid personality, equally at ease in teaching and writing classical Arabic; practicing architecture and engineering in Chicago, Cairo and Beirut; and building in stone as well as in reinforced concrete.

Born in Deir al Qamar, Lebanon, Aftimus studied and taught the Arabic language at the Syrian Protestant College (later the American University of Beirut). In 1893, he graduated in civil engineering from the United States and had the opportunity to work with Max Herz, a pioneer of neo-Mamluk architecture, on the Egyptian Exhibit at the Chicago World Fair. In 1894, he studied architecture in Antwerp, Belgium, before establishing his own firm in Beirut in 1895.

Based on research by Abdul Halim Kaissy

Aftimus in Egypt, where he w
contractor and member of th
Order of Engineers and Arch
between 1904 and 1910.

The Hamidiya fountain.

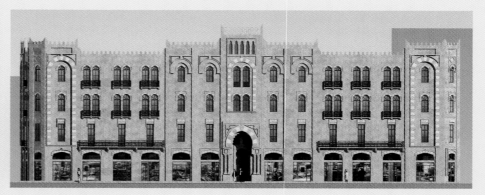

The Municipality building.

Mardiros H. Altounian

Architect of the Young Republic

unian, painter and architect,
is Paris studio.

Mardiros H. Altounian (1889–1958) belongs to the leading generation of architects educated at Ecole des Beaux-Arts in Paris who were entrusted to build the first civic monuments of the young republic of Lebanon. His masterworks include three major national symbols: the Parliament building and the Etoile Square clock tower, completed in 1934, during the French Mandate; and the Nahr al Kalb commemorative stela, commissioned by President Bechara al Khoury in 1945, during the early Independence years, to celebrate the impending withdrawal of the French troops.

The Parliament building may be considered as a landmark of the 'early Lebanese national style', which would disappear with the spread of international modernism in the 1940s and 1950s. To quote the architect's son and biographer, Achot Altounian, "It was strictly recommended to him to erect a building inspired by the purest Lebanese style, for which my father searched in the Shouf, in the palaces of the amirs." The actual outcome is a Beaux-Arts building with an Oriental-revivalist style, which articulates historical regional references around a strong symmetrical and monumental composition. This search for a national style by looking at historical precedents and regional traditions is a common trend of the colonial period, from Cairo to Istanbul. It expresses an attempt at accommodating East and West while searching for a local architectural identity.

Born in Bursa, Turkey, Altounian studied art and architecture in Paris between 1910 and 1919, then moved to Beirut in the early 1920s, and was assigned to the post of architect at the Ministry of Public Works. His professional career in Lebanon spanned the French Mandate and the first decade of the Independence period. He designed key civic and religious buildings, as well as private residences; his work extended beyond Lebanon to Jordan, Iraq and India.

Etoile Square clock tower.

Nahr al Kalb
commemorative stela.

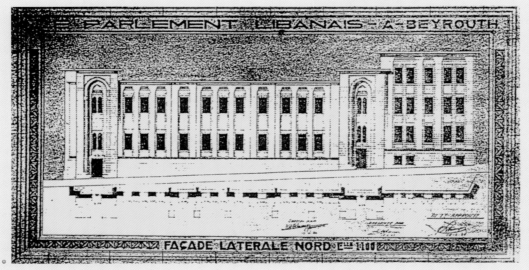

Upper left and bottom
Original drawings of Parliament building,
front and lateral elevations.

Figure 7.108
Lots 1300, 1327 and 168
walk-through passageway.

Figures 7.109, 7.110, 7.111
Building entrances.

Figures 7.112, 7.113, 7.114
Transition between ground floor
and first floor.

Figures 7.115, 7.116, 7.117, 7.118, 7.119, 7.120, 7.121
Shop openings.

Figures 7.122, 7.123, 7.124, 7.125
Balconies.

Figure 7.126
Early modern and neo-Ottoman
adjoining fronts.

Figure 7.127
Elevations on Parliament and
Mgsr Toubia Aoun streets.

The Foch-Allenby and Etoile model illustrates how an urban design idea applied in the 1920s was brought to its full potential three quarters of a century later, through Solidere's redevelopment of Beirut Central District (BCD). The following sections of this book go over the details of this achievement. Sections Two and Three describe the reconstitution and enhancement of the public and private domain in the area. The legal and institutional framework through which this result could be attained is explained in Section Four.

Destined to be the showcase of France in the Levant, the early twentieth-century modernization of the old city center was conceived along the Beaux-Arts and Haussmannian design principles that exemplified nineteenth-century Paris. Throughout the decades that followed, the townscape of Foch-Allenby and Etoile retained to a notable degree its original cohesiveness, despite the modifications imposed during the 1960s and 1970s and the heavy destruction inflicted by the 1975-1990 Lebanon war. The 1994 BCD Master Plan, having designated Foch-Allenby and Etoile as a part of the Conservation Area, reinstated and further emphasized it as Beirut's 'showcase' district. As such, it represents the most prominent instance in Beirut's recent history of concern for quality with regard to both the public domain and individual buildings. The public realm was enhanced in the entire BCD through the adaptation of the hardscape, softscape and signscape design to the general character of the district and the specific character of its sectors, as well as to contemporary environmental and civic design standards.

This section traces the process of frontage and streetscape enhancement. Chapter 8 describes the shaping of street frontage in Foch-Allenby and Etoile and outlines the various measures and regulations governing the external composition and treatment of individual buildings. In particular, façade controls and design guidelines are presented. This is followed, in Chapter 9, by an overview of the landscape framework, street equipment and public signage as enhancers of the district character.

Note 8.1

Nineteenth-century Paris downplayed the individual character of buildings in favor of the
street's visual continuity. A notable example is
the uniform and aligned frontages of Haussmann's
grand boulevards, characterized by a neo-classical revivalist style and the absence of overhangs. In 1823, modifications to the building
code allowed for strictly regulated protrusions
in terms of entablatures, cornices and other
projections. Construction of balconies with an
80-centimeter maximum depth was restricted
to façade areas six meters above street level
and was subject to official permission (fig. 8.1).

The resulting streetscapes, deemed harmonious
and orderly at the time by Paris residents and
visitors, were to be criticized by the turn of the
century as wearisome and too regimented. The
1882-1884 decrees allowed for a high variety of
protrusions on streets of 20- and 30-meter widths
(fig. 8.2), paving the way for the appearance of
the bay window. Furthermore, the 1902 law (fig.
8.4) introduced new façade regulations based
on the building envelope, or gabarit, instead of
the specific dimensioning of façade elements.
This allowed architects more freedom to design
elevations with embellishments and overhangs,
as well as to reshape attic floors and increase
their height (fig. 8.3).

The new flexibility of building codes, coupled
with the municipal façade competition tradition
(1897-1919), led to highly diversified and ornamented streetscapes (fig. 8.5). The austere
Haussmannian building, blending into boulevard
frontage, was gradually eclipsed by the turn-
of-the-century eclectic building, which tended
to stand out while respecting the overall street
composition. Closed and open protrusions like
balconies and bay windows, acknowledged by
the 1893 legislation, became an integral part
of exuberant façade compositions. These eclectic stone façades became the prototype of late
nineteenth-century Paris and, a quarter of a
century later, of Beirut's Foch-Allenby and
Etoile area.

Chapter 8

Shaping the Street Frontage

Street frontage or building elevations confer identity, architectural character and scale to the public domain. They also provide a wealth of information about the area's history. Functionally, the external openings and commercial frontages of buildings constitute a permeable front and a mediating device between public and private space.

Frontages were historically dependent on the way the public domain was perceived. Streets and open spaces were either considered as a leftover space, or as basic structuring elements of the city layout.

In the first case, their role was mainly to provide access for individual buildings with no consideration of the esthetic quality of street frontages. This is illustrated by the organic patterns and façade irregularity of the surviving historic cores of Tripoli and Sidon. In the second case, streets acquired visual primacy over individual buildings, whose elevations were subordinated to a street frontage ordering system. Haussmannian Paris is a prime example of this approach, which was diffused and emulated worldwide. The Foch-Allenby and Maarad buildings were initially articulated along the lines of this tradition of nineteenth-century Paris, where façade esthetics was considered as a prime enhancer of the visual quality of cityscapes. The present recovery of Foch-Allenby and Etoile, while following a similar approach, focuses on the entirety of the building envelope and subscribes to special design requirements for building streetwalls, rooftops, shopfronts and signage.

Figure 8.1
The Haussmannian uniform
and aligned frontages:
Portalis Street, Paris.

© Bibliothèque Musée des Arts Décoratifs Collection, Paris

Figures 8.2, 8.3
The 1882–1884 decrees:
Drawings by Louis Bonnier of the
allowed protrusions on the
20- and 30- meter wide streets.

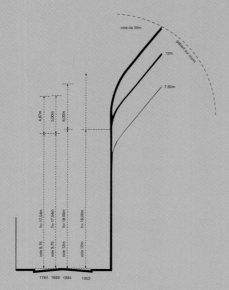

Figure 8.4
The Parisian building profile following
the 1902 regulations.

Figure 8.5
The post-Haussmannian diversified and
ornamented frontages — Rapp Avenue, Paris.

Streetwall Controls: Rise and Decline

Two sets of tensions lie at the heart of the process of shaping the public frontage: the first lies between the integrity of single buildings and the continuity of street-walls; and the second, between the building envelope and the public domain, in terms of setbacks and encroachments. The buildings of Foch-Allenby and Etoile were originally conceived as individual structures that were designed to form a coherent street frontage. A façade design competition had been launched by the Municipality of Beirut under the French Mandate, along the lines of the competition held once a year in turn-of-the-century Paris. The purpose of the competition was to promote the public image of the newly developed area, while also cultivating high esthetic standards. As indicated by the reviews of municipal façade designs of the time, the criteria for building permit approval included 'the use of cut stone', contribution to the 'beauty of the street' and the 'image of the square', and 'harmony' between street elevations.

The regulations imposed by the design façade competition were first imported from Paris (*Note 8.1*) to Beirut via Istanbul. In 1896, as part of the new Ottoman reforms (Tanzimat), a new building law was introduced in Beirut. Streets were classified into five categories, with building height regulated in accordance to street width, reaching a maximal limit of 24 m on wide streets. Enclosed and open protrusions located on the buildings' street elevations were restricted to the upper floors, and balcony widths were constrained to one third of the building frontage. Protrusions ranged from 83 cm (one zira') to 125 cm (one and a half zira'). Precise dimensions were specified for small projections such as window frames and other ornaments. A 1930 regulation 'concerning projecting balconies and closed protrusions' slightly modified this range. The depth of protrusions was regulated as follows (Governor of Beirut Resolution 199, dated February 24, 1930, concerning open and covered protrusions, i.e. balconies):

- Protrusion over the public domain:
  - 1.31 m onto public places.
  - 1.13 m onto streets of at least 9 m width.
  - 0.94 m onto streets of 7.5 m width.
  - 0.75 m onto streets of 6 m width.
- Distance from ground level: above 3.75 m.
- Protrusion area: not to exceed two thirds of façade width.

In 1960, enclosed protrusions over the public domain were abolished, putting an end to bay window and balcony space projections beyond the street line. As a result of the visual hegemony brought about by such modernist idioms, and by the application of zoning regulations as the main framework for urban growth, the concern for public frontage gradually waned. In the following decades, a major break in the continuity of street façades was brought about by the introduction of modern vertical extensions to some unfinished Foch-Allenby buildings that were set back from the ground floor frontage. The modernization of certain elevations further contributed to the disruption of the architectural unity of the area. In 1939, the concept of gabarit or building envelope was introduced in Lebanon. In the Beirut city center, it progressively began to undermine the continuity of the public frontage. It also resulted in exposing the flanking walls of adjoining structures and interrupting the building roofline. Gabarit controls, still applicable outside the Beirut Central District, allow for setbacks from property line in exchange for gaining additional building height. Although the maximum building height outside the BCD is not fixed in absolute terms, it is restricted to twice the width of the street, i.e. the distance between opposite building façades.

Figure 8.6
Building condition, 1994.

BCD boundary
In good condition
Lightly damaged
Partially damaged
Partially destroyed
Demolished

Once the Foch-Allenby and Etoile area had been identified by the BCD Master Plan as a Conservation Area, a
field investigation and a building-by-building survey
were conducted by Solidere as part of the process
to define a comprehensive conservation framework for
the area (*fig. 8.6 - 8.8*). The analysis of Foch, Allenby and
Maarad, in section and elevation, brought forth their
common features (*fig. 8.9*):

• Façades are built to property line and are clearly articulated into three sections: base, body and crown — a subdivision reminiscent of the turn-of-the century Parisian
immeuble de rapport, i.e. speculative or rental building.

• Protrusions (maximum 1.50 m) consisting of balconies
and bay windows are confined to the middle section of
the building and do not project by more than 1.50 m over
the public domain.

• Façade openings do not exceed 20 per cent of the
wall surface.

In order to ensure continuity between the existing historic context and new development, a set of unifying and
restrictive façade regulations or streetwall controls have
been established for the wide range of street frontage in
the BCD (*fig. 8.10a - 8.10b*). These controls are the result
of the formal analysis of retained buildings in Foch-
Allenby and Etoile and follow the tripartite division of
existing elevations into:

• A base including the ground floor and mezzanine up to a
horizontal expression line.

• A body encompassing the midsection of the building up
to a cornice line.

• A crown formed by the recessed upper stories up to a
maximum height plane.

The difference between small, intermediate and large-
scale streetwalls resides in the proportions assigned to
the tripartite subdivision.

Small-scale streetwalls are set for the historic core.
Building height is limited to 24 meters with a horizontal
expression line between 6 and 8 meters delimiting the

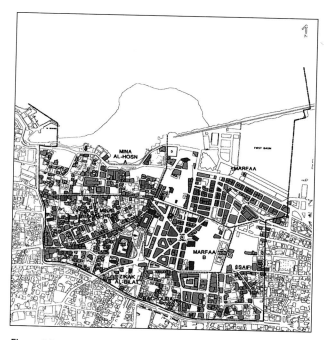

Figure 8.7
Heritage and townscape value, 1994.

⊟ BCD boundary
▨ Religious building
■ High value building
▨ Medium value building
▢ Low value building
□D□ Demolished high value building
⊟ Cadastral boundaries

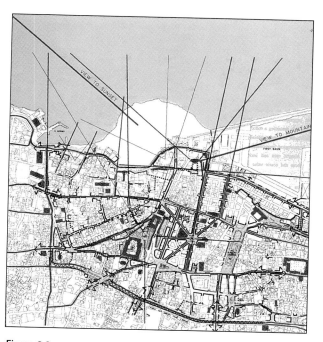

Figure 8.8
Townscape analysis, 1994.

▨ Key building
⊕ Landmark
✳ Monument
▭ Main route
⟩⟩⟩ Steep slope
▢ Public activity space
⋯ Pedestrian route
⟨⟩ Gateway link
▭ Important frontage
◺ Important frontage (destroyed)
▭ Edge
∿ Barrier
▭ Port enclosure/entrance
▭ Vista
◁ Panoramic view

base. A cornice line between 19 and 20 meters delimits the midsection or body of the building. No setbacks are allowed on the Maarad axis (SWA1), in order to preserve a consistent street alignment. A colonnade, with a minimum width of 3 meters, is a required feature. A setback or a jetty of 1.7 meter, is allowed on the remaining streets (SWA2), the jetty being mandatory for Foch Street.

Middle-scale streetwalls (SW3/SW4) are intended for mid-rise development. The maximum height plane reaches 40 meters and upper stories above the cornice line are mandated to set back a minimum of 3 meters from the property line so as to reduce the apparent height of the building.

Large-scale streetwalls (SW5) are reserved for high-rise development of up to 160 meters. In some cases, streetwalls are subdivided into two sections, a podium and a tower. A minimum 9-meter setback is required above the horizontal expression line to make the tower less apparent from the street. This measure is adopted to ensure street enclosure and façade continuity while optimizing site exploitation.

Both in the Conservation Area and its related periphery, like the Allenby and Foch extensions, Martyrs' Square and Riad al Solh Square, high restrictions are imposed on the use of materials (natural stone finish) and on other considerations such as wall-to-window proportions. Controls for high-rise buildings are more flexible and are mainly concerned with retaining basic façade proportions.

The Master Plan adopted these design features as a model to formulate a set of urban design controls specific to infill development and to the rebuilding of structures deemed to be unsound. The original streetwall controls in the area of Foch-Allenby and Etoile were translated into two diagrammatic sections: SWA1 for the Maarad axis and SWA2 for the Foch-Allenby area.

Provisions relating to these two types of streetwalls defined the building height and the required architectural treatment of its façades. Solid to void ratios, proportions of façade openings and construction materials were specified. Natural stone finish was mandatory, except for the building crown to be selected according to Solidere specifications.

In the case of middle- and large-scale elevations, located along the extensions of Foch and Allenby streets outside the historic core, streetwall controls SW1/SW2, SW3/SW4 and SW5 were formulated around the same tripartite division and setback approach, to guarantee visual continuity between the old and new sections of the streetscapes.

Roofscapes

Special attention was given to the roofscape in Foch-Allenby and Etoile and other BCD sectors. In both new and extant buildings, the crown above the cornice line was subject to the following constraints: a minimum setback of 1.5 m from the façade plane; and a building height limit of 24 m for the two types of streetwalls applied to the Conservation Area. No structure (access stairs, satellite dishes, telecommunication towers, etc.) was to be allowed beyond this limit, with the exception of pitched tiled roofs. These had to comply to a minimum inclination of 25 degrees, which added another 2.5 meters to the building height.

To ensure a harmonious skyline, the rooftop was approached as a fifth façade. It was specified that mechanical equipment — such as lift machinery, water tanks and chillers — be concealed behind an enclosure and incorporated within the overall building mass. In many instances, claustra parapets and wooden pergolas were used to that effect (fig. 8.11-8.15). Roof gardens and terraces were encouraged, both in the general BCD planning regulations and in the specific development/ restoration briefs. Accordingly, a number of restored buildings have incorporated landscape features into their roofscape design.

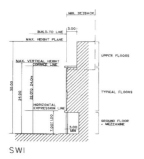
SWI

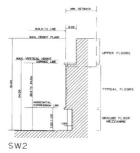
SW2

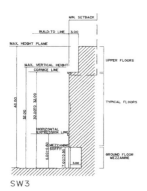
SW3

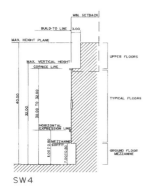
SW4

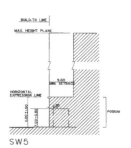
SW5

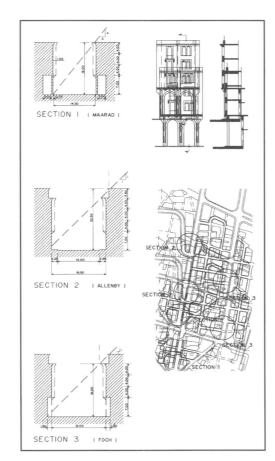

Figure 8.9
Streetwall analysis, Foch–
Allenby and Etoile area.

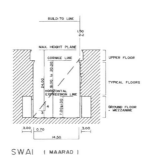
SWAI (MAARAD)

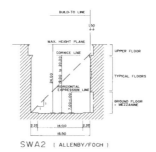
SWA2 (ALLENBY/FOCH)

Figures 8.10a, 8.10b
Streetwall controls adopted in
the Master Plan.

Figures 8.11, 8.12, 8.13, 8.14, 8.15
Claustra parapet wall and pergolas.

Shop Fronts and Private Signage

A signage manual issued by Solidere sets detailed guidelines for private signage in the BCD that complement the provisions of the Lebanese building code. Specifications as to the positioning, size, scale and proportions of signage ensure its adaptation to the shape of architectural openings and street elevations. Other specifications relate to such features as lighting and color.

Required identification signs for each building consist of its name, mailing address, parking entrances and exits, and access for the handicapped. The names and logos of building occupants are confined to the main entrance hall (*fig. 8.16-8.17*). External signage is generally limited to the building base, defined by the horizontal expression line. No identification signs are allowed above this line, except for the names of major corporations and institutions occupying the entirety of the premises. In that case, wall-mounted letters without background are required to prevent distracting from building elevation and architectural details. Shop signs are integrated into the shop frontage (*fig. 8.18-8.24*). A homogenous background is recommended, in line with the rolling shutter color or the general façade color scheme. In view of its scale relative to other districts, the Conservation Area uses smaller signage lettering. Projecting signs and luminous boxes are prohibited.

Establishing these guidelines was particularly significant in the case of the Conservation Area, where the integrity of the historic townscape is an urban design priority. The policy of public and private signage coordination aimed at avoiding visual clutter and creating harmony. Signage design and implementation continue to be closely monitored by Solidere through a review process involving detailed drawings and samples of materials.

Figures 8.16, 8.17
Exterior and interior nameplates.

Figures 8.18, 8.19, 8.20, 8.21, 8.22, 8.123, 8.24
Signs for institutions and shops.

Figures 9.1, 9.2
Foch Street landscaping
Flower planter and landscaped street median.

Figures 9.3, 9.4, 9.5
Etoile Square landscaping
Ficus nitida, ficus australis, laurus nobilis.

Figure 9.6
Small garden facing the Municipality of Beirut.

Figure 9.7
Amir Munzer Mosque with landscaped placette.

Chapter 9

Adapting Streetscape to District Character

The 'area-based' revitalization approach adopted for the BCD attaches special importance to the provision of high-quality public space. In Foch-Allenby and Etoile, the public domain was deemed more than a spatial background, as it is mainly from a pedestrian perspective that the area is approached and perceived. Accordingly, it was enhanced by a judicious choice of trees and plants, paving materials and landscape design, as well as by the harmonious design of signage, street lighting and all other street furniture. While street paving and decorative lighting were adapted to the character of the historic core, street furniture and signage design conformed to a unified contemporary style that would establish visual continuity throughout the city center.

Landscaping

Relatively little emphasis has been placed on landscaping in Foch-Allenby and Etoile, compared to the rest of the BCD, in keeping with its original French Mandate character. The choice of trees and plants aimed mostly at differentiating between the two sub-areas by enhancing the character of each.

In Foch-Allenby, the dominant landscape feature consists of flower planters adorning pedestrian roads or marking their entrances (fig. 9.1). A landscaped median in Foch Street acts as a visual relief from excessive hardscaping (fig. 9.2).

In the Etoile area, trees have been introduced. The initial idea of planting palm trees was abandoned due to the potential interference of their roots with the infrastructure. Instead, ficus nitida was selected for the base of the clock tower; ficus australis for the periphery of the square; and laurus nobilis for the radiating streets (fig. 9.3-9.5).

Three small gardens, distributed along Weygand Street, complement the landscaping of streets and squares within the intermediate zone between the Foch-Allenby and Etoile sub-areas. A small garden in front of the Municipality annex highlights the entrance of the Conservation Area from the adjoining Martyrs' Square. An open space at the intersection of Foch, Weygand and Ahdab streets provides a visual link between three major BCD landmarks: al Omari Mosque, Amir Assaf Mosque and the Municipality building (fig. 9.6). A small placette behind Amir Munzer Mosque, formerly part of Souk Bazerkan, has been landscaped into an intimate and shaded open space (fig. 9.7).

Hardscaping

The paving scheme implemented in the historic core complements the rich stonework on building elevations. The choice of street-finishing materials distinguishes between vehicular and pedestrian roads, thus visually articulating the hierarchy of the traffic network. Narrow pedestrian streets and crossings are paved with basalt cobblestones recycled from the city center, while vehicular and wide pedestrian streets are covered with new uniformly cut basalt (see fig. 4.7a). Overall, this treatment provides visual continuity between pedestrian and vehicular surfaces and encourages outdoor activities and events (fig. 9.8-9.9).

The majority of sidewalks, curbs and trims (outlining pedestrian areas) have been executed in granite. Striped bands of polished granite have been integrated at regular intervals into the paving of the Maarad arcaded passages (fig. 9.10). Concrete has also been used in sidewalk paving, either in its natural gray color or mixed with fine black gravel, as in the northern section of Allenby Street.

Figure 9.8
Street hardscaping and shops in
the Foch-Allenby area.

Figure 9.9
Sidewalk cafés in the Maarad area.

Figure 9.10
Polished granite bands of Maarad arcade.

Figure 9.11
Zaghloul-Foch intersection emphasizing
pedestrian street paving and the
positioning of flower planters and bollards.

Street Lighting

In line with the historical character of the area, 1920s and 1930s lanterns, brackets and decorative lampposts were replicated at the original manufacturer in France, Fonderie de l'Est, to be used along main and secondary streets of Foch-Allenby and Etoile.

Five variations of lighting were created, according to street type and width:
- Lightposts with banner holders were mounted in the Foch Street median to complement its formal avenue layout (*fig. 9.12*).

- Lightposts with twin cantilevered lanterns were installed around Etoile Square (*fig. 9.13*).

- Lightposts with single cantilevered lanterns were placed along Allenby Street as well as main and secondary pedestrian-priority roads (*fig. 9.14*).

- Wall-mounted cantilevered lanterns were used for narrow passages (*fig. 9.15*).

- Suspended lanterns were fixed to the keystones of the Maarad arcade (*fig. 9.16*).

Furthermore, traditional scroll-shaped brackets and small lanterns were used for Foch-Allenby and Etoile, where as cast-iron Art Deco brackets with large lanterns were employed in the rest of the historic core. The richly decorated base of the Foch and Allenby lampposts carries a badge featuring the cedar and the Phoenician trireme.

Figure 9.12

Figure 9.13

Figure 9.14

Figure 9.15

Figure 9.16

Other Street Furniture

Besides lighting, street furniture in the BCD consists of bollards, trash bins, culvert ventilation towers, newsstands, bus shelters, police kiosks, traffic barriers, telephone booths, flagpoles, benches, planters and shielded trash containers. Some of these elements are designed for a dual purpose: culvert ventilation towers allow for the display of advertisements, general information or artwork; newsstands also serve as tourist information points. Landscaping and street furniture elements are clustered together and/or aligned in order to facilitate pedestrian movement and create a barrier-free environment for the disabled (*fig. 9.17 - 9.21*).

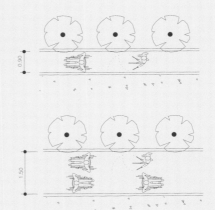

Figure 9.17
Barrier-free environment for the disabled.

■ Street Furniture

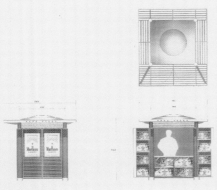

Figure 9.18
Newsstand.

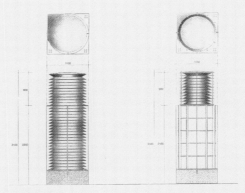

Figure 9.19
Ventilation tower.

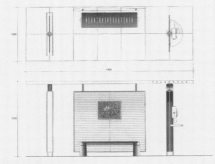

Figure 9.20
Bus shelter type 1.

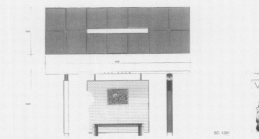

Figure 9.21
Bus shelter type 2.

Public Signage and Way-Finding

While BCD traffic signs are a Solidere responsibility, other public signage falls under the Municipality's umbrella. A unified, distinctive signage was formulated by Solidere, in agreement with the Municipality and the international French-speaking cities association AIMF (Association Internationale des Maires et Responsables des Capitales et Métropoles Partiellement ou Entièrement Francophones), which contributed to the financing of directional signs in Beirut.

The signage system in two languages — Arabic and French — involves, in addition to traffic signs, a comprehensive pedestrian and vehicular way-finding system composed of directional signs and street names and also provides guidelines for private signage.

All BCD signs, locally manufactured in line with international conventions and standards, sought to improve on prevailing esthetics without compromising legibility. The adopted design succeeded in resolving the main visual problems associated with installing traffic signs citywide. Because the shapes of standard traffic signs — square, rectangle, hexagon, triangle and circle — do not correspond when positioned back to back, a simple but visually effective solution was devised, which consisted in laying out all signs on similar rectangular or square-shaped plates of petroleum blue in background color (fig. 9.22). The installation of directional signs was governed by two innovative requirements:

- The introduction of orientation maps for pedestrian use.

- The allowance of clear passage around pedestrian signs for the convenience of wheelchair users. This requirement mandated fixing vehicular directional signs on a single pole instead of two, to reduce clutter on sidewalks and liberate a minimum 90-cm clear passage for the disabled.

Directional signs

The design of directional signs is based on a modular system, sustained by two vertical poles that are conically shaped and which can also accommodate cantilevered car signs. Pedestrian orientation panels are 50 x 70 cm (the standard size of a poster) and their reverse side can be used as a billboard (fig. 9.24-9.27). In the historic core, each panel is fixed on a bronze oval base plate, featuring a high relief of wheat stems, the Phoenician symbol for fertility. Outside the historic core, the identifying symbol changes to a bas-relief map of the BCD.

In Foch-Allenby and Etoile as in the rest of the Conservation Area, street names are engraved on rectangular granite plates with bronze fixation clamps. In other parts of the BCD, blue-glazed porcelain is expected to be used, as in the rest of the city. Street and sector names and numbers are grouped on the same plate to limit cluttering of walls (fig. 9.23).

Figure 9.22
New design of traffic regulation sign with blue background and fixation clamps.

Figure 9.23
Street name panel for historic core.

Figure 9.24
Single directional sign.

Figure 9.25
Double directional sign.

Figure 9.26
Pedestrian orientation panel.

Figure 9.27
Directional signs are designed to be accessible for the disabled.

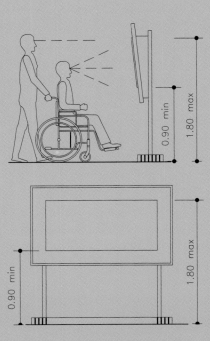

The recovery of streets, squares and architectural frontages forming the public domain has restored the formal urban character of the Foch-Allenby and Etoile area. At the same time, building interiors, the main components of the private domain, have been modernized and brought to par with the contemporary standards of comfort and efficiency imposed by market demand. These two concurrent processes — conservation and rehabilitation from the outside in, modernization from within — constituted the second important stage in the development of the office building in the traditional center of Beirut. The first stage had occurred in the 1920s and 1930s. It was then that the office building was introduced as a new building type, in response to the emergence of Foch-Allenby and Etoile as the capital's modern business district. Today, three quarters of a century later, those office buildings have been recovered and upgraded through the reemergence of Foch-Allenby and Etoile as Beirut's new historic district. This section traces this two-stage evolution by outlining continuity and change in the morphology of plans and the physiognomy of the office buildings.

Between the mid-nineteenth and early twentieth centuries, port-related sites and districts in Beirut, as in other colonial outposts around the Eastern Mediterranean, underwent a rapid process of development that involved three types of change: extension through land reclamation; regularization of the urban fabric; and a progressive shift from traditional building types (such as khans) to a new breed of specialized structures (such as office buildings, department stores, hotels, banks, customs houses and warehouses). The early, pre-1920 offices of the Beirut city center were generally accommodated in residential buildings of the prevalent central hall type with its pitched roof and triple arch. In the following decades, with the enlargement of the port, the expansion of trade and the development of Foch-Allenby and Etoile, a distinctive office building type emerged. Responding to the functional demands of the times, it provided workspace dedicated to commerce, banking and shipping. In order to accommodate a wide range of functions, this transitional office type consisted of a central hall layout suitable for both commercial and residential use. It was characterized by an eclectic stone façade that reflected prevailing European stylistic trends. The dialectic relationship between traditional interior and westernized exterior marked the 1920s and 1930s as a transitional period between tradition and modernity in architecture.

The present recovery of Foch-Allenby and Etoile has reversed this paradigm. From wrapping a modern envelope around traditionally built interiors, the objective has evolved to preserving traditional envelopes around modern interiors. On the outside, the interventions included simple renovation, faithful reconstitution, informed reinterpretation, creative remodeling and contextual infill. Inside, the choice was either to integrate modern facilities within the existing structure or to demolish the internal structure and build a new modern core. Chapter 10 explores the building conservation strategies that were adopted for the rapid recovery of Foch-Allenby and Etoile, using specific examples from the area.

It investigates the challenging task of repairing war-damaged frontages and emphasizes issues of scale and stone craftsmanship. It also looks at the process of modernizing interiors to bring them up to contemporary standards of efficiency, security and comfort. Chapter 11 focuses on stone repair as one of the most important aspects of the recovery process, owing to the high prevalence of stone buildings and the wide range of stone types and stone damage. It outlines the evolution of stone repair techniques applied throughout the project, and shows how local skills and the latest international techniques and standards were combined to revive a vanishing craft. Finally, Chapter 12 discusses the issue of integrating modern features in old structures to meet contemporary standards. It takes building 131, a shell structure that has been completely reconstructed from within, as a representative case to point out the range of constraints involved in conservation work. The chapter raises the question of how to bridge the gap between conservation choices and actual implementation, an issue that will be addressed in Section Five.

Chapter 10

Recovering Building Exteriors

Within the context of the Solidere-led reconstruction and development of the BCD, the Maarad axis presented relatively few challenging conservation choices, given the uniformity of its streetwalls, the predominance of stone elevations, and the contained damage inflicted by the war on the building fabric. Foch-Allenby, by contrast, with its eclectic architectural character and the greater level of war damage, presented a vast array of conservation options. An overall preservation strategy was therefore articulated from the start, based on an assessment of the condition of each building and the extent to which it related to the overall street frontage. This contextual approach allowed for existing structures to be upgraded to their original design; for new infill development to match the neighboring structures; and for the overall street profiles to read as a harmonious entity. Although preservation strategies and guidelines were established at an early stage of the project, the design and actual implementation turned out to be, as will be seen, an incremental process based on progressive adjustments to local constraints and international standards.

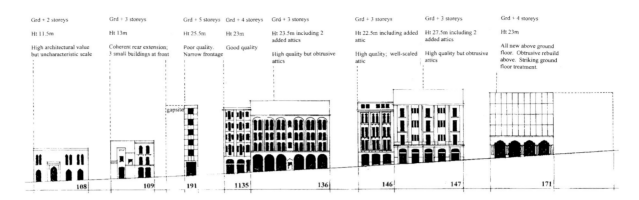

Figure 10.1
Allenby Street east elevation.

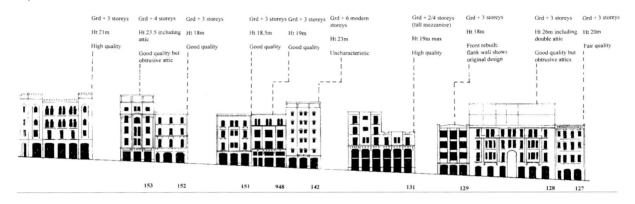

Figure 10.2
Foch Street west elevation.

Conservation Issues

In 1993 and 1994, Solidere commissioned a number of technical studies in preparation for the BCD reconstruction, which allowed for the immediate start of operations upon the company's inception in 1994. With the Conservation Area ranking highest on the priority list in Phase One of the Master Plan, a streetscape and architectural survey of Foch-Allenby and Etoile was one of the first studies conducted, along with a three-dimensional photogrammetric recording of retained buildings. In the assessment of each building, a distinction was made between the original structure and later additions, and attention was given to maintaining visual continuity between the buildings and street fronts. The study, critical in formulating a comprehensive restoration strategy, was based on the following observations (*fig 10.1 - 10.10*):

Some structures had not been completed to their intended heights. By remaining significantly lower than the adjoining structures, they created a gap in the street frontage. These buildings usually consisted of a retail ground floor and one or two additional stories (Foch Street, lot 131; Allenby Street, lots 108 and 109). In one case, the building was originally intended as a two-story structure, with an entablature clearly marking its crowning (Moutrane Street, lot 137).

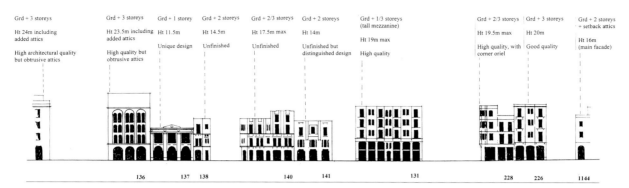

Grd + 3 storeys	Grd + 3 storeys	Grd + 1 storey	Grd + 2 storeys	Grd + 2/3 storeys	Grd + 2 storeys	Grd + 1/3 storeys (tall mezzanine)		Grd + 2/3 storeys	Grd + 3 storeys	Grd + 2 storeys + setback attics
Ht 24m including added attics	Ht 23.5m including added attics	Ht 11.5m	Ht 14.5m	Ht 17.5m max	Ht 14m	Ht 19m max		Ht 19.5m max	Ht 20m	Ht 16m (main facade)
High architectural quality but obtrusive attics	High quality but obtrusive attics	Unique design	Unfinished	Unfinished	Unfinished but distinguished design	High quality		High quality, with corner oriel	Good quality	

136   137   138   140   141   131   228   226   1144

Figure 10.3
Moutrane Street north elevation.

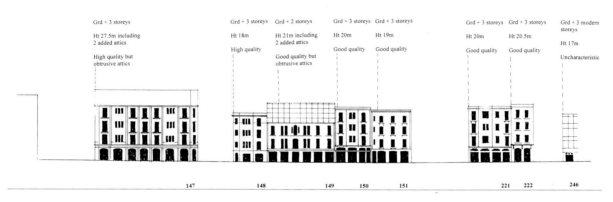

Grd + 3 storeys	Grd + 3 storeys	Grd + 2 storeys	Grd + 3 storeys	Grd + 3 storeys	Grd + 3 storeys	Grd + 3 storeys	Grd + 3 modern storeys
Ht 27.5m including 2 added attics	Ht 18m	Ht 21m including 2 added attics	Ht 20m	Ht 19m	Ht 20m	Ht 20.5m	Ht 17m
High quality but obtrusive attics	High quality	Good quality but obtrusive attics	Good quality	Good quality	Good quality	Good quality	Uncharacteristic

147   148   149   150   151   221   222   246

Figure 10.4
Saad Zaghloul Street north elevation.

Some structures had been extended vertically during the 1950s and 1960s, usually to reach the maximum height allowed under zoning and building regulations. In a few cases, a whole modern body was superimposed on the ground floor, sharply contrasting with the original style of the building and its immediate context (Allenby Street, lot 171; Uruguay Street, lot 246; Foch Street, lot 142).

Attic floors had sometimes been added in a style that was unsympathetic with the rest of the building. While they were visually unobtrusive when set back from the building envelope, they were visible from the street, especially along wide streets like Foch and Allenby and when aligned with the building elevation (Allenby east side, lots 136 and 147; Foch east side, lots 153 and 128).

Poor quality repairs might have been undertaken in earlier phases of conservation, as in the 1980s and especially on the Allenby-Maarad axis. Furthermore, some structures built on substandard lots needed to be either demolished or integrated with adjoining developments (Allenby, lot 191).

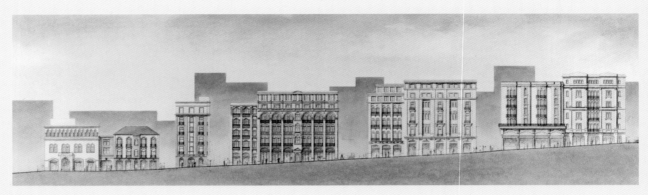

Figure 10.5
Proposed Allenby Street east elevation.

Figure 10.6
Proposed Foch Street east elevation.

Figure 10.7
Allenby Street west elevation
before restoration.

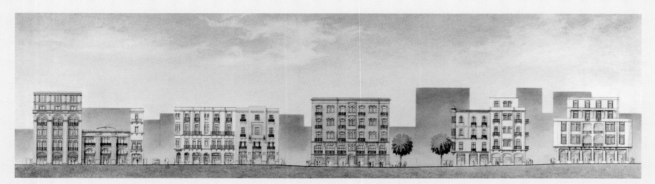

Figure 10.8
Proposed Moutrane Street north elevation.

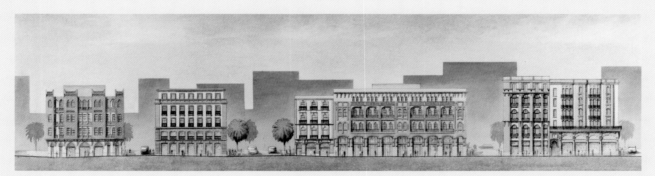

Figure 10.9
Proposed Saad Zaghloul Street south elevation.

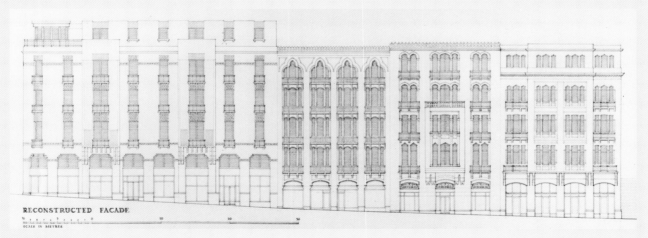

RECONSTRUCTED FACADE

SCALE IN METRES

Figure 10.10
Proposed Allenby Street west elevation.

Conservation Strategies

Based on this technical study, five approaches to building conservation were defined: restoration, refurbishment, renovation, rebuilding and remodeling. For each approach, a level and type of action was recommended for façade repair, stylistic treatment and permitted additions. These were integrated into the guidelines and schematic proposal included in the restoration and development briefs that were later prepared for each building (see page 191). These briefs were provided to the owner and his architect to orient the articulation of a preliminary design and restoration strategy. The final scheme was then refined in consultation with Solidere to reflect the architect's interpretation and/or response to economic and time constraints.

Renovating and restoring

According to the conservation guidelines, renovation and restoration involve the meticulous repair of retained buildings "as nearly as possible to their known original state." Renovation applies to partially damaged buildings that required minor repairs to their façades "due to the effect of time and environment" and "basically involves cleaning the existing fabric, using any special techniques." Restoration is concerned with more severely damaged buildings in need of an elaborate repair work that involves "removing accretions, reassembling existing components, repairing or replacing damaged or missing components with matching new materials and matching decorative details." This conservation approach, which was extended to religious and public buildings (the 'exempt' buildings), applied mainly to high-quality office structures that had been built according to their original design and despite partial destruction retained their stylistic integrity. In fact, most of the buildings in Foch-Allenby and Etoile belonged to this category. They were either restored or renovated, and in each case were to revert as nearly as possible to their prewar condition. A notable example of restoration is lot 27, northwest of Allenby, the only Art Deco building in the area (see *fig. 7.56*). Despite the deteriorated condition of its elevation, the building was reconstituted together with its adjoining structures to the minutest detail. The result represents one of the best examples of a unified frontage in the area. The same may be said about some of the buildings or groups of buildings to the east and west of Foch Street (*fig. 10.11 - 10.18*) and the majority of the arcaded buildings along the Maarad axis. Structures that had suffered only partial damage, such as those from the 1950s and 1960s in the area between Etoile and Riad al Solh Street, were simply renovated.

Renovation and restoration guidelines left little margin for creative solutions. This was particularly so when the surviving structure provided clear evidence of the original materials and ornaments. Cases that involved the reconstitution of original details by using contemporary techniques and materials, or the reproduction of missing pieces based on prototypes from other surviving buildings, presented a special challenge. The standard problem was to retrace wrought iron or cast stone balustrades and gates in the absence of surviving fragments or prewar photographs. Informed guesses were based on extensive research and on detailed knowledge of the building morphologies of that period, both inside and outside the BCD. Other methods included the review of Western catalogues of the period. Another challenge was the identification of matching stones for replacement and patching and developing the construction skills needed to carry out masonry repairs. In sum, public frontage restoration, as opposed to interior renovation, mainly required technical knowledge and managerial skills and left little scope for design creativity on the part of the architect.

Lot 228 Marfaa

Architects
Pierre Neema and
Meguerditch Yapoudjian

Structural Engineer
Souheil Shehfe

Contractor
Owners

Type of stone
Yellow limestone

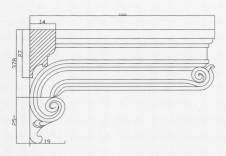

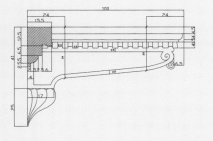

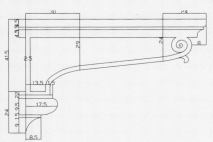

Figures 10.11, 10.12, 10.13, 10.14, 10.15
Corbel details.

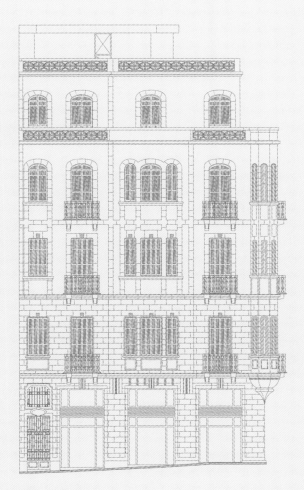

Figure 10.16
Elevation on Foch Street.

Figures 10.17, 10.18
Detail before and after restoration.

■ Lot 24 Marfaa

Architects
R & K Consultants sarl

Structural Engineer
Karim Karam

Contractor
Société du Lot 24

Type of stone
Original: Abou dhifr
New: Mansouriya

Figures 10.19, 10.20
Before and after restoration.

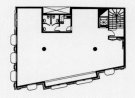
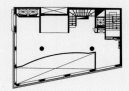
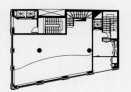

Figures 10.21, 10.22, 10.23
Plans.

Figures 10.24, 10.25
Arch detail before and
after restoration.

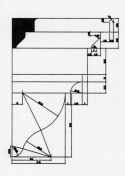
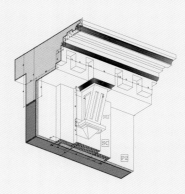

Figures 10.26, 10.27
Corbels details.

Figures 10.28, 10.29
Lot 171 before and after restoration.

Rebuilding

As stated in the conservation guidelines: "A limited number of the buildings retained for conservation have been subjected to such severe damage, or even partial or total destruction, as to require reconstitution, according to the elevations specified in their respective restoration brief. These are to be based, as nearly as possible, on archival material or record drawings of the buildings." Such buildings were preserved either for their historic, architectural or townscape value or for "other reasons". In the former case, they had to be rebuilt to their original condition; in the latter, any modification had to remain within the confines of the building's original style. An interesting example of rebuilding is lot 24, a partially destroyed small structure on the north side of Fakhry Bey Street (*fig. 10.19 - 10.27*), which has been rebuilt to its original state and carefully integrated with the adjoining structures. Another example is lot 171 at the intersection of Allenby and Weygand (*fig. 10.28 - 10.29*). The ground floor of the building constitutes the most elaborate example of Orientalist style in the area. The upper section, a modern addition with curtain walls, was highly damaged during the war; it has been rebuilt in a neo-Orientalizing style, in tune with its lower section.

Figures 10.30, 10.31
Lot 1154 before and after restoration.

Figures 10.32, 10.33
Lot 287 before and after restoration.

Completion as per original design

Conservation guidelines do not develop a specific approach to address the restoration of buildings which were never completed. However, they do recognize the possibility of intervening in the restoration of "existing exterior façades of retained buildings as nearly as possible to their known original state"; concurrently, they encourage adaptation to "the building's surrounding context, or similar buildings in the area."

Some of the buildings along the Maarad axis had not originally been completed to their intended height, as construction had been interrupted after the first, second or third floor. Such buildings, situated at the southern end of the Maarad axis, towards Amir Bachir Street, have been extended vertically to restore streetwall visual continuity (*fig. 10.30 - 10.35*). The Foch Street frontage was also interrupted by two incomplete structures, lot 225 at the corner of Azmi Bey Street (*fig. 10.36 - 10.39*) and lot 131 between Beyhum and Moutrane streets. Both of those structures have been extended to the permitted height of 24 meters, using the original architectural language deduced from existing building sections. In the state thus acquired, they constitute striking examples of fully integrated elevations, in which it is difficult to differentiate between the original sections and the vertical additions.

Figures 10.34, 10.35
Lot 1142 before and
after restoration.

Lot 225 Marfaa

Architects
Saïd Bitar,
Ingénierie et Urbanisme

Structural Engineer
Saïd Bitar,
Ingénierie et Urbanisme

Contractor
Berytus

Type of stone
Mansouriya as existing

Figures 10.36, 10.37
Before and after restoration.

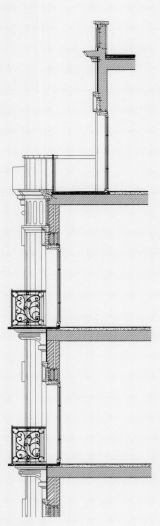

Figure 10.38
Wall section.

Figure 10.39
Pediment detail.

Figures 10.40, 10.41
Lot 142 before and after restoration.

Figures 10.42, 10.43
Lot 149 before and after restoration.

Figures 10.44, 10.45
Lot 246 before and after restoration.

Remodeling

While rebuilding and completion required strict adherence to the original building appearance, leaving limited room for interpretation on the part of the architect, remodeling was geared to providing "new façades or building enclosures to an existing structure." This gave the architect the opportunity to investigate both existing site evidence and the predominant character and range of architectural styles in the area in order to come up with a contextual answer. The task of selecting a particular style that conformed to the existing context therefore demanded a complex and highly subjective decision. This was especially the case in Foch-Allenby, where eclecticism dominated. Such decisions were also subject to economic considerations, since remodeling offered a variety of solutions, ranging from simple rendering to elaborate stone carving.

In Foch-Allenby, remodeling was mainly applied to structures whose upper floors were completed in the International style of the 1950s and 1960s. An example is lot 142 (fig. 10.40-10.41) on the intersection of Foch and Moutrane streets. The building originally consisted of a ground floor executed in carved stone. The upper floors, added at a later date, had a flat rendered elevation and simple rectangular openings. In his design, the architect extrapolated the syntax of the whole elevation based on the stonework at the building base. As the building stands now, the façade reads as an integrated whole, and it is difficult to distinguish between the old base and the remodeled upper section. A similar approach was applied to lot 149 on Zaghloul Street, where a vertical addition dating back to the 1960s was wrapped in an elaborate limestone façade matching the original 1920s base both in material and detailing (fig. 10.42-10.43). A unique solution in Foch-Allenby was adopted for lot 246, at the intersection of Uruguay and Azmi Bey streets. The glass-reinforced concrete (GRC) elements applied to the existing modern elevation of the upper floors were designed in a contemporary retro style in keeping with the Art Deco cast concrete base (fig. 10.44-10.45).

The roof section of buildings, though less visible from the street level, entailed a more delicate remodeling process. The existing attic floors, aligned with the façade and extending vertically to more than one floor, constituted a heavy mass that clearly clashed in style and surface treatment with the rest of the building. Restoration, which comprised stone-cladding and an integrated treatment of window surrounds, managed to reduce the visual difference between the building roof and body. A good example is lot 1080 in Etoile Square (fig. 10.49). Other solutions, involving the simple rendering of the surface and the addition of a stone frame around openings, as in lots 153 and 173 in the Foch-Allenby area, were not as effective visually (fig. 10.50-10.51).

In cases where the attic floor was recessed from the main elevation, a structural frame was used to link the two planes together. The elaborate treatment of this frame, with the addition of handrails and parapet, constituted a successful strategy to crown the building and provide a visual transition between the main and the recessed façades (fig. 10.46-10.48). A more straightforward treatment consisted of adding a pediment to further emphasize and demarcate the main elevation from the recessed plane (fig. 10.52).

A unique example of roof remodeling applied to two adjoining Art Deco and neo-Islamic buildings, situated on the western side of Allenby and acquired by the same owner (fig. 10.53). There, a similar treatment of the two parapets and recessed attic floors helped link the two structures visually, combining their styles in the eclectic spirit of the Foch-Allenby area.

Finally, a unique case of façade remodeling associated with a new addition is illustrated by a block-scale development at the intersection of Beyhum and Tijara streets. The block consists of the two lots 1462 and 119, the former vacant and the latter occupied by a stone-clad early modern building that had been severely impacted by the war. The remodeling extended the existing building to create a new addition on the adjoining site, and the two structures were wrapped in a sober neo-colonial elevation. A similar approach was used in the building on lot 1202, situated on Uruguay Street behind al Dabbagha Mosque. An early modern elevation was decorated with stone detailing, such as rusticated corners and window surrounds, to simulate a neo-colonial façade. In both cases also, the structures posed the basic problem of concealing the original building character and date of construction, in an effort to adapt to the predominant architectural character of the area.

Figures 10.46, 10.47, 10.48
Lots 136, 147, 201 roof treatment.

Figure 10.49
Lot 1080 with reduced visual difference
between roof and body.

Figures 10.50, 10.51
Lots 153, 173 with visible difference
between roof and body.

Figure 10.52
Lot 149 roof top treatment.

Figure 10.53
Lot 104-27 roof top treatment.

Lot 1455 Marfaa, The Atrium

Architects
Builders Design Consultant

Structural Engineer
Ghassan Salibi

Contractor
Mouawad Engineering and Partners

Type of stone
Hajar forni

Figure 10.54
The Atrium building.

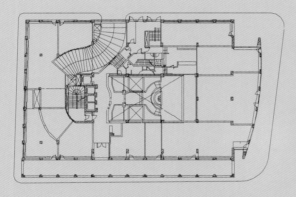

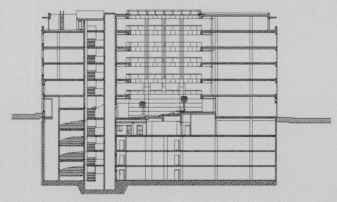

Figures 10.55, 10.56
Ground floor plan and section.

Figure 10.57
Interior view of the Atrium building.

Figure 10.58
Deputies' offices building.

Contextual Infill

Empty lots in Foch-Allenby and Etoile are both rare and randomly distributed. Because they are located in a historic context, their space utilization is severely constrained by existing street alignments, building envelopes, street-wall controls and the area's predominant architectural character. The main question that confronts any infill development on such sites is: to what extent should it reveal its contemporary identity and to what extent should it blend in with the existing historical context.

The Atrium building, and the Deputies' offices building on Etoile Square, provided two different answers to that challenging question: the former was carefully integrated into its surroundings, while the latter was boldly set apart.

The Atrium building (*fig. 10.54 - 10.57*) is strategically situated on lot 1455 at the intersection of Weygand Street and the Maarad axis, facing al Omari Mosque. Its new eastern elevation both incorporates and ends the Maarad axis by providing an abstract interpretation of its frontage. The elevation and arcaded profile of the ground floor are in keeping with the treatment of the Maarad arcade, while the walls and openings use a simplified ornamental language. In the roof section, the cantilevered metallic pergola crowning the building clearly contrasts with the solid stone elevation. The northern elevation on Weygand presents a curtain wall subdivided into a central transparent bay flanked by an elongated glazed opening, a clear allusion to the hierarchical ordering of the bay window elevations of Foch-Allenby. This approach may be described as 'serial contextualism', since each elevation mirrors the adjoining street character. It is also an attempt to conform to the ordering principles of the historical façades of the area, while providing a modern interpretation of the façades by the use of new materials and architectural details.

The Deputies' offices building (*fig. 10.58*) is a block-scale development on lot 1156, fronting the southern elevation of the Parliament. It is built on three assembled lots that include the former Banco di Roma site. The building con-

sists of an irregular stone base and an upper section of dark opaque glass, which acts as a mirror while outlining the simple massing of the building. Historical elements, like arched windows, are randomly distributed on the elevation, alluding to the surrounding architectural language. Unlike the Atrium building, the Deputies' offices building does not invite a detailed reading of its elevations. The whole envelope reads as a single entity, the emphasis being more on massing than on architectural detailing. At the same time, its form clearly contrasts with that of the Parliament building. To the symmetry and monumentality of the latter structure, it opposes an informal balance between architectural elements and a marked contrast between materials. This difference reduces the visual competition between the two buildings, although it does not necessarily make them complementary.

Incremental Learning Process

The above diversity of solutions, ranging from simple restoration to contextual infill, invites reflection on the importance of built-in flexibility in design and in design control. The responsiveness of the design review process, the necessary trade-offs between esthetic and economic considerations and the competing philosophies of meticulous conservation versus free interpretation of building style were issues to be discussed and resolved on a building-by-building basis. This called for constant readjustments in the monitoring and decision-making process. The differences between the initial guidelines provided by the restoration/development briefs and the final outcome, i.e. the restored building itself, clearly testify to that. Such an incremental adjustment and learning process did not stop at the design approval phase, but continued throughout the implementation phase. This is best illustrated in the evolution of the stone restoration techniques witnessed throughout the process of recovering the Foch-Allenby and Etoile buildings, which resulted in the quality repair of stone elevations.

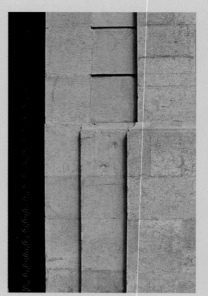

Figures 11.1, 11.2
Lots 152, 147, hard and soft limestone.

Figure 11.3
Lot 148, soft limestone.

Figure 11.4
Lot 148, hard limestone carved into decorative shapes.

Figure 11.5
Lot 287, hajar forni.

Chapter 11

Stone Works

Perhaps the most notable aspect of the restoration of Foch-Allenby and Etoile is the high quality repair of its building façades. Although traditional masonry restoration is still in demand, given the high prevalence of stone use in historic monuments and domestic buildings, it is today a vanishing craft. Different restoration options of masonry façades were considered by Solidere for Foch-Allenby and Etoile. The first was the use of artificial stone, which several European companies were marketing as an economical substitute. The second consisted of setting up a stone masonry school for the training of local craftsmen. The developers themselves suggested the third option, which was ultimately adopted. It consisted of identifying a large body of experienced stonemasons both in Mount Lebanon and Aleppo. By following a systematic process of identifying the different stone typologies in the Conservation Area and investigating their local availability, and by bringing in a formally educated stone conservator to help in field supervision, it was possible to develop a new trade that combined local craftsmanship and international standards of quality.

Stone Typology

The process of masonry restoration began with a three-dimensional photogrammetric recording of retained buildings, together with a visual assessment of the levels of damage and types of repair needed for each structure. This was followed by a detailed survey of the different stone typologies used in the Conservation Area, which identified eleven different types of limestone, along with compatible stone quarries around the country. The inventory, constituting the first and most extensive survey of Lebanon's stone types undertaken to date, sheds light on the building materials and techniques of the 1920s and 1930s and will continue to serve as an indispensable reference for quality stone restoration.

Among the types of limestone identified, the most common is of the beige and compact variety (locally referred to as abou dhifr), which was used for the elevation base because of its strength and known resistance to impact. Soft yellow limestone, easy to carve, was reserved for the façade's decorative details. This combination of hard and soft limestone was used in about half the buildings in the Conservation Area (*fig. 11.1 - 11.4*). In some cases, however, hard limestone was used for the entire façade, despite the difficulty of carving it into decorative patterns.

Most of the Foch-Allenby façades consist of stone and cement lime render. By contrast, those in the Etoile area are mostly built with yellow oolitic limestone (hajar mbarghal asfar, or hajar forni) (*fig. 11.5*). This variety is neither hard nor soft and is both hard-wearing and easy to carve, as shown by the elaborate façade detailing of most buildings in that area (*fig. 11.6 - 11.7*).

Different types of limestone were favored in different periods. Old churches, mosques and buildings of the Ottoman period used either white limestone as in the St Elie Greek-Catholic Church, or soft and porous limestone with lime render as in the al Omari and Amir Munzer mosques (*fig. 11.8 - 11.9*). Most buildings erected after 1950 used beige and fine-grained limestone (*fig. 11.10*). In general, the 1920s and 1930s remain the most creative period for the eclectic and decorative use of limestone. Among the different stone types and colors incorporated for carved ornamentation and decorative elements were white and rosy marble (shahm wa lahm) or granite (*fig. 11.11 - 11.12*) and red and white masonry for ablaq arches and bands to highlight specific parts of the façade (*fig. 11.13 - 11.14*).

Figures 11.6, 11.7
Lot 203 details.

Figures 11.8, 11.9
Al Omari and Amir Munzer mosques,
soft and porous sandstone.

Figure 11.10
Lot 130, beige and fine-grained
limestone.

Figure 11.11
Lot 171 columns carved in white
and rosy marble (shahm wa lahm).

Figure 11.12
Lot 136 entrance columns carved
in granite.

Figures 11.13, 11.14
Lots 157 and 173, ablaq arches
and bands in elevation.

Stone Damage Categories

The field survey of surviving buildings identified, in parallel with the structural condition, four categories of stone condition (*fig. 11.15*).

- The category with stone in good condition (*fig. 11.16 - 11.17*).

- The lightly damaged category, which mostly needed stone patching of bullet holes, eroded pockets and moldings, with only a limited amount of stone repair (*fig. 11.18 - 11.19*).

- The partly damaged category, which needed advanced repair of stone surfaces and protruding architectural elements, with limited stone replacement (*fig. 11.20 - 11.21*).

- The partly destroyed category, which needed stone addition, as well as the replacement and repair of structurally defective walls and severely damaged structures.

The last category was prevalent in the Foch-Allenby area. The first category was mostly represented by the buildings between Etoile Square and Riad al Solh Street, which include the Parliament, the Central Post office building and a large number of banking headquarters.

Evolution of Stone Restoration Techniques

A range of restoration techniques was then elaborated to cover the various types of repair, from surface touch-up to the removal and rebuilding of severely damaged sections of a building façade. In the early phase of restoration, Western standards for restoration were applied as a guiding framework. In order to come up with a comprehensive strategy tailored to local needs, Solidere commissioned three of its buildings, in parallel, to different architects. A manual on methods of restoration was prepared by Solidere staff members responsible for on-site quality control, in conjunction with the three architects who contributed their own experience in the field. Intended as reference for architects and building contractors, the manual summarized the most common stone repair problems and solutions. For example, while the use of lime mortar had first been considered as a cheap alternative to stone for bullet hole patch-up work, it later proved to be a difficult and time-consuming process. To ensure good quality results, the process required the application of successive layers of mortar filling, with two or three days between each layer to allow it to cure slowly.

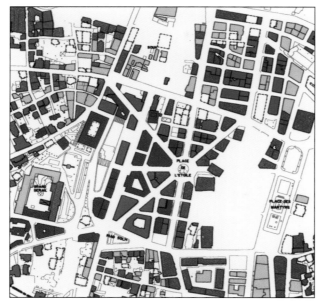

In good condition
Lightly damaged
Partly damaged
Partly destroyed

Figure 11.15
Building condition in the Conservation Area.

Figures 11.16, 11.17
Building in good condition:
lots 168, 203 before and after restoration.

Figures 11.18, 11.19
Building lightly damaged:
lots 201, 820 before and after restoration.

Figures 11.20, 11.21
Building partly damaged:
lots 1123, 1124 before and after restoration.

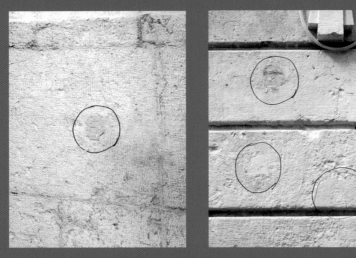

Figures 11.22, 11.23
Stone restoration techniques: patching.

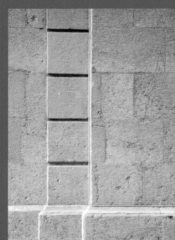

Figures 11.24, 11.25, 11.26, 11.27
Stone restoration techniques: piecing in.

Figures 11.28, 11.29
Dealing with stone patina: traces of bullets.

Figure 11.30
Dealing with stone patina: third-degree burns.

Neither was it cost-effective or even guaranteed in the long term, for the pigmented mortar could change color with aging and clash visually with its stone background.

Therefore, the patching method (*fig. 11.22-11.23*) was replaced by 'piecing in' (*fig. 11.24-11.27*), a technique that uses matching or reclaimed stone for the repair of small areas. With time, this technique was perfected through improvements in craftsmanship and the enforcement of high standards of quality, especially in relation to color, joints and fitting methods.

Strict procedures

Both piecing in and stone replacement work required strict sampling, testing and approval procedures. These consisted of:

• Visual identification of comparable stone types.

• Visual on-site comparison for approval.

• Testing of samples of original stone and proposed replacement for compressive strength, absorption and porosity.

• Clearance of test results.

• Forwarding a reference sample to Solidere.

• Ordering the materials and making sure that the quarry could supply the quantity needed to complete the work.

This last requirement was added at a later stage in order to avoid using different quarries for the same building, thereby compromising the homogeneity of stone elevations. The type, thickness and anchorage of the stone used for a work of restoration were all checked on site.

Dealing with Stone Patina

The experience gained triggered new attitudes towards stone restoration methods, most notably by favoring the preservation of age marks on stone surfaces over the systematic repair or erasure of traces of usage and weathering. As a result, one can see delicate shades of abrasion on restored façades, as well as traces of bullet holes (*fig. 11.22-11.29*) and dark red patches of third-degree burns (*fig. 11.30*). Not all age marks and traces of war damage were left intact, however: surfaces that had been 'eaten' by dense bullet marks were scraped and redressed to look like new, even though they lost some 15 mm of stone facing. More gentle techniques like washing were chosen to remove dirt and stain without causing abrasion to the surface. Washing techniques included medium pressure water jets and the use of fork instead of nozzle jets, as well as 'misting' and spraying. Combined water jet and sand were used to clean surfaces soiled by pollution and, in the case of severely stained stone, the surface was hammered in keeping with its original texture. These techniques were particularly favored over mechanical and chemical cleaning.

Re-Emerging Trade

The easy accessibility to stone quarries and the availability of experienced stonemasons made stone replacement a more economical alternative than piecing in or patching with mortar. The new methods, the increasing versatility in stone repair and the rapid improvement in the quality of work, as witnessed in all the renovation phases, point to the revival and development of an old trade, previously limited to traditional methods of stonemasonry. This will inevitably have an impact on stone restoration work in other projects, both nationally and regionally.

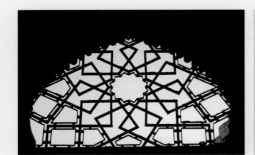

Figure 11.31
Pattern in broken arch.

Figure 11.32
Pattern in orientalist arch.

Figure 11.33
Pattern in flattened arch.

Figure 11.34
Pattern in round arch.

Figure 11.35
Pattern in lancet arch.

Figure 11.36
Traditional.

Figure 11.37
Scroll traditional.

Figure 11.38
Scroll traditional.

Figure 11.39
Scroll.

Figure 11.40
Scroll.

Figure 11.41
Scroll.

Figure 11.42
Scroll composite.

Figure 11.43
Geometric.

Figure 11.44
Geometric.

Figure 11.45
Composite.

Figure 11.46
Composite.

Figure 11.47
Scroll Art Deco.

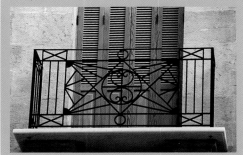

Figure 11.48
Art Deco – Art Nouveau.

Figure 11.49
Art Deco – Art Nouveau.

Figure 11.50
Art Deco – Art Nouveau.

Figure 11.51
Art Deco late transitional.

Figure 11.52
Art Deco late transitional.

Figure 11.53
Various styles.

Figure 11.54
Various styles.

Figure 11.55
Various styles.

Figure 11.56
Modern.

Figure 12.1
Building 150 interior.

Figure 12.2
Building 150 entrance.

Figure 12.3
Building 148 interior.

Chapter 12

Modernizing Building Interiors

The first generation of modern office buildings erected in the 1920s and 1930s was characterized by a simple layout and finish, which contrasted with the elaborate interiors of the domestic architecture of the time. While their façades were decorated with richly carved stone, their concrete skeletal structure was simple, repetitive and at the same time geared towards functionality and flexibility of use. In the current restoration process, the renovation of interiors was essential in order to bring them up to par with contemporary standards in space utilization and internal design, as well as in the provision of utility services and modern technology.

Accommodating Modern Needs

With respect to space utilization and internal design, the absence of historically significant interiors worth preserving allowed for changes in layout, color scheme and materials. In modernizing the office buildings, opting for an open plan layout was therefore considered as an alternative to preserving internal partitioning (fig. 12.1 - 12.3). While the latter would provide a more economical solution, which could be particularly appropriate when the office space was being recuperated by the original tenants, the open space alternative offered a more flexible solution favored by new owners, developers or tenants. In some instances, however, this solution was limited by the constraints of building codes. Existing codes for example stipulated that fenestration openings should be no less than one-tenth of the floor area, to ensure adequate ventilation and lighting. Hence, compliance with the codes could sometimes necessitate an enlargement or change in the shape of windows, which would jeopardize the integrity of the historical façade. Such conflicts between restoration practice and building codes prompted the updating of current codes to accommodate the demands of authentic conservation practice.

One common problem faced in the process of modernizing office space was the unobtrusive installation of up-to-date utility services. These include plumbing, electrical wiring, lighting, ventilation, heating and cooling, and security systems. The application of fire safety codes, the creation of a barrier-free environment for the disabled,

and the provision of adequate, mainly underground, storage and parking space presented the same problem. Other challenges pertaining to the building as a whole included the accommodation of ramps, adequate-size elevators and wheel-chair landings, all of which were difficult to plan and construct, given the narrow dimensions of existing entrance halls and staircases, especially in the smaller buildings.

The installation of air-conditioning units was deemed disruptive to the decorative character and architectural detailing of building façades. Similar considerations meant that heating-cooling systems that required the installation of towers on the roof often could not be added. In some buildings, such limitations were overcome by gutting out the interior core, then rebuilding it to modern standards. This process, referred to as shell structures, constituted one of the most original conservation solutions to be adopted for the first time in Lebanon. Finally, in telecommunications, a fiber optic network is planned to provide BCD buildings with a direct connection to high-capacity broadband services.

About half the buildings in Foch-Allenby were originally designed with a basement floor. The introduction of concrete during the early 1920s and the subsequent use of skeleton structures freed the ground floor from vaulting masses and bearing walls. This allowed for excavations to go below ground level and introduced new basements to be used as storage space for shops (see fig. 6.13). In the process of the BCD conservation and renovation, these

Lot 131 Marfaa

Architects
Ziad Akl Architecte

Structural Engineer
Rodolphe Mattar

Contractor
Batitec

Type of stone
Yellow limestone

Figure 12.4
Lot 131 under construction.

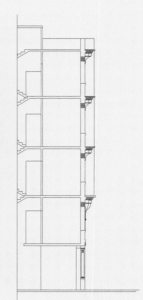

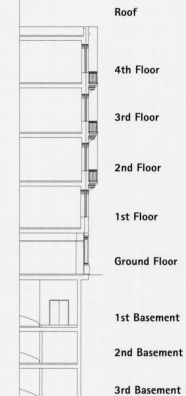

Roof

4th Floor

3rd Floor

2nd Floor

1st Floor

Ground Floor

1st Basement

2nd Basement

3rd Basement

Figures 12.5, 12.6
Wall section before
and after restoration.

Figures 12.7, 12.8
Lot 131 elevation and detail.

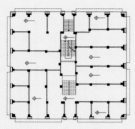

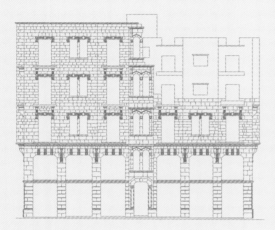

Figures 12.9, 12.10
Lot 131 ground floor plan and existing south elevation before restoration.

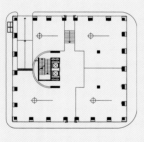

Figures 12.11, 12.12
Lot 131 ground floor plan and proposed south elevation after restoration.

basements were waterproofed and utilized for storage and service installations. Their use as parking space was not always possible; in many cases, it was hindered by the small size of the building footprint, the position of the structure and/or the difficulty in creating access ramps. Consequently, parking space was accommodated for the most part around the periphery of the Conservation Area.

Shell Structures

When developers insisted on the convenience of on-site parking, this meant extending the buildings below ground and adding basement floors. A case in point is building 131 on Foch Street (*fig. 12.4 - 12.12*). Its restoration involved the complete demolition of all its core, except for the façade, and excavating below ground level for the accommodation of three levels of parking. The building was also extended above ground to bring it up to its originally intended height. Since the complete demolition of retained buildings was prohibited by BCD regulations, the external envelope was kept and reinforced by steel bracing, and the new functional core was rebuilt from scratch. This tour de force, carried out within a saturated urban setting, posed substantial structural and operational challenges, since it involved straight-sided excavations and sheet piling carried to substantial depths. Concurrently, digging and building below the water table (around 8 m in Foch-Allenby) necessitated the subsurface drainage of basement walls and elaborate waterproofing.

Five other buildings underwent a similar process. Among them is building 157 (*fig. 12.13 - 12.14*), co-owned by Solidere, which was completely transformed from within, by the adoption of an atrium layout with a central entrance hall crossing the building from side to side and the addition of one basement floor. Building 137 was freed from its internal partitions and replanned into a symmetrical layout for pub and restaurant use (*fig. 12.15 - 12.21*).

■ Lot 157 Marfaa

Architects
Saïd Bitar
Ingénierie et Urbanisme

Structural Engineer
Saïd Bitar
Ingénierie et Urbanisme

Contractor
Joe Chiha

Type of stone
Yellow limestone

Figure 12.13
Lot 157 entrance.

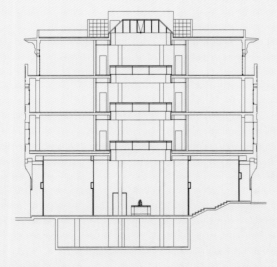

Figure 12.14
Lot 157 section.

Integrating Historic Fronts and Modern Interiors

Building 131 illustrates clearly the different roles building façades and interiors play when located in a historic setting. First, the façade emphasizes the dual nature of the building envelope, both as a protective shell enclosing the private domain and as a surface demarcating the boundary of the public domain. And second, the interior shows how new functional requirements may completely reshape the building core with regard to layout flexibility and the integration of modern services.

The first generation of speculative commercial buildings, which originated in Foch-Allenby and Etoile in the 1920s and 1930s, reflected the same dichotomy between exterior and interior. Their stone façades read as solid bearing walls that exhibit the styles and techniques of the period; from within, they stood as independent concrete structures, defining an optimal multifunctional layout. The current recovery and restoration have further reinforced this duality, emphasizing the historicity of the outside and the modernity of the inside. In both periods, the front becomes an economic asset that conveys unique status to the building and the interior offers functionality, comfort and efficiency. Both are a response to market demand in an upscale urban setting.

The restoration of building 131 elicits a question concerning the extent to which it is appropriate to tamper with the internal layout and external appearance of an old building. It is a clear reminder that buildings may be historically significant, but their survival and extended use remain dependent on contemporary realities. Those realities include: the extent of constant or renewed interest and respect for historic settings; the client's specifications and the possibility of accommodating them within the confines of existing buildings; compliance with government regulations; the merging of traditional crafts with contemporary techniques; and above all, in the absence of public subsidies, real estate economics. On the design level, these realities and constraints generate dissonance between the functional requirements of private space and the esthetic considerations regarding public fronts.

On the management level, they necessitate the creation of a coordinated framework capable of resolving legislative, technical and economic hurdles that may hamper the implementation of the developer's program.

Lot 137 Marfaa

Architects
AAA, Atelier des
Architectes Associés

Structural Engineer
Nabil Hennaoui

Contractor
Maken sarl

Type of stone
Yellow limestone

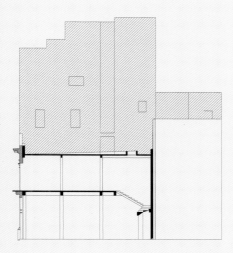

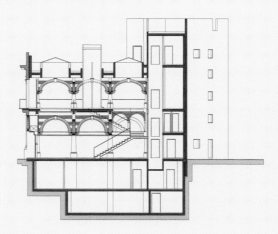

Figures 12.15, 12.16
Lot 137 ground floor plan and
section before restoration.

Figures 12.17, 12.18
Lot 137 ground floor plan and section
after restoration.

Figure 12.19
Lot 137 proposed elevation.

Figure 12.20, 12.21
Lot 137 before and after restoration.

The postwar reconstruction of the Beirut Central District is a highly symbolic act as well as an important catalyst for the initiation of economic recovery at the level of both city and nation. The product of a grand design vision, its realization was conditional on the setting up of an adequate legal and institutional framework. At the basis of the enacted legislation is Law 117 of 1991, which regulates the creation of private real estate companies for the purpose of redeveloping war-damaged areas according to an officially approved master plan. It is in accordance with this law that Solidere was established in 1994 and entrusted by the State with the implementation of the ratified BCD Master Plan, in coordination with the public authorities and the private sector.

The Master Plan (1993, updated 1994) together with Solidere constitute the legal and institutional backbone of the BCD reconstruction. After a review of the main features of the plan, this section outlines the mechanisms of implementation that have been put in place to guarantee suitable development in terms of speed, quality and cost, along with emphasis on the special provisions devised for the Conservation Area. The intention is to spotlight the originality of this planning and operational framework, especially when compared to earlier planning of the war and prewar periods. The section also points at some postwar urban revitalization initiatives at the country-wide level, and argues that the diverse planning attempts may lead for the first time in Lebanon to a homegrown approach to urbanism.

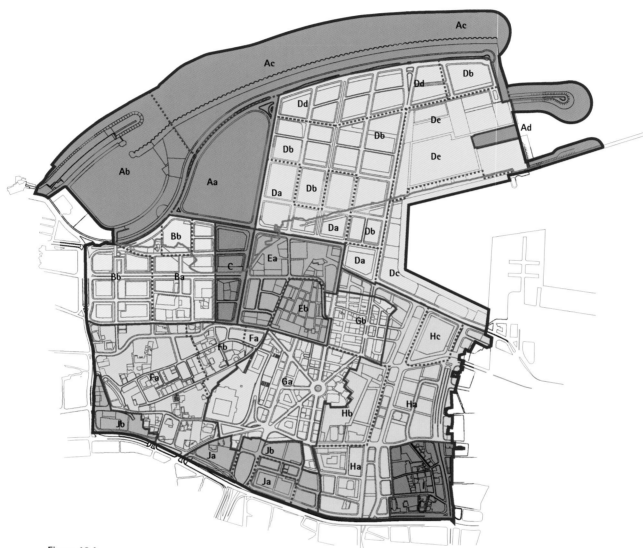

Figure 13.1
BCD planning sectors and subsectors, with targeted floor area and land use.

—— BCD boundary

—— Traditional BCD boundary (old seashore line)

—— Sector boundary

- - - Sub-sector boundary

A Park and waterside 15,000 sq m
Recreation, culture, commerce

B Hotel district 655,000 sq m
Hotels, offices, housing, recreation

C Serail corridor 94,000 sq m
Housing, commerce

D New waterfront district 1,574,000 sq m
Offices, commerce, housing, culture

E Souk district 240,000 sq m
Commerce, offices, housing, culture

F Wadi Abou Jamil 450,000 sq m
Housing, commerce

G Conservation Area 325,000 sq m
Commerce, offices, culture, recreation, housing

H Martyrs' Square 815,000 sq m
Commerce, offices, culture, recreation, housing

I Saifi 160,000 sq m
Housing, commerce

J Ghalghoul 362,000 sq m
Offices, commerce, housing

Upper case letters refer to sectors
Lower case letters refer to subsectors

Chapter 13

Institutional and Operational Framework

The Master Plan

The Solidere Master Plan, backed by the Lebanese planning and building codes, provides the regulatory framework for the BCD reconstruction. In 1992, a number of decrees issued by the Council of Ministers defined the BCD boundaries and its constituting lots and ratified the initial master plan, that had been prepared in 1991 shortly after the end of hostilities. This initial plan was modified later to reflect a more comprehensive and contextual approach, which revolved around historic identity, mixed-used development and responsiveness to market forces. Some of its basic concepts were also revised to reach a better integration with the surviving urban fabric of the BCD:

- The strong impact of the grade-separated infrastructure on the urban fabric was reduced by downgrading through-traffic arteries into urban boulevards and resizing underground parking.

- The bold shaping of the waterfront into a high-density business island with decked development was replaced by a peninsula protected by a sea defense system and invested with a large park and seaside corniche.

- The notion of conservation was reinforced by expanding the selection of preserved buildings and giving consideration to archeological finds. The new Master Plan was ratified by the Council of Ministers in two documents: the Detailed Master Plan for Beirut Central District (1993, updated 1994) and the Regulations and Planning of Beirut Central District and its Sectors (1993). Both were later the subject of several amendments.

The Master Plan covers the total area of 185 hectares that comprises 'the traditional BCD', namely Beirut's historic core and its adjoining areas; and the New Waterfront District, which consists of approximately 60 additional hectares of land reclaimed from the sea.

The Master Plan subdivides the BCD into 10 planning sectors. This subdivision takes into consideration several factors, such as the BCD natural landform, visual corridors, traffic and open space networks. The Master Plan, complemented by detailed sector studies as opposed to blanket zoning, is governed by a set of formative ideas aimed at the functional and formal integration of the planning sectors, as well as the phasing of their development (*fig. 13.1*).

BCD planning sectors

Sector A, the Park and Waterside, comprises leisure facilities; two marinas; a 74,000-square-meter waterside park, the largest in municipal Beirut; and a Corniche, or landscaped seaside promenade, stretching from the St George's Bay to the first basin of the Beirut port.

Sector B, the Hotel District, is a high-density area planned to accommodate a broad mix of commercial, office and residential uses, together with a limited number of prominent hotels. It is intended as the natural extension of what constituted the hotel and entertainment hub of the capital before the war. This new district is in keeping with the scale of the hotel area situated on its western edge.

Sector C, the Serail Corridor, is a mixed-use area of medium density that forms a transition between the historic core (Sector G) and the new Hotel District. Its strict controls on building height and its tiled roofscape are designed to preserve a visual corridor from the Serail hill to the sea and the waterside park.

Sector D, the New Waterfront District, is a high-density, mixed-use area to be developed on reclaimed land. A rectilinear grid of broad landscaped avenues with relatively high-density development and carefully located high-rise buildings distinguishes this new district. Its envisioned bold silhouette is shaped by block-scale buildings, which include towers of up to 160-meter height, the tallest in Beirut. The area is to become an upmarket office, commercial, residential and recreational district, with office development mainly targeted for use as regional and international business headquarters.

Sector E, the Souks, is named after the late Ottoman markets that once occupied most of the sector's site. The new Souks of Beirut are planned as the focus of commercial and shopping activities in the BCD. In addition to traditional shops, they will accommodate an international department store, an entertainment complex and a large underground car park serving the Souks as well as the adjoining Conservation Area. The western part of the sector is a new mixed-use area of medium density.

Sector F, Wadi Abou Jamil, is a medium-density residential area with a relatively high number of retained buildings. Because of its character, it is designated as a Special Policy Area. Here, urban design concepts focus on low-scale construction primarily dedicated to residential use.

Sector G, the Conservation Area, is another Special Policy Area in the BCD. Forming the political, financial, religious and cultural focus of the city center, it possesses a rich late Ottoman and French Mandate heritage and constitutes a zone of high archeological opportunity.

Sector H, the Martyrs' Square axis, is a mixed-use district extending along the prewar Martyrs' Square to the port. Planned around a highly symbolic civic space, it aims at reconnecting the city, reactivating its city center and enhancing the relationship with the waterfront. Its detailed design, the subject of an international competition, is expected to highlight both its new spatial identity and preferred land-use pattern as a visitors' destination and a focus of cultural and high tech activities.

Sector I, Saifi, is a medium-density residential, Special Policy Area, with a high concentration of retained residential buildings. The recently implemented 'Saifi Village' is planned around a network of pedestrian links, play areas, small squares and landscaped streets to recreate the milieu of traditional urban neighborhoods.

Sector J comprises two sub-areas of high density: the **Ghalghoul** area and **Beirut Trade Center** area, which are bounded on their southern edge by Fouad Chehab Avenue, the section of the inner ring road that links East and West Beirut. Some gateway buildings are planned along this strategically located edge, marking key entries to the BCD.

Master Plan formative ideas

- **Maintaining existing scale and enclosure**
  Special design guidelines were devised for new and infill development to ensure harmony between the historic core and surrounding sectors. In order to create a sense of enclosure while respecting human scale, techniques such as build-to-line and streetwall controls were introduced. These include three categories of streetwalls shaped after the Foch, Allenby and Maarad cross-sections.

- **Defining density areas according to sector character**
  Low densities are reserved for residential neighborhoods, while medium densities characterize the historic core and adjoining transitional areas (Sectors C and E). The highest densities are distributed among the newly developed sectors to create a bold contemporary urban scale and mark key access points to the BCD. Though the permissible floor area for each sector is defined, built-in flexibility — a significant and innovative feature of the Master Plan — allows the transfer of up to 10 percent of floor space from one sector to another.

- **Accommodation of a broad mixture of uses**
  The Master Plan considers functional diversity a precondition for the BCD to regain its prewar strategic role. The envisioned land-use mix consists of offices (33.7 percent), commercial (12 percent), residential (41.8 percent), hotels (4.2 percent) and cultural facilities and government offices (8.2 percent). Although each BCD sector has a range of permissible activities, the overall planning strategy is articulated around a flexible and market-responsive use of land and parceling framework, supported by a robust infrastructure able to accommodate change in development type and intensity. While each sector is assigned a predominant function or vocation, a range of complementary uses is also recommended. In particular,

residential space is considered a component in each sector. The neighborhood character of Wadi Abou Jamil and Saifi (Sectors F and I) is enhanced by the provision of the largest residential use in the BCD.

Special provisions for the Conservation Area

To guide restoration and contextual development, Solidere devised additional regulatory provisions, to be observed in conjunction with the Master Plan and the sector plans. 'Design Guidelines' were prepared for each sector by independent consultants, which led to the establishment of a set of Development and Restoration Briefs for each BCD building. These documents constitute binding components of the agreement between Solidere and the developer or recuperating party.

- The Development Briefs specify the physical and regulatory controls imposed on parcels, including permitted, prohibited and recommended land uses. Design recommendations are illustrated through massing schemes, to be further elaborated by developers in the detailed project design.

- Based on Restoration Guidelines issued by the Directorate General of Urbanism (DGU), the Restoration Briefs detail the types of repair required for façade restoration, and the specifications relating to permissible additional built-up areas. They include schematic plans and elevations that clarify urban design intentions, and stand as the main reference for all restoration and conservation work.

- Other planning and design provisions relate to seismic design dispositions, site regulations, safety rules and fire safety codes, as well as to disabled access, signage and landscape guidelines.

The planning provisions regarding retained buildings in the Conservation Area are quite specific. Based on the 1994 building survey that preceded the Master Plan (see *fig. 8.6-8.8*), the General Planning Regulations of Beirut Central District and its Sectors distinguished between two main categories (Article 5). The first comprises "buildings retained due to their historic or architectural value, or because they belong to a group of buildings having a specific townscape quality." The second category consists of buildings "retained for reasons other than those listed above." In the former case, the regulations stipulate strict compliance with the original character and materials; in the latter, modifications in the decorative elements are allowed, provided they comply with the building's original architectural style. Façades with "no architectural value" may be altered and renewed, provided they abide by the detailed Master Plan.

The Stakeholders and their Respective Roles

Key stakeholders in the BCD project, together with their mutual responsibilities and rights, constitute the institutional framework underlying the reconstruction process. As the vehicle established for implementing the project, Solidere is the most important stakeholder in the BCD reconstruction. Other key stakeholders are, on the one hand, the relevant public authorities, mainly the Directorate General of Urbanism (DGU) and the Beirut Municipality; and, on the other hand, the buying or recuperating parties, i.e. new property developers and former property right holders who have recuperated their built lots.

Solidere

Solidere is a private joint-stock company of property right holders and investors. Its share capital is made up of two types of common stock: A shares, issued to property right holders against their real estate property contributions in kind; and B shares, issued to investors against their cash subscriptions. The shares are publicly traded on the Beirut Stock Exchange.

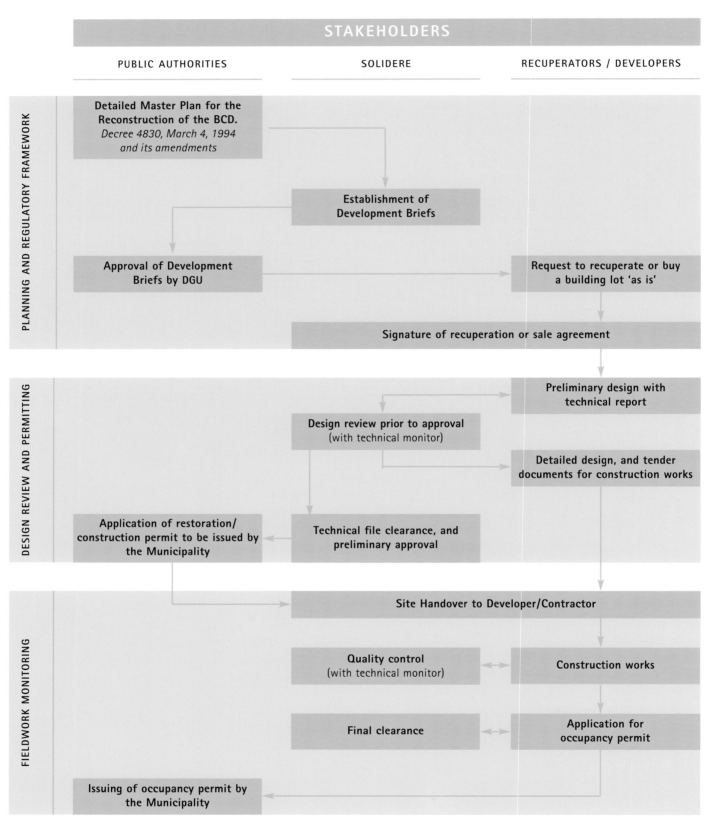

STAKEHOLDERS

PUBLIC AUTHORITIES　　　　　SOLIDERE　　　　　RECUPERATORS / DEVELOPERS

PLANNING AND REGULATORY FRAMEWORK

Detailed Master Plan for the Reconstruction of the BCD.
Decree 4830, March 4, 1994 and its amendments

Establishment of Development Briefs

Approval of Development Briefs by DGU

Request to recuperate or buy a building lot 'as is'

Signature of recuperation or sale agreement

DESIGN REVIEW AND PERMITTING

Preliminary design with technical report

Design review prior to approval (with technical monitor)

Detailed design, and tender documents for construction works

Application of restoration/ construction permit to be issued by the Municipality

Technical file clearance, and preliminary approval

FIELDWORK MONITORING

Site Handover to Developer/Contractor

Quality control (with technical monitor)

Construction works

Final clearance

Application for occupancy permit

Issuing of occupancy permit by the Municipality

Figure 13.2
Operational framework.

Solidere was granted title of all development land and all retained buildings in the traditional Beirut Central District, except for government-owned land and 26 public and religious buildings classified as exempt from the Master Plan. In consideration of BCD infrastructure and management costs incurred as part of its agreement with the State, the company was granted development rights in the New Waterfront District. For a period of two years following the company's inception, right holders of retained buildings were encouraged by Solidere to recuperate and restore their property by relinquishing the A shares that had been initially allocated to them in lieu of their property rights. This led to the retirement of 17 million shares and the company's capital now stands at US$1.65 billion.

The company is entrusted with land and real estate development throughout the BCD. It has the tasks of developing vacant land and non-recuperated built lots; selling part of the final developments; keeping and managing the rest as part of its property portfolio; and supervising restoration and real estate development by third parties. Its responsibilities consist of:

- **Master Plan development and enforcement**
This includes complementing the BCD Master Plan through the preparation of detailed sector and sub-sector studies, updating and amending the Master Plan when needed, and ensuring the compliance of all BCD development with the Master Plan.

- **Infrastructure development**
Solidere is responsible for financing and executing on behalf of the State all infrastructural works in the traditional BCD area and its extension on reclaimed land. This includes road networks, pavement, open public space, street furniture, power transformer units and public parking areas, as well as the treatment of the landfill zone, the installation of seawall protection and the development of seaside promenades and marinas.

- **Real estate development**
Solidere is a 'lead developer' responsible for the rehabilitation and restoration of all buildings retained for conservation, except for those that are recuperated by their original owners and/or tenants or sold to a third party. The company undertakes real estate development projects and sells the development rights on remaining parcels to other developers, in accordance with the Master Plan and market demand.

- **Property and services management and operation**
Solidere's responsibilities include leasing, maintaining and operating its property portfolio. The company may offer such services to other property owners and is also equipped to provide management and operation services for BCD infrastructure, marinas, public utilities, car parks and open areas.

Public authorities and developers

Public authorities retain the right to control and intervene on behalf of the State. The Directorate General of Urbanism holds the power to approve and, if need be, amend BCD regulations. Like elsewhere in the country, the DGU is authorized to review and approve the architectural design of special and large projects in the area. For existing buildings, the DGU has the discretionary power to stop restoration works on any building in the event of inadequate or improper execution. The Beirut Municipality, acting as the executive agency that reports to Beirut's administrator (Mohafez), controls adherence to building regulations in accordance with Lebanese codes and issues construction, restoration and occupancy permits. In any case of discrepancy between restoration pratice and building codes, resolution of the issue or any consequent regulation amendment has to be endorsed by a decree issued by the Council of Ministers.

The recuperating or buying party is bound to both Solidere and the public authorities with regard to permit issuance and execution. Whether for restoration or new construction, Solidere enforces its control through a binding contract with the owner-developer, which gives the company the legal right to enforce the design guidelines and reviews and to ensure quality control. It also allows Solidere to impose tight schedules and financial guarantees, thus ensuring that only serious developers with a clearly defined project, timetable and end-users in mind operate in the BCD.

A set of processes for design review, permit issuance and fieldwork monitoring provides an operational framework for the implementation of the BCD Master Plan and its regulations and ensures quality construction and restoration (*fig. 13.2*).

Design review and permitting

To ensure harmonious and contextual development, Solidere devised a set of design control procedures. The design review deals with qualitative issues related to esthetic, environmental and functional considerations. Given that these concerns cannot be rigidly framed within a mechanical checking procedure, the essence of the design review process lies in the interactive process of negotiation between the Solidere technical and professional staff, the appointed architect and the developer.

Design review focuses on the project's adherence to the BCD Master Plan and its general planning regulations, contextual development and technical issues related to fire safety and accessibility for the disabled. For key sites and large projects, a mass plan is required, together with the preliminary design file. Following review by Solidere, the massing study is forwarded to the DGU for final approval. The design has to be developed in close coordination between the appointed architect, Solidere, the Beirut Municipality and, if necessary, the DGU.

In the case of retained buildings, the first phase consists of preparing a measured drawing of the building, assessing its structural and architectural condition, and verifying its compliance with planning regulations. A restoration report is also required, specifying materials, repair works, restoration methods and guidelines for the rehabilitation of façades. The report forms the basis of a preliminary design proposal that is submitted to Solidere for approval. The proposal includes the architectural design, a description of the building and engineering systems, and a preliminary cost estimate. The second phase, which leads to the contracting of restoration works, consists of preparing a detailed design and working drawings. Solidere requests that it review and approve the details of selected external design features, such as windows, shutters, balustrades, decorative elements, canopies, sun breakers, shop windows, rolling shutters, awnings, signage design, roof parapet and pergolas, mechanical plant treatment, landscape treatment, etc. The technical file is submitted to Solidere for clearance, and then to the

Municipality for the issuing of a restoration or building permit. Solidere acts as a facilitator for the issuing of building permits. Its professional team reviews the file in order to ascertain that it contains no technical discrepancies that might delay the permit. In an effort to resolve problems at an early stage, Solidere may consult the relevant public authorities in a joint meeting with the architect in charge of the project.

Fieldwork monitoring

Solidere ensures proper implementation through a close quality control and monitoring process. Whether for new or retained buildings, it requests that all developers appoint technical monitors to verify and certify compliance with fire safety codes, guidelines for disabled accessibility and seismic standards.

The contractor is requested to submit for Solidere approval samples of façade materials, color scheme, signage, shop rolling shutter, window framing and glazing and other elements as may be necessary for each building. For the retained buildings of Foch-Allenby and Etoile, stone sampling and testing is of particular relevance to guarantee appropriate matching before the start of repair work.

Upon completion of construction or restoration work, the technical monitor has to approve the 'as-built' drawings as well as the building maintenance manual prepared by the contractor, before submitting them to Solidere for the issuance of a final clearance form for the building. The cleared file is then submitted to the Beirut Municipality and the Civil Defense Fire Department for review and approval, after which the occupancy permit and fire safety certificate are granted. Compliance with the built-up or floor area as specified in the construction permit is a main condition for the Municipality to issue an occupancy permit. Specifications for adequate and timely maintenance of the building, its façade and external works are detailed in the maintenance manual and are subject to the approval of the Municipality. Periodic renewal of the fire certificate is determined by the Municipality and the Civil Defense Fire Department.

Figure 13.3
Aerial view of Etoile Square.

Conclusion

Assessing the Solidere Model: The Foch-Allenby and Etoile Experience

The Master Plan devised for the reconstruction of the Beirut Central District and the mechanism chosen for its implementation — with Solidere as the main stakeholder spearheading and coordinating the project — introduced an innovative approach to town planning and development control in Lebanon. It was an approach that invited controversy, and during the inception stage the very concept of a private real estate company becoming the vehicle for reconstruction was subject to extensive public debate.

However, from both a public and business perspective the merits of the approach became apparent with the unfolding of the Master Plan and the testing of project implementation on the ground. This notably revealed the capacity of Solidere to control the quality of design and execution, and also to promote land and real estate development. New planning, design and operational approaches were articulated around international experience, especially as related to city centers; they were adapted to local conditions, addressing, among others, incompatibilities with local building and planning codes and practices. The Solidere model invites reflection on how a private-led redevelopment approach compares with the previous and current models of urbanism applied in Lebanon on city and national levels; and how far these models reflect both imported trends and local adaptation in terms of urban design ideology, planning legislation, operational processes and the private-public relationship. In view of the diversity of postwar reconstruction approaches witnessed in the Beirut Central District and elsewhere in Lebanon, a legitimate question arises: Is urban planning and design in this country shifting from imported models to homegrown solutions?

Imported Urban Models and their Local Adaptation

Since the second half of the nineteenth century and following the industrial revolution in Europe, city centers East and West have been laboratories of spatial and formal experimentation, in tune with the economic signs of the time. As such, they took the lead in applying new models of urban design, whether locally generated or imported. With the spread of shifting urban design ideologies, from Beaux-Arts to modernism to postmodernism, city centers tended to exhibit remarkable similarities. These ideologies may be apprehended with reference to their attitude towards the past, their assumption about the role of the city center, their formal approach, their implementation mechanisms and their adaptation to the different styles of governance.

Between Grand Design and Modernist Traditions

The Grand Design tradition, inspired by the baroque precedents in Europe and propelled mainly by Haussmannian Paris, considered city centers as a dignified symbol of public life. The redevelopment of city centers was based on two premises: reinforcing civic pride and responsibility and creating an attractive and exclusive commercial and cultural environment for thriving businesses and entertainment activities.

Commissioned by local governments, beautification schemes were welcomed by the business elite as adding value to their properties and other investments. In Western metropolises, the purpose was to clean up city centers from the visual blight of industrial activities; and in colonial outposts, the aim was to infuse order into the 'chaotic' patterns of pre-industrial towns. Extensive restructuring of the urban fabric was therefore emphasized, based on universal geometric composition schemes and open space prototypes, such as rectilinear streets and grand squares, sometimes star-shaped, articulated around public monuments. A clear illustration of the latter case in Beirut is the emergence of the Foch-Allenby and Etoile area. There, the late Ottoman and French Mandate powers superimposed a formal geometric layout over the organic fabric of the intramural town. While intended to express the city's new administrative status, this action also aimed at providing a suitable framework for private development. In this regard, the public sector was simultaneously ahead of and in tune with the private sector.

On the formal level, the current approach to the recovery of Foch-Allenby and Maarad represents a contemporary reinstatement of this Grand Design tradition, along the lines of the neo-rationalist movement that emerged in Europe during the 1960s and evolved through the 1970s. This movement considered cities as "theaters of memory". According to Delovoy: "The fundamental types of habitat: the street, the arcade, the square, the yard, the quarter, the colonnade, the avenue, the boulevard" are to be reinstated, so "that the city can be walked through. So that it becomes a text again. Clear. Legible." On the other hand, as explained by Nan Ellin: "To design by analogy means borrowing past city forms (morphology) and building forms (typology) — the formal esthetic of the past — without their meanings because the meanings of these forms have changed with time... The significance of a place, for Rossi, lay not in its function, or even in its form, but in the memories associated with it."

The advocates of modernism and the functionalist ideology, a trend that historically occurred between Beaux-Arts and postmodern neo-rationalism, shared the same view of the city center as an enforcer of civic consciousness, in tune with the Grand Design tradition. Despite the segregation of functions (residence, work, leisure and circulation networks) called for in the functionalist model, the city center was often conceived as a domain for pedestrian movement and the locus for an organized mix of activities — a role that went beyond its perceived economic function as an efficient machine to produce wealth and as a node for human and merchandise traffic. While significant heritage buildings were deemed worthy of preservation, the historic fabric itself was generally judged unfit for contemporary use and lacking in adequate sunlight, fresh air and open spaces. This negative assessment led in practice to three main consequences. The first was the urban renewal movement, which favored wiping out decaying sections of city centers and replacing them with mega-structures. The second was the segregation of downtown areas from their immediate surroundings, through the establishment of bold circulation networks designed for decongestion and improved accessibility. The third was the creation of new towns to accommodate urban growth.

In Lebanon, imported versions of those three orientations were reflected in the urban schemes for different city and town centers that were generated in the 1950s and 1960s by international consultants and local architects. Notable examples in Beirut were the two redevelopment schemes that aimed at transforming the Saifi and Ghalgoul sectors of the traditional Beirut city center into modern, high-rise districts; the construction of the Fouad Chehab ring road that created a strong edge between the city center and adjoining sectors; and the envisioning of Beirut as a polynuclear structure, with a new town and a new government city in the periphery. Elsewhere in Lebanon, reconciling archeology and urban growth in the historic towns of Sidon and Baalbeck — both World Heritage sites — led to radical schemes based either on the axial segregation between the old and the new city, in the case of Sidon; or in the juxtaposition of the archeological city next to a new city, in the case of Baalbeck.

Those radical schemes were anchored in the belief that urban form creates social order; that the shaping of urban form is a task confined to the technician and specialist, i.e. the architect and the engineer; and that urban schemes have to be imposed and implemented by a powerful and centralized public administration. However, those plans were often thwarted, owing to the ignorance of the architects behind them "of the real forces that were struggling to strengthen their control over the territories (religious institutions, political feudal lords, landowners and financial corporations), as well as their amazing lack of knowledge of the powers that resisted the implementation of their plans," as argued by Jad Tabet. Even when adopted, those plans failed to materialize; or when they did, they failed to reach their intended goals of social equity and environmental quality. High land prices stood in the way of the public sector, preventing it from acquiring private property for large-scale development projects (except for roads and basic public utilities), as well as areas of high archeological potential surrounding historic sites. It was partly to avoid these pitfalls that a public-private partnership was deemed necessary. A major step in this direction was a law issued in 1963 for the constitution of mixed (private and public) capital real estate companies, with the government holding 25 percent of equity and the private landowners holding the remaining 75 percent. Law 117 of 1991, which formed the basis for the Beirut city center reconstruction, was an extension and amendment to that legislation and aimed at reconstructing areas destroyed by the war through private real estate companies.

Market-driven Urbanism

Despite introducing substantial changes, the Master Plan of 1994 was driven by the same ambitions as the prewar and wartime plans: to revive Beirut's leading role in the Arab Middle East; to renew the image and function of downtown Beirut and reinforce its centrality; to modernize it through contemporary urban design and planning models and state-of-the-art infrastructure; and, last but not least, to enhance the real estate asset value of the city center.

However, instead of the customary reactive-remedial approach, the Master Plan is based on a promotional-proactive approach to urbanism with an extensive involvement of the private sector. This deliberate approach, deemed controversial at the time, was conditioned by the urge to circumvent obstacles to the Beirut Central District reconstruction, and to incorporate emerging global trends in privatization, commercialization and deregulation.

Among the principal arguments invoked in favor of adopting a private real estate company as the vehicle to manage BCD reconstruction were the high level of war destruction and the extreme fragmentation of property rights, coupled with absenteeism. Furthermore, the prospects for reconstruction were dimmed by the severely limited capacities of the public sector following fifteen years of war. Thus, for the first time in Lebanon, the establishment of a private-sector managed and funded city development corporation shifted planning responsibility from the public to the private sphere.

Although this choice stemmed from complex and unusual local circumstances, it reflected at the same time the general reorientation towards market-driven urbanism witnessed in Europe and the United States in the 1980s. At the heart of the world trend to privatize planning is a dual incentive. On the one hand, there is the common reaction to the failure of public-led urbanism in reaching the ideals of social equity and environmental quality; and, on the other hand, there is the renewed pursuit of a broader vision, related to late capitalism, to reconvert city cores into efficient corporate centers within a national, regional and global network. As pointed out by Berry and McGreal: "A common theme (in planning systems) is the desire to combine local economic development objectives with those of the international investor. In this context, the interaction between planning and other regulatory measures and land and property markets in both Western and Eastern European cities is of paramount importance." Until now, bureaucratic planning had been unable to keep up with the dynamism of the private sector. The discrepancy between high idealistic discourse and low performance in practice has been equally observed within strong or weak governance systems, in Western as well as in developing countries. A case in point is Lebanon, where past master plans managed by the public sector often proved to be an after-the-fact reactive tool aimed at validating the fait accompli, while at the same time being subject to manipulation by private and sectarian interests and also plagued by a chronic weakness of bureaucratic credibility and efficiency.

Towards Homegrown Urbanism

Emergency response planning, imposed by Lebanon's postwar reconstruction, has put into question the adequacy of conventional public-led planning, especially in terms of its weak bureaucratic performance. To that could be compared the Solidere experience in the Beirut city center as an efficient model of private-led redevelopment planning. Ranging between those poles, various approaches to revitalization and renewal of city and town centers have recently been tested on both city and country level.

The Directorate General of Urbanism has been engaged in a serious assessment and revision of the national planning and building codes in the light of past performance, driven by such considerations as environmental quality and action-led legislation. Concurrently, the Council for Development and Reconstruction (CDR) and the World Bank have launched studies for tourism development, economic revitalization and heritage conservation in such key historic cities and towns as Tripoli, Sidon and Baalbeck. The terms of reference for these studies involve a serious investigation of public-private partnership in urban renewal, taking into consideration relevant stakeholders as well as pertinent implementation mechanisms.

On the city level, various degrees of success have been registered in areas of Beirut adjoining the BCD. In Furn al Hayek to the south, ad hoc individual decision-making within the context of existing bureaucratic planning was able to generate a chain of day-and-night activity throughout the area. Meanwhile, in Gemmayzeh to the east, the tendency to 'facelift' non-repaired stucco and stone elevations with a pastel coat of paint (provided by an NGO in coordination with the Municipality) has been destroying the original character of the historic neighborhood, owing to the low quality of façade rehabilitation. These attempts, in their diversity and unequal results, represent a novel approach to local experimentation. Beyond the pragmatic picking and choosing among imported theories and precedents which characterized previous attempts, they illustrate the tendency towards homegrown solutions as an important dynamic in reconstruction.

Meanwhile, the debate around the BCD Master Plan and its implementation vehicle has evolved. In particular, the limitations of a debate focusing on two main positions — a market-led versus a market-critical stance towards urbanism — have become obvious after a decade of reconstruction. Breaking away from such polarized attitudes, the approach has widened to include diverse processes operating in Lebanon under private and/or public initiatives. The creation of Elissar for the redevelopment of the Beirut southern suburb is one example of a government-led redevelopment project. The ongoing CDR-World Bank project is a joint private-public project. The involvement of NGOs with municipalities in filling their planning and management needs is yet another example of private-public cooperation.

A dialogue between entrepreneurial planning within and conventional planning outside the BCD was recommended by the author in 1996 with a view to improve the sharing of responsibilities, interests and practices. By learning from the reconstruction of the Beirut historic core, as well as from the ongoing CDR-World Bank project, pericenter districts may be able to integrate valuable strategies of implementation to widen the scope and upgrade the quality of their restoration work. In turn, Solidere may achieve functional and esthetic complementarity in relation to its surroundings by participating in the conservation and revitalization of its immediate periphery. Even more importantly, it could enhance Beirut's civic image in preserving the memory of the city beyond the limits of its jurisdiction.

Such coordination can be instrumental in ensuring an innovative transition to a more flexible and responsive urbanism in Lebanon, with obvious advantages over earlier approaches. Formerly, urban designers and planners in their specialist-regulatory functions used to impose universal formulas for the development of towns and city centers. Nowadays, each project is considered within the context of its temporal, geographical and economical specificity. It is hoped that as a result a real, homegrown synthesis will soon materialize. As such, the 1990s and the turn of the twenty-first century may be considered in the near future as one the richest and most dynamic periods in the recent history of urban design and planning in Lebanon — in brief, a turning point breaking half a century of modernist dogma and idealistic discourse.

ARCHITECTU
RAL SURVEY
ARCHITECTU
RAL SURVEY
ARCHITECTU
RAL SURVEY
ARCHITECTU

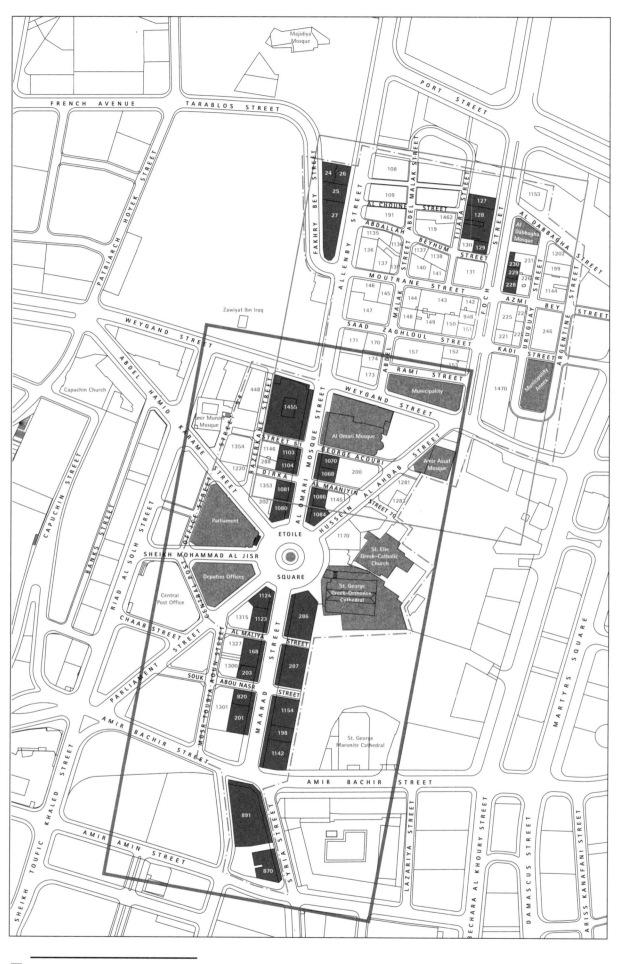

Majidiya
Mosque

FRENCH AVENUE   TARABLOS STREET   PORT STREET

PATRIARCH HOYEK STREET

FAKHRY BEY STREET

24 26
25
27
ALLENBY STREET
AL CHOUNE   STREET
108
109
191   1462
ABDALLAH   119
1135
136   1136
137   1138 1137
1138
140 141
139
MOUTRANE STREET
ABDEL MALAK STREET
BEYHUM STREET
TIJARA STREET
127
128
130 129
FOCH STREET
AZMI STREET
231
230
229
228
226
199
URUGUAY STREET
1153
1202
1144
AL DABBAGHA STREET
Al
Dabbagha
Mosque
ARGENTINE STREET

WEYGAND STREET

Zawiyat Ibn Iraq

Capuchin Church

ABDEL HAMID KARAME STREET

Amir Munzer
Mosque

MALAK STREET
146 145
147
SAAD ZAGHLOUL STREET
144 143
148   149
150 151
948
142
171 170
157   152
174   153
173   RAMI STREET
ABDEL KADI STREET

Municipality

225
221 222
246
KADI STREET
1470

Municipality
Annex

448
STREET 51
1455
1354
1146
1103
1104
288
1220
BAZERKANE STREET
DIRKA STREET
1353
1081
202
1080
AL OMARI MOSQUE STREET
GEORGE ACOURI
1070
1068   200
AL MAANIYIN
1086 1145
1084
Al Omari Mosque
Amir Assaf
Mosque
HUSSEIN AL AHDAB STREET
1281
1287
STREET 70

Parliament

OFFICE STREET

CENTRAL POST OFFICE STREET

SHEIKH MOHAMMAD AL JISR

Deputies Offices

ETOILE
1170
SQUARE

St. Elie
Greek-Catholic
Church

St. George
Greek-Orthodox
Cathedral

Central
Post Office

BANKS STREET

RIAD AL SOLH STREET

CHAAB STREET

PARLIAMENT STREET

SOUK TOUBA ADUN STREET

1124
1123
1315
1327
1300
1301
AL MALIYA STREET
168
203
ABOU NASR STREET
820
201
MAARAD STREET
286
287
SYRIA STREET
STREET
1154
198
1142
St. George
Maronite Cathedral

MARTYRS SQUARE

LAZARIYA STREET

AMIR BACHIR STREET

CAPUCHIN STREET

SHEIKH TOUFIC KHALED STREET

AMIR BACHIR STREET

891

870

AMIR AMIN STREET

AMIR BACHIR   STREET

BECHARA AL KHOURY STREET

DAMASCUS STREET

ARISS KANAFANI STREET

☐ Architectural Survey, Foch–Allenby

☐ Architectural Survey, Etoile

■ Building Groups

▨ Public and Religious Buildings

☐ Other Buildings

– – Conservation Area Boundary

0   1   4
⊢⌐⌐⌐⌐⌐⊣ Elevations
01   4
⊢⌐⌐⌐⌐⊣ Plans

*All plans and elevations are
in the indicated scales
throughout the architectural
survey unless noted.*

ARCHITECTURAL SURVEY

FOCH-ALLEN
BY FOCH-ALL
ENBY FOCH-
ALLENBY FO
CH-ALLENBY

Marfaa Lots 129-130, 128, 127

Marfaa Lots 230-231, 229, 228

Marfaa Lots 104-27, 25, 26

Marfaa Lots 24, 25, 27-104

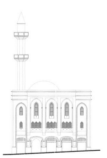

Al Dabbagha Mosque

Municipality

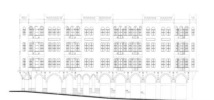

Municipality Annex

Marfaa Lot 157

Marfaa Lot 1153

Marfaa Lot 136

Marfaa Lot 225

Marfaa Lot 1137

Marfaa Lot 119

Marfaa Lot 147

Marfaa Lot 143

Marfaa Lot 246

Marfaa Lot 173

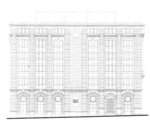

Marfaa Lot 191

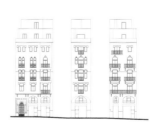

Marfaa Lot 1136

Marfaa Lot 1135

Marfaa Lot 146

Marfaa Lot 1202

Marfaa Lot 149

Marfaa Lot 131

Marfaa Lot 1144

Marfaa Lot 171

Marfaa Lot 129-130

Marfaa Lot 221-222

Marfaa Lot 153

Marfaa Lot 152

Marfaa Lot 140

Marfaa Lot 1138

Marfaa Lot 170

Marfaa Lot 230-231

Marfaa Lot 145

Marfaa Lot 144

Marfaa Lot 142

Marfaa Lot 199

Marfaa Lot 224

Marfaa Lot 148

Marfaa Lot 150

Marfaa Lot 948

Marfaa Lot 151

Marfaa Lot 138

Marfaa Lot 174

Marfaa Lot 226

Marfaa Lot 141

Marfaa Lot 137

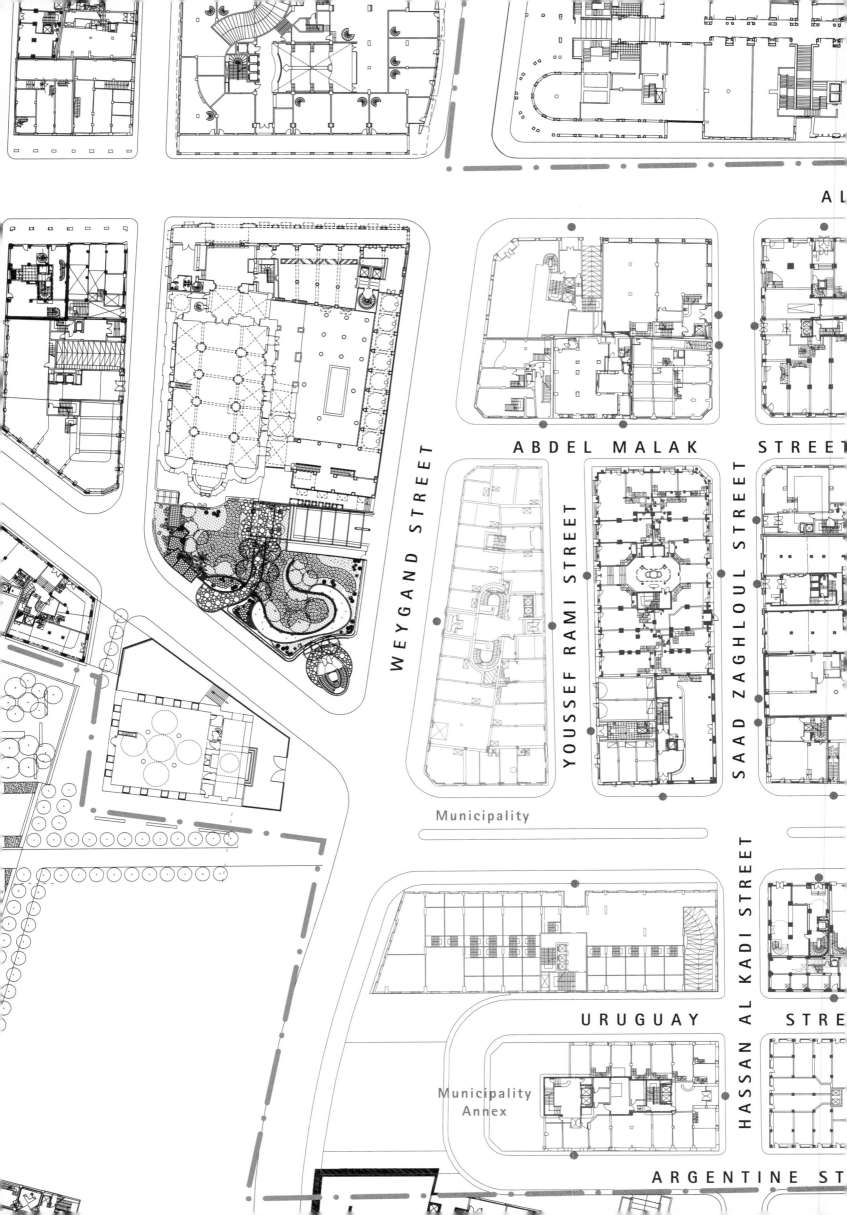

ABDEL MALAK STREET

AL

WEYGAND STREET

YOUSSEF RAMI STREET

SAAD ZAGHLOUL STREET

STREET

Municipality

HASSAN AL KADI STREET

URUGUAY STRE

Municipality
Annex

ARGENTINE ST

FAKHRY BEY STREET

STREET

MOUTRANE STREET

BEYHUM STREET

ABDALLAH

FOCH STREET

Al Dabbagha
Mosque

AZMI BEY STREET

AL DABBAGHA MOSQUE STREET

Public and Religious Buildings

Retained Buildings

Infill Buildings

Conservation Area Boundary

Building Entrance

■ Building Groups

Marfaa Lots
129–130, 128, 127

230–231, 229, 228

104–27, 25, 26

24, 25, 27–104

■ STREET 66 – FOCH

Marfaa Lots 129–130, 128, 127

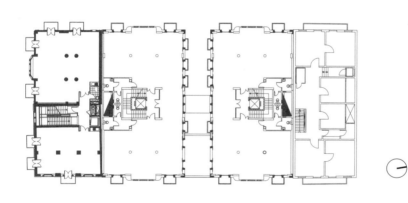

STREET 33 – WEYGAND

Lot 179
Municipality

STREET 75 – YOUSSEFF RAMI

Lots 153, 152

STREET 73 – SAAD ZAGHLOUL

Lots 151, 948, 142

STREET 71 – MOUTRANE

Lot 131

STREET 69 – A. BEYHUM

Lots 129, 128, 127

Marfaa Lots 230–231, 229, 228

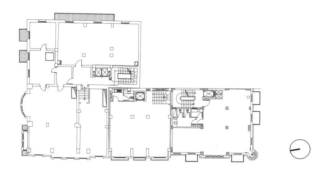

STREET 1

Lot 1153

STREET 51 – AL DABBAGHA

Lot 1152
Al Dabbagha
Mosque

STREET 53 – JAAFAR AL SADEQ

Lots 230, 229, 228

STREET 55 – AZMI BEY

Lots 225, 221

STREET 57 – HASSAN AL KADI

Marfaa Lots 104–27, 25, 26

Al Dabbagha Mosque

Municipality

Municipality Annex

Al Dabbagha
Mosque ·
Municipality ·
Municipality Annex ·

Al Dabbagha Mosque

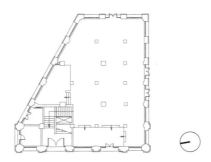

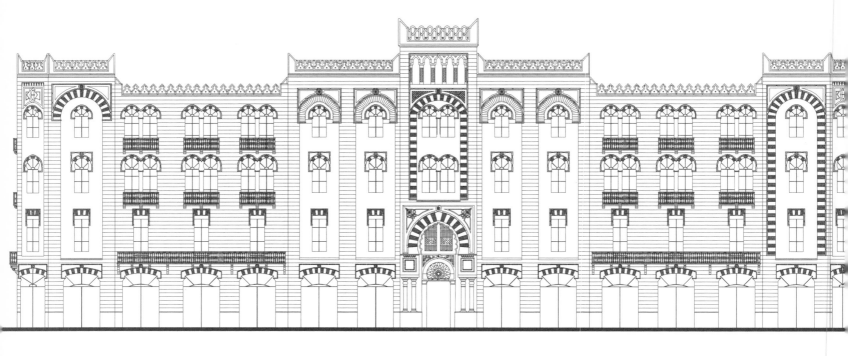

■ STREET 33 – WEYGAND

Municipality

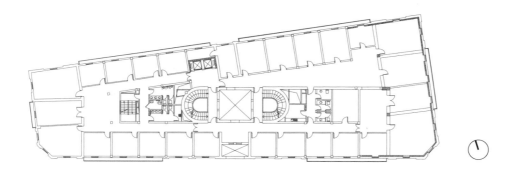

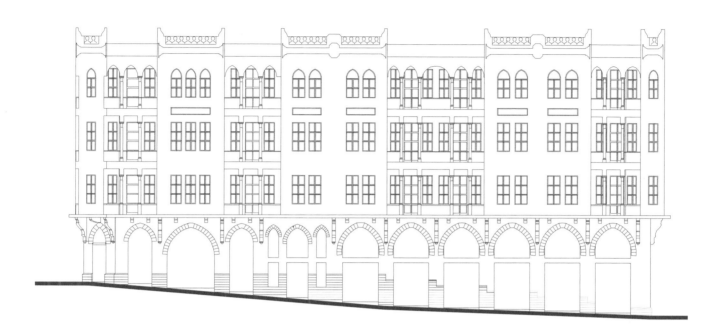

STREET 52 – ARGENTINE

Municipality Annex

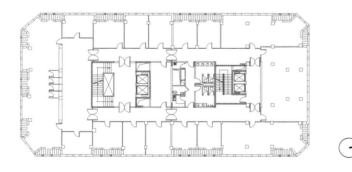

■ Other Buildings

Marfaa Lots	129–130
157	221–222
1153	153
	152
136	
	140
225	1138
1137	170
	230–231
119	
147	145
	144
143	
246	142
	199
173	
191	224
	148
1136	
1135	150
	948
146	
1202	151
	138
149	
131	174
	226
1144	
171	141
	137

STREET 73 – SAAD ZAGHLOUL

Marfaa Lot 157

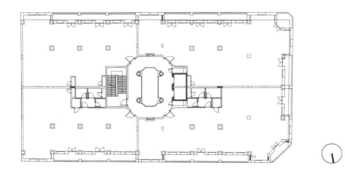

Marfaa Lot 1153

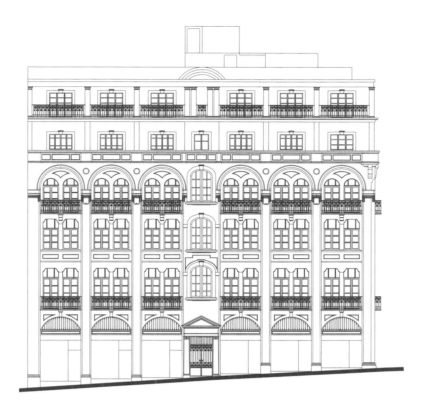

STREET 60 – ALLENBY

Marfaa Lot 136

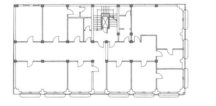

■■■ STREET 66 – FOCH

Marfaa Lot 225

Marfaa Lot 1137

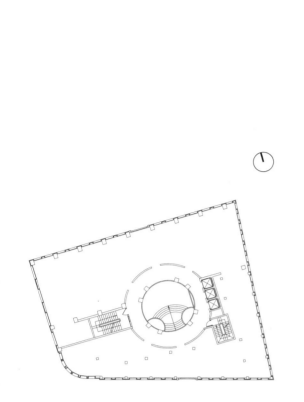

STREET 69 – ABDALLAH BEYHUM

Marfaa Lot 119

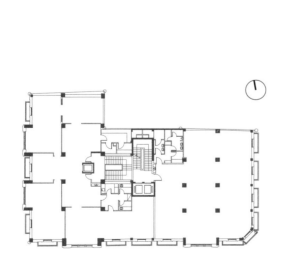

STREET 73 – SAAD ZAGHLOUL

Marfaa Lot 147

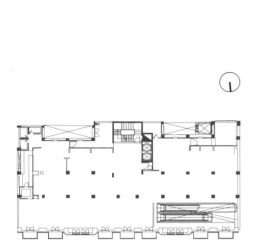

STREET 71 – MOUTRANE

Marfaa Lot 143

STREET 52 – ARGENTINE

Marfaa Lot 246

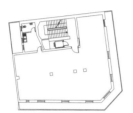

■ STREET 33 – WEYGAND

Marfaa Lot 173

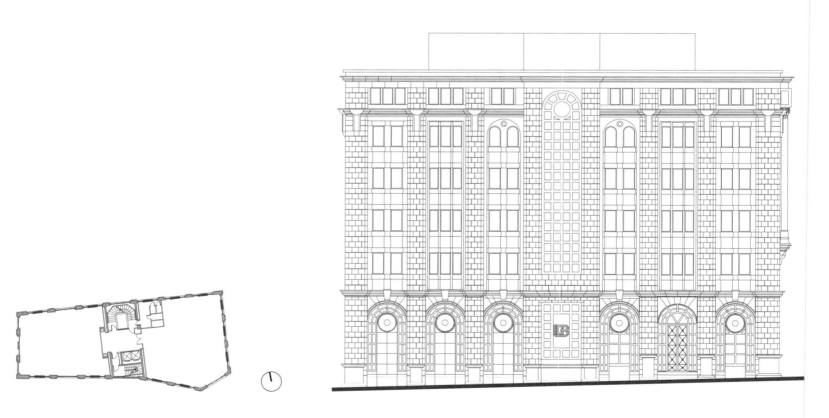

■ STREET 69 – ABDALLAH BEYHUM

Marfaa Lot 191

STREET 62 – ABDEL MALAK

Marfaa Lot 1136

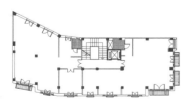

STREET 69 – ABDALLAH BEYHUM

Marfaa Lot 1135

STREET 71 – MOUTRANE

Marfaa Lot 146

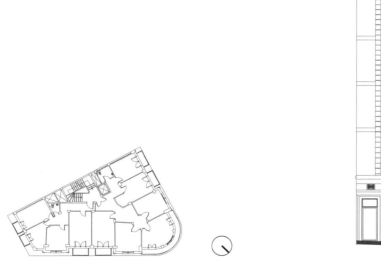

STREET 51 – AL DABBAGHA MOSQUE

Marfaa Lot 1202

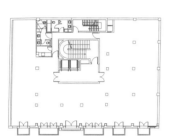

STREET 73 – SAAD ZAGHLOUL

Marfaa Lot 149

STREET 71 – MOUTRANE

Marfaa Lot 131

STREET 52 – ARGENTINE

Marfaa Lot 1144

STREET 60 – ALLENBY

Marfaa Lot 171

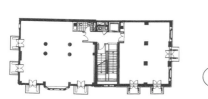

STREET 69 – ABDALLAH BEYHUM

Marfaa Lot 129-130

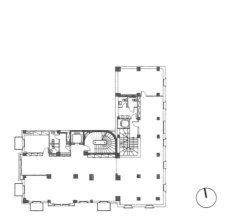

STREET 57 – HASSAN AL KADI

Marfaa Lot 221-222

STREET 75 – YOUSSEF RAMI

Marfaa Lot 153

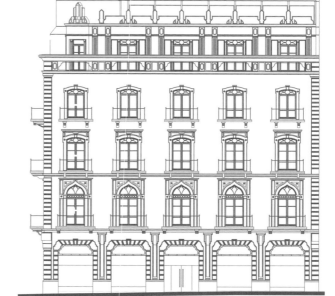

STREET 73 – SAAD ZAGHLOUL

Marfaa Lot 152

■ STREET 71 – MOUTRANE

Marfaa Lot 140

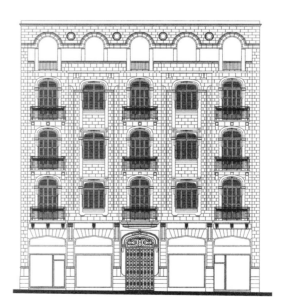

■ STREET 69 – ABDALLAH BEYHUM

Marfaa Lot 1138

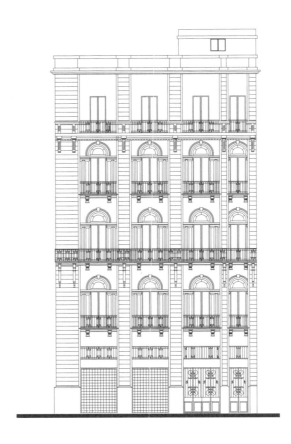

STREET 73 – SAAD ZAGHLOUL

Marfaa Lot 170

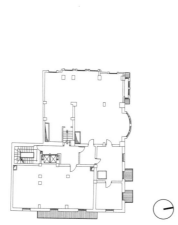

STREET 50 – URUGUAY

Marfaa Lot 230-231

■ STREET 62 – ABDEL MALAK

Marfaa Lot 145

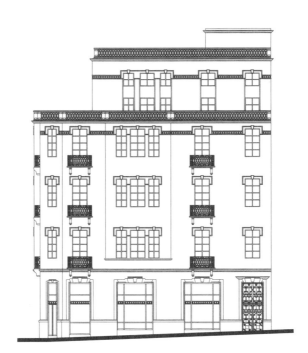

■ STREET 62 – ABDEL MALAK

Marfaa Lot 144

STREET 66 – FOCH

Marfaa Lot 142

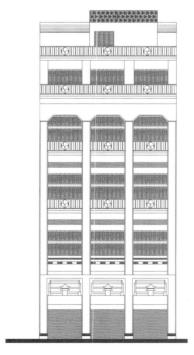

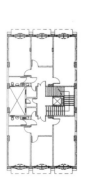

STREET 50 – URUGUAY

Marfaa Lot 199

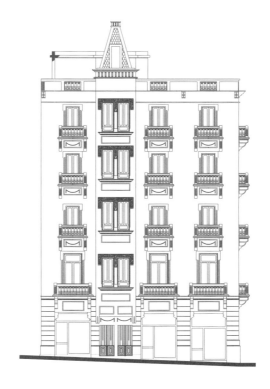

STREET 50 – URUGUAY

Marfaa Lot 224

STREET 73 – SAAD ZAGHLOUL

Marfaa Lot 148

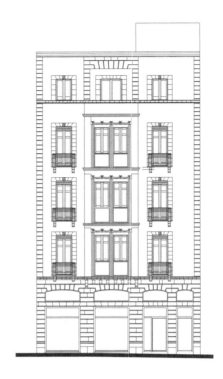

STREET 73 – SAAD ZAGHLOUL

Marfaa Lot 150

STREET 66 – FOCH

Marfaa Lot 948

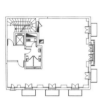

STREET 73 – SAAD ZAGHLOUL

Marfaa Lot 151

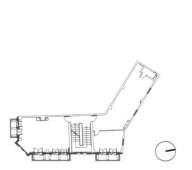

STREET 62 – ABDEL MALAK

Marfaa Lot 138

STREET 62 – ABDEL MALAK

Marfaa Lot 174

STREET 55 – AZMI BEY

Marfaa Lot 226

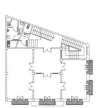

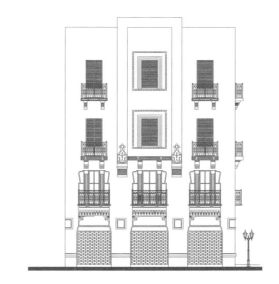

STREET 71 – MOUTRANE

Marfaa Lot 141

STREET 71 – MOUTRANE

Marfaa Lot 137

ARCHITECTURAL SURVEY

ETOILE ETOIL
E ETOILE ET
OILE ETOILE
ETOILE ETOI
LE ETOILE ET

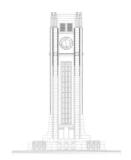

Clock Tower

Parliament

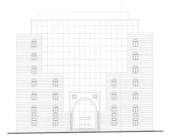

Deputies Offices

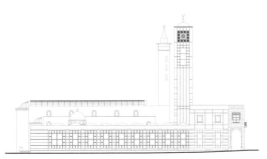

Al Omari Mosque

St George Greek-Orthodox Cathedral

Amir Assaf Mosque

St Elie Greek-Catholic Church

Marfaa Lot 1301

Marfaa Lot 202

Marfaa Lot 1354

Marfaa Lot 1353

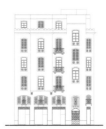

Marfaa Lot 1145

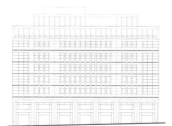

Marfaa Lot 448

Marfaa Lot 1220

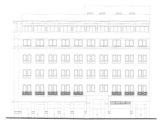

Marfaa Lot 200

Marfaa Lot 1315

Marfaa Lot 1170

Marfaa Lot 1283

Marfaa Lot 1327

Marfaa Lot 1300

Marfaa Lot 1146

Marfaa Lot 1281 Rear Elevation

Marfaa Lot 288

Building Groups

Bachoura Lot
891

Marfaa Lots
201, 820, 203, 168, 1123, 1124

1080, 1081, 1104, 1103, 1455

418, 1070, 1068, 1086, 1084

286, 287, 1154, 198, 1142

Bachoura Lot 891   Grand Theatre

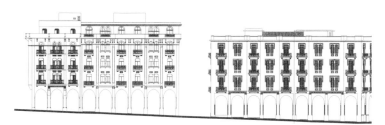

Marfaa Lots 203, 168   Marfaa Lots 1123, 1124

Parliament   Marfaa Lots 1080, 1081

Marfaa Lots 1104, 1103   Marfaa Lot 1455

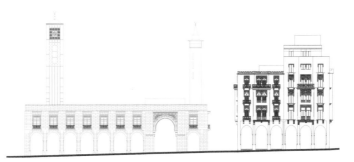

Marfaa Lot 418   Al Omari Mosque   Marfaa Lots 1070, 1068

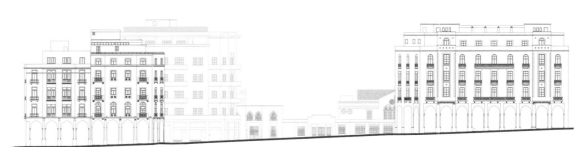

Marfaa Lots 1086, 1084   St Elie   St George   Marfaa Lot 286
Greek-Catholic Church Greek-Orthodox Cathedral

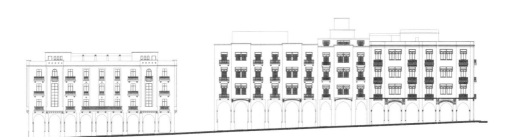

Marfaa Lot 287   Marfaa Lots 1154, 198, 1142

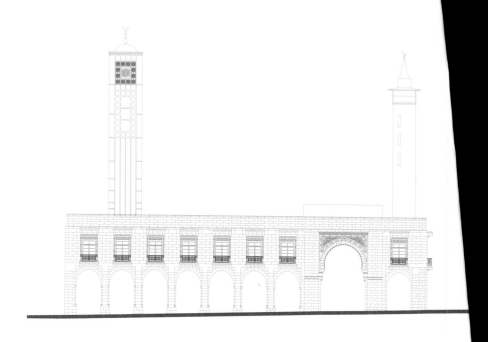

Al Omari Mosque

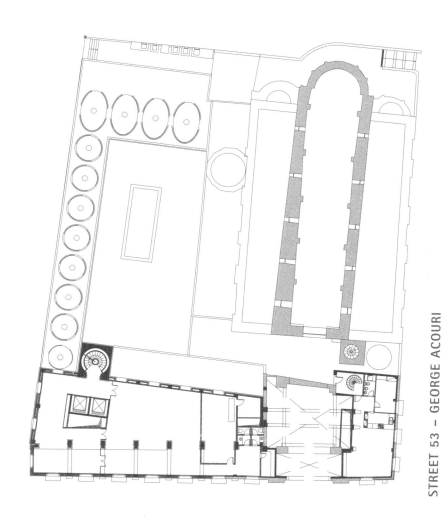

STREET 33 – WEYGAND

STREET 53 – GEORGE ACOURI

Lot 418

Lot 1

St Elie
Greek-Catholic
Church

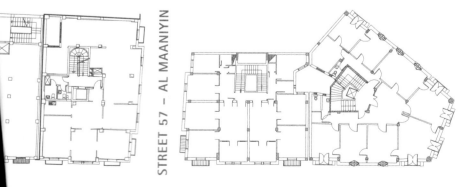

STREET 57 – AL MAANIYIN

070   Lot 1068   Lot 1086   Lot 1084

ETOILE SQUARE

01 ___ 4

St George
Greek-Orthodox
Cathedral

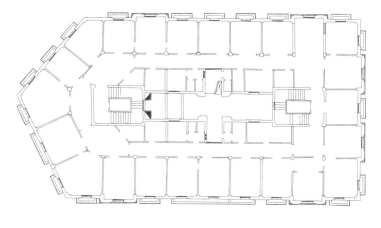

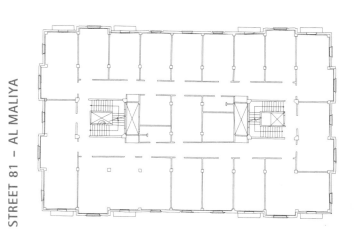

STREET 81 – AL MALIYA

Lot 286

Lot 287

STREET 85 – ABOU NASR

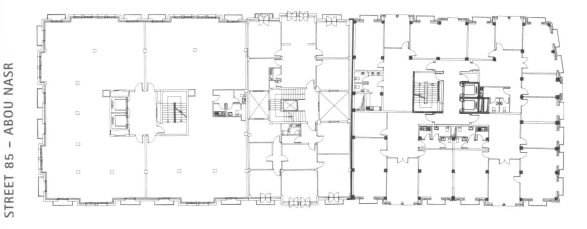

STREET 12 – AMIR BACHIR

Lot 1154   Lot 198   Lot 1142

01   4

Public and Religious Buildings

Clock Tower

Parliament

Deputies Offices

Al Omari Mosque

St George Greek–Orthodox Cathedral

Amir Assaf Mosque

St Elie Greek–Catholic Church

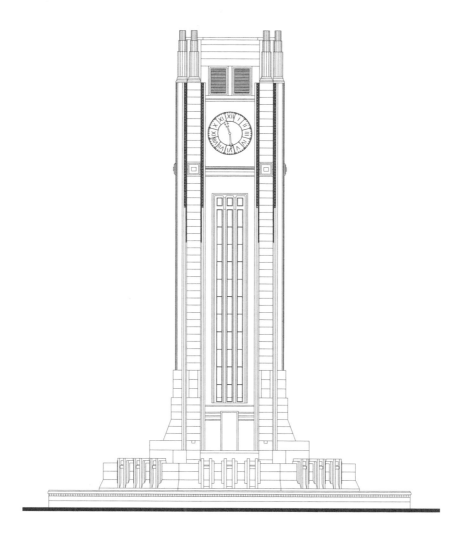

ETOILE SQUARE

Clock Tower

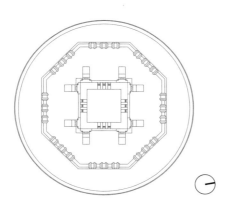

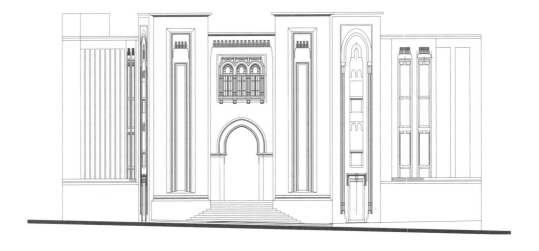

Parliament

Plan not available

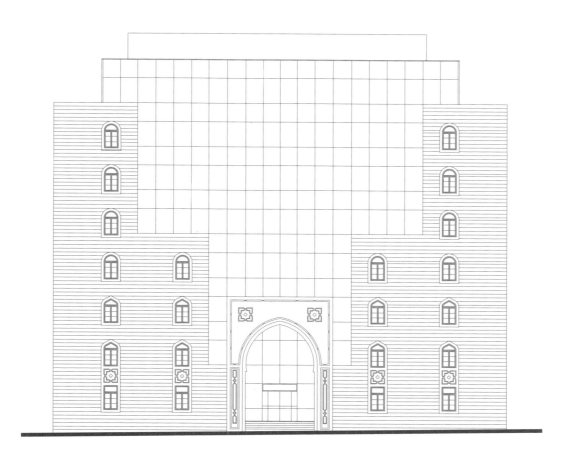

STREET 90 – CENTRAL POST OFFICE

Deputies Offices

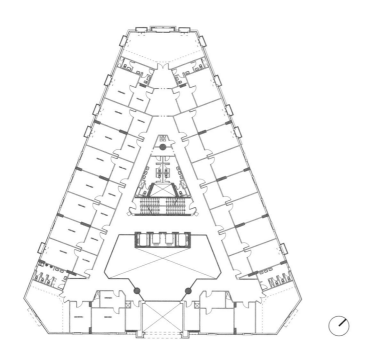

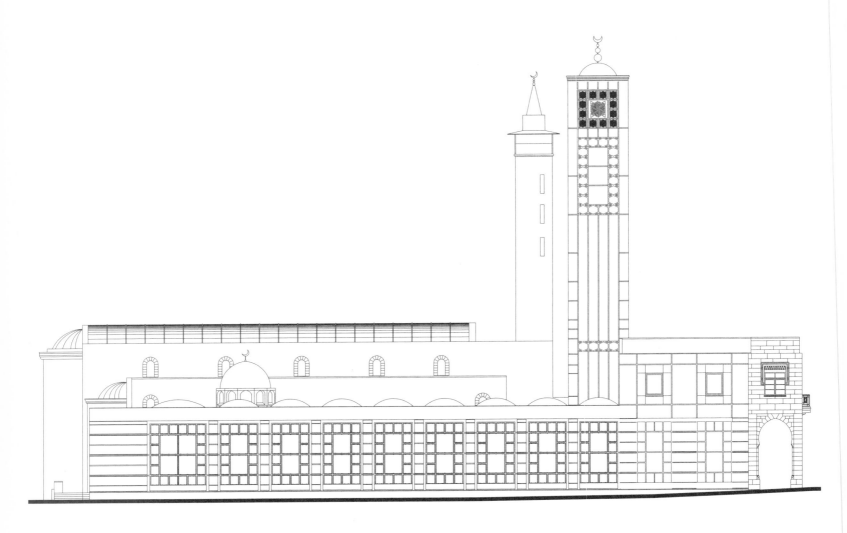

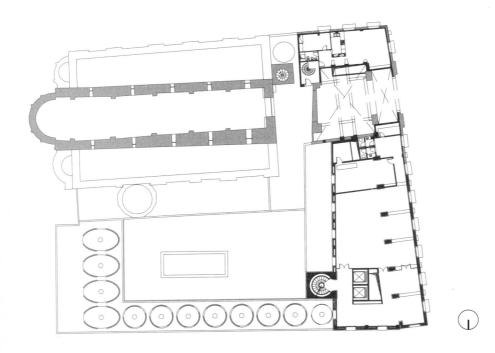

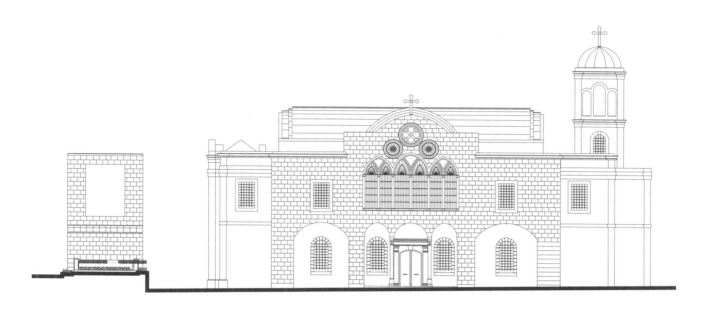

St George Greek-Orthodox Cathedral

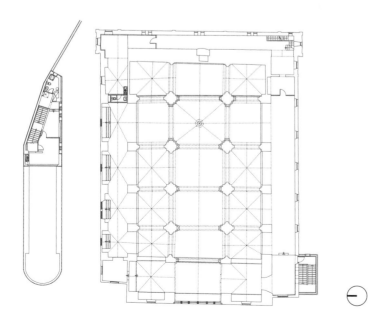

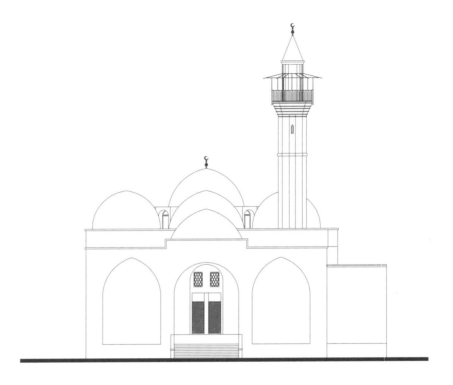

Amir Assaf Mosque

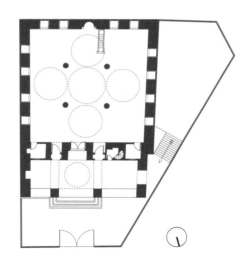

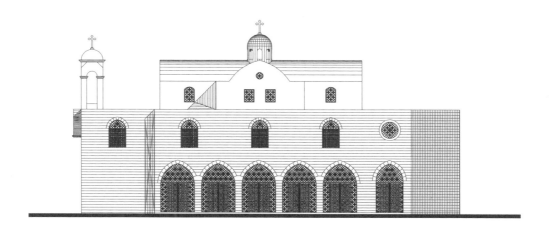

St Elie Greek-Catholic Church

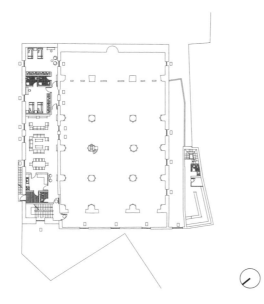

Other Buildings

Marfaa Lots

1301

202

1354

1353

1145

448

1220

200

1315

1170

1283

1327

1300

1146

1281

288

1301 · 202 ·
1354 · 1353 ·
1145 · 448 ·
1220 · 200 ·
1315 · 1170 ·
1283 · 1327 ·
1300 · 1146 ·
1281 · 288 ·

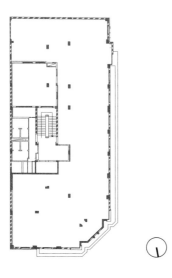

STREET 85 – SOUK ABOU NASR

Marfaa Lot 1301

STREET 50 – ABDEL HAMID KARAME

Marfaa Lot 202

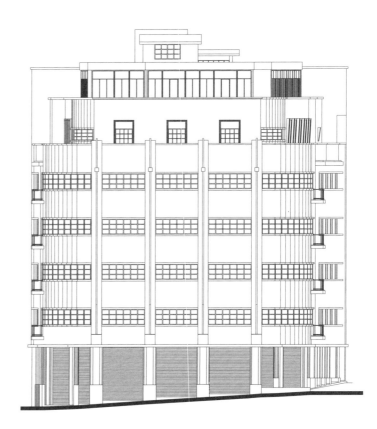

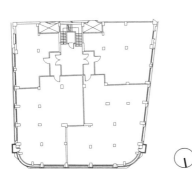

STREET 51

Marfaa Lot 1354

STREET 55 – DIRKA

Marfaa Lot 1353

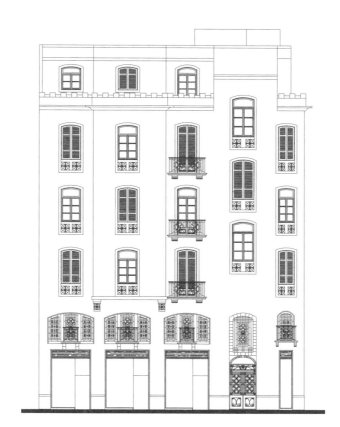

STREET 62 – HUSSEIN AL AHDAB

Marfaa Lot 1145

STREET 54

Marfaa Lot 448

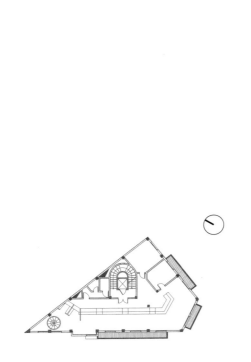

STREET 50 – ABDEL HAMID KARAME

Marfaa Lot 1220

STREET 53 – GEORGE ACOURI

Marfaa Lot 200

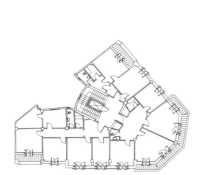

STREET 88 – PARLIAMENT

Marfaa Lot 1315

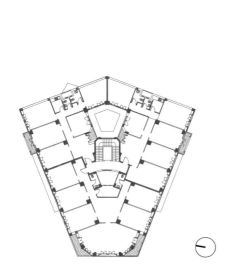

STREET 62 – HUSSEIN AL AHDAB

Marfaa Lot 1170

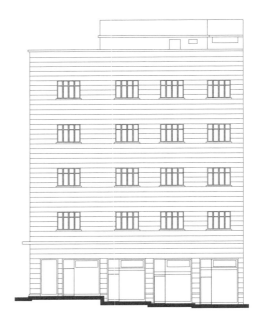

STREET 70

Marfaa Lot 1283

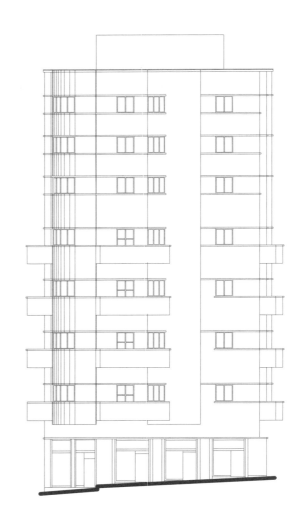

STREET 86 – MGSR TOUBIA AOUN

Marfaa Lot 1327

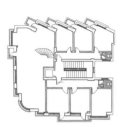

STREET 85 – SOUK ABOU NASR

Marfaa Lot 1300

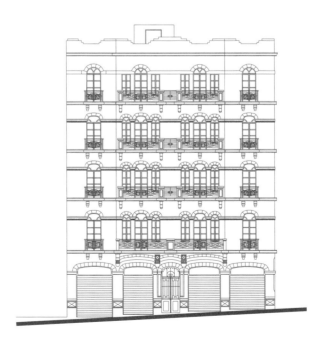

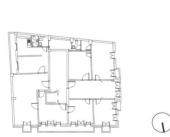

STREET 51

Marfaa Lot 1146

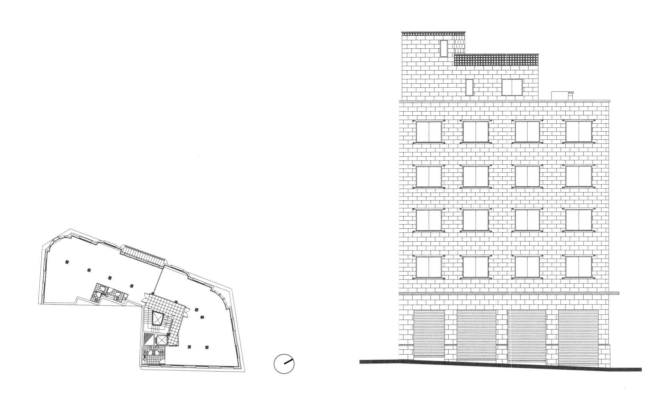

STREET 62 – HUSSEIN AL AHDAB

Marfaa Lot 1281 Rear Elevation

STREET 55 – DIRKA

Marfaa Lot 288

Index

Numerals appearing in black indicate items found in the main text, green in picture captions and numerals in brown are items found in the architectural survey.

Bibliography

Altounian, Achot. *A la recherche du temps retrouvé avec mon père*. Beirut: Sipan Printing Press, 2000. (AA)

Attoe, Wayne and Donn Logan. *American Urban Architecture: Catalysts in the Design of Cities*. Berkeley: University of California Press, 1989.

Babikian, Christine. "Développement du Port de Beyrouth et Hinterland." In *Beyrouth, Grand Beyrouth*. Les Cahiers du CERMOC, No 16. Beirut: Centre d'Etudes et de Recherches sur le Moyen-Orient Contemporain, 1997.

Berry, James and Stanley McGreal, ed. *European Cities, Planning Systems and Property Markets*. London: E & FN Spon, 1995.

Boeri, Stefano. "Mediterranean Ports: Functional Metissage", *L'Architecture d'Aujourd'hui*, vol. 332, January-February 2001.

Borruey, René. "Paris sur Marseille", *L'Architecture d'Aujourd'hui*, vol. 332, January-February 2001.

Borruey, René and Mario Fabre. "Marseille et les Nouvelles Echelles de la Ville Portuaire." In *Les Cahiers de la Recherche Architecturale*. Marseille: Editions Parenthèses, 1991.

Brindley, Tim, Yvonne Rydin, and Gerry Stoker. *Remaking Planning: The Politics of Urban Change in the Thatcher Years*. London: Unwin Hyman, 1989.

Çelik, Zeynep. *The Remaking of Istanbul: Portrait of an Ottoman City in the Nineteenth Century*. Seattle: The University of Washington Press, 1986.

Daher, Gaby. *Le Beyrouth des Années 30*. Beirut: 1994. (GD)

Danger Frères - La Société des Plans Régulateurs de Villes. *Ville de Beyrouth: Rapport d'Enquête et Justificatif*. Paris: 1932.

Davie, May. *Beyrouth et ses Faubourgs: 1840 -1940*. Les Cahiers du CERMOC, No 15. Beirut: Centre d'Etude et de Recherche sur le Moyen-Orient Contemporain, 1996. (MD)

Davie, Michael F. "Maps and the Historical Topography of Beirut", *Berytus*, Vol. XXXV. Beirut: American University of Beirut, 1987. (MFD)

--------- . "Trois Cartes Inédites de Beyrouth. Eléments Cartographiques pour une Histoire Urbaine de la Ville", *Annales de Géographie*, vol. 5, 1984. Beirut: Université Saint-Joseph, Faculté des Lettres et des Sciences Humaines. (USJ)

de Dumast, Maxime. *Le Port de Beyrouth*. Conference at the Centre d'études géographiques du Proche-Orient. Beirut: 1951.

Debbas, Fouad C. *Beirut Our Memory: An Illustrated Tour in the Old City from 1880 to 1930*. Paris: Folios, 1986. (FD)

Delovoy, Robert, ed. *The Reconstruction of the European City*. Brussels: Architecture Rationelle, 1978.

Direction Générale de l'Urbanisme. *Plan Directeur de la Ville de Beyrouth*. Beirut: 1968.

--------- . *Schéma Directeur de la Région Métropolitaine de Beyrouth*. En collaboration avec le Conseil du Développement et de la Reconstruction and la Mission Franco-Libanaise pour l'Aménagement de la Région Métropolitaine de Beyrouth. Beirut: 1986.

Ecochard, Michel. *Le Port de Beyrouth*. (Rapport aux services d'urbanisme). Beirut: 1943.

El Khazen, Joseph. "Quel Port pour quelle Economie?," *Le Commerce du Levant*, July 1991.

Ellin, Nan. *Postmodern Urbanism*. Cambridge: Blackwell Publishers Inc., 1996.

Evenson, Norma. *Paris, a Century of Change: 1878 -1978*. New Haven: Yale University Press, 1979.

Fawaz, Leila Tarazi. *Merchants and Migrants in Nineteenth-Century Beirut*. Cambridge: Harvard University Press, 1983.

Gavin, Angus and Ramez Maluf. *Beirut Reborn: The Restoration and Development of the Central District*. London: Academy Editions, 1996. (G&M)

Hanssen, Jens. "Your Beirut Is on My Desk: Ottomanizing Beirut under Sultan Abdulhamid II (1876 -1909)." In Rowe, Peter G. and Hashim Sarkis, ed. *Projecting Beirut: Episodes in the Construction and Reconstruction of a Modern City*. Munich: Prestel, 1998.

Kabbani, Oussama. "Al mousalaha bayn al yabissa wal bahr: Mathaf bayrout, bawabat al bahr." In *el Bourj: Place de la Liberté et Porte du Levant*. Beirut: Dar an-Nahar, 2000.

--------. *Prospects for Lebanon: the Reconstruction of Beirut*. Oxford: Centre for Lebanese Studies, 1992.

Labaky, Ramzi. "Port of Beirut: Project Aborted", *Business Life*. Spring 2001.

Laugénie, Jean. "Le Port de Beyrouth", *La Revue de Géographie de Lyon*, No 4, 1956. (JL)

Lebanese Republic, Council for Development and Reconstruction. *Beirut Central District Master Plan*. Report by Dar Al-Handasah Consultants (Shair and Partners). Beirut: 1991.

------. *Beirut Central District. Detailed Plan Report: Planning and Urban Design.* Report by Dar Al-Handasah Consultants (Shair and Partners). Beirut: 1994.

------. *Recovery Planning for the Reconstruction and Development of Lebanon.* Report prepared by International Bechtel Inc. and Dar Al-Handasah Consultants (Shair and Partners). Beirut: 1991.

Lebanese Republic, Ministry of Public Works and Transport. *La Cité Gouvernementale.* Report prepared by Technikon Graphein Doxiadis. Athens: 1959.

Lebanese Republic, Municipality of Beirut. *Plan Directeur d'Aménagement du Centre de Beyrouth, 1977.* Atelier Parisien d'Urbanisme (APUR). Beirut: 1977.

Lebas, Jean-Paul. "Revitaliser le Centre-Ville de Beyrouth en Intégrant la Mémoire des Lieux dans la Reconstruction." In Akl, Ziad and Michael F. Davie, ed. *Questions sur le Patrimoine Architectural et Urbain au Liban.* Beirut and Tours: ALBA-URBAMA, 1999.

Loukaitou-Sideris, Anastasia and Tribid Banerjee. *Urban Design Downtown: Poetics and Politics of Form.* Berkeley: University of California Press, 1998.

Meyer, Han. *City and Port: Urban Planning as a Cultural Venture in London, Barcelona, New York and Rotterdam; Changing Relations Between Public Urban Space and Large-Scale Infrastructure.* Utrecht: International Books, 1999.

Mission Franco-Libanaise d'Etudes et d'Aménagement de la Région Métropolitaine de Beyrouth. *Perspectives de Développement du Port et Conséquences de son Fonctionnement sur l'Aménagement Urbain de Beyrouth.* Port Autonome de Marseille, November 1984.

------. *Le Schéma Directeur de la Région Métropolitaine de Beyrouth.* Beirut : Conseil du Développement et de la Reconstruction et Direction Générale de l'Urbanisme, June 1986.

Pitlenko, Igor. *Annuaire d'Architecture de Syrie et du Liban.* Beirut: 1934.

Rossi, Aldo. "Rational Architecture." Catalogue for the Triennale of Architecture, Venice. Reprinted in *Oppositions,* 1975.

Ruppert, Helmut. "Beirut, eine westlich geprägte Stadt des Orients." *Erlanger Geographische Arbeiten,* Erlanger, 1969; translated into French by Eric Verdeil. *Beyrouth, Une Ville d'Orient Marquée par l'Occident.* Les Cahiers du CERMOC, No 21. Beirut: Centre d'Etudes et de Recherches sur le Moyen-Orient Contemporain, 1999. (HR)

Sader, Helen. "Ancient Beirut: Urban Growth in the Light of Recent Excavations." In Rowe, Peter G. and Hashim Sarkis, ed. *Projecting Beirut: Episodes in the Construction and Reconstruction of a Modern City.* Munich: Prestel, 1998.

Saliba, Robert. "Emergency Preservation of Beirut's Peri-Center Districts: A Framework for Debate and Action." In Davie, Michael and Ziad Akl, ed. *Le Patrimoine Urbain et Architectural au Liban; pour qui, pourquoi, comment faire?,* Beirut: CNRS-URBAMA and Institut d'Urbanisme de L'ALBA, 1998.

------. "The Mental Image of Downtown Beirut, 1990: A Case Study in Cognitive Mapping and Urban Form." In Davie, Michael, ed. *Beyrouth, Regards Croisés.* Villes du Monde Arabe, No 2. Tours: URBAMA, 1997.

------. *Beirut 1920 -1940: Domestic Architecture between Tradition and Modernity.* Beirut: The Order of Engineers and Architects, 1998.

Salibi, Kamal. *A House of Many Mansions: the History of Lebanon Reconsidered.* Berkeley: University of California Press, 1988.

Sarkis, Hashim. "Al sahat al mouajalat: A'rd litataour sahat al chouhada' abr al tasamim al maoudouat laha fi ta'rickaha al hadith." In *el Bourj: Place de la Liberté et Porte du Levant.* Beirut: Dar an-Nahar, 2000.

Silvetti, Jorge. "Beirut and the Facts of Myth." In Rowe, Peter G. and Hashim Sarkis, ed. *Projecting Beirut: Episodes in the Construction and Reconstruction of a Modern City.* Munich: Prestel, 1998.

Soffer, Arnon and Shimon Stern. "The Port City: A Sub-group of the Middle-Eastern City Model." *Ekistics,* January-April 1986.

Solidere. See Solidere documents.

Tabet, Jad. "From Colonial Style to Regional Revivalism: Modern Architecture in Lebanon and the Problem of Cultural Identity." In Rowe, Peter G. and Hashim Sarkis, ed. *Projecting Beirut: Episodes in the Construction and Reconstruction of a Modern City.* Munich: Prestel, 1998.

Thoumin, Richard. *Géographie Humaine de la Syrie Centrale.* Paris: Librairie Ernest Leroux, 1936.

Wilson, Ariane. "Villes-Ports: Quand l'Urbain prend le Large", *L'Architecture d'Aujourd'hui,* vol. 332, January-February 2001.

Solidere Documents

Chapman Taylor Partners, Architects, London / Saïd Bitar, Architect, Beirut. *Restoration Master Plan of the Foch-Allenby District.* Beirut: 1994 (CTSB).

Davie, May. *The History and Evolution of Public Spaces in Beirut's Central District.* Beirut, 1997.

Kamal Turk Consultants, Architects. *Restoration Master Plan of the Maarad / Nejmeh Square District.* Beirut: 1994.

Laboratoire d'Etude des Matériaux avec Prospective et Patrimoine. *Observation, Sampling and Testing of the Retained Buildings in BCD.* Strasbourg: 1994.

-------. *Guidelines for the Restoration of Five Buildings Façades in Allenby District.* Strasbourg: 1994.

Solidere, Land Development Division, Area Management Section. *Restoration Methods.* Beirut: 1997

-------, **Land Development Division, Urban Management Department: Area Management Section.** *On-Premise Signage Guidelines.* Beirut: 1998.

-------, **Land Development Division, Urban Management Department: Area Management Section.** *Site Administration, Safety, Health and Environmental Regulations.* Beirut: 1998.

-------, **Land Development Division, Urban Management Department: Town Planning Section.** *Accessibility for the Disabled: A Design Manual for a Barrier Free Environment.* In collaboration with ESCWA, and the approval of the Ministry of Social Affairs. Beirut: 1998.

-------, *Annual Reports, 1994 - 2002.*

-------, *General Planning Regulations of Beirut Central District and its Sectors.* English Translation of decree 4830, 1994, as published in the Lebanese Official Gazette. Beirut: 1994.

Pictures Credits

New Photographs

Gabriele Basilico
1991: pages 15, 16, 17, 18, 19, bottom
2003: pages 15, 16, 17, 18, 19, top, 152

Digital Globs page 44

Fares Jammal
inside front and back covers, pages 10, 20-21, 22, 124, 210, 250, 278, 285

Youmna Medlej
figures 7.6, 7.32, 7.35, 7.58, 7.100, 7.101, 7.102, 7.103, 7.104, 7.106, 8.17, 8.19, 9.4, 9.5, 9.12, 9.15, 10.58, 11.13, and pages 116, 129, 178-179

Roger Moukarzel
figures 4.10, 4.12, 9.2, 12.13 and pages 142, 180, 186-187, 195

Samir Saddi
figures 6.28, 7.1, 7.2, 7.5, 7.7, 7.8, 7.9, 7.10, 7.12, 7.13, 7.14, 7.15, 7.16, 7.18, 7.27, 7.38, 7.39, 7.40, 7.41, 7.54, 7.55, 7.56, 7.59, 7.60, 7.62, 7.63, 7.64, 7.65, 7.66, 7.67, 7.71, 7.78, 7.79, 7.80, 7.82, 7.85, 7.87, 7.89, 7.90, 7.92, 7.93, 7.94, 7.95, 7.96, 7.97, 7.98, 7.99, 7.107, 7.109, 7.110, 7.112, 7.113, 7.115, 7.116, 7.117, 7.118, 7.119, 7.120, 7.122, 7.124, 9.1, 9.3, 9.10, 9.11, 9.16, 10.46, 10.47, 10.50, 10.53, 10.54, 11.11, 12.7, 12.8 and pages 2, 97, 110-111, 114-115, 149, 150, 274

Solidere's photographers:

Mosbah Assi
figures 4.2, 4.3, 7.3, 7.4, 7.11, 7.17, 7.28, 7.29, 7.30, 7.31, 7.33, 7.34, 7.36, 7.37, 7.42, 7.57, 7.61, 7.68, 7.69, 7.70, 7.72, 7.73, 7.74, 7.75, 7.81, 7.83, 7.84, 7.86, 7.88, 7.91, 7.111, 7.114, 7.121, 7.123, 7.125, 7.126, 8.16, 8.18, 8.20, 8.21, 8.22, 8.23, 8.24, 9.6, 9.7, 9.9, 9.14, 10.20, 10.29, 10.31, 10.33, 10.35, 10.37, 10.41, 10.43, 10.45, 10.48, 10.49, 10.51, 10.52, 11.12, 11.14, 11.17, 11.19, 11.21, 11.30, 12.4 and pages 104, 120, 127, 137, 146, 147, 170, 172

Roger Bou Jaoude
figure 9.13.

Archives

An Nahar Research Center for Documentation figure 6.38 and page 81

Solidere
figures 10.14, 10.15, 10.17, 10.18, 10.19, 10.24, 10.28, 10.30, 10.32, 10.34, 10.36, 10.40, 10.42, 10.44, 10.57, 11.16, 11.18, 11.20, 11.22, 11.23, 11.24, 11.25, 11.26, 11.27, 11.28, 11.29, 12.20, 12.21 and page 122 bottom right

Museums and Private Collections

Achot Altounian (AA)
page 123 top left and middle right

Gaby Daher (GD)
figures 5.6, 5.37

Fouad Debbas (FD)
figures 2.2, 2.3, 2.4, 5.1, 5.2, 5.3, 5.4, 5.10, 5.11, 5.12, 5.13, 5.14, 5.17, 5.18, 5.22, 5.23, 5.26, 5.27, 5.28, 5.31, 5.32, 6.1, 6.2, 6.3, 6.5, 6.6, 6.7, 6.8, 6.9, 6.10 and pages 122 bottom left, 123 middle center

Jamal and Samia Junblat
figure 2.1

Musée des Arts Décoratifs, Paris
figures 8.2, 8.3

Bureau Stephan
figures 5.36a, 5.36b

Publications

Pierre Fournié and Jean-Louis Riccioli,
La France au Proche-Orient, Belgium: Editions Casterman, 1996
figures 5.24, 5.29, 5.30, 5.42

L'illustration 15/12/1860, n° 929, France
figure 5.7

Nina Jidejian, *Beirut Through the Ages,*
Beirut: Librairie Orientale, 1997
figure 5.5

François Loyer, *Paris XIX Siècle, l'immeuble et la rue,*
Paris: Editions Hazan, 1987
figures 8.1, 8.5

Order of Engineers and Architects of Beirut,
Al Mouhandess, vol 11. Beirut: 2000
page 122 top right

Gwendolyn Wright, *Politics of Design in French Colonialism,* USA: University of Chicago Press, 1991
figure 1.1

Graphics Credits

Archives

APUR, Atelier Parisien d'Urbanisme
figures 3.5, 8.4

CTSB
pages 154, 155, 156, 157

**Dar Al-Handasah Consultants
(Shair and Partners)**
figures 3.6, 3.7, 3.8, 3.9, 3.10, 8.6, 8.7,
8.8, 8.9, 8.10a, 8.10b, 11.15

**Direction des Affaires Géographiques de
l'Armée Libanaise**
figure 1.2

Institut Géographique National (IGN), France
figures 5.20, 5.21 base map

Service Historique de l'Armée de Terre, France
figure 5.15

Solidere
figures 2.5, 4.4, 4.5, 4.6, 4.7a, 4.7b, 4.7c, 4.9, 4.11, 6.4, 9.17, 9.27,
10.11, 10.12, 10.13, 10.16, 10.21, 10.22, 10.23, 10.25, 10.26, 10.27,
10.38, 10.39, 10.55, 10.56, 12.5, 12.6, 12.9, 12.11, 12.14, 12.15,
12.16, 12.17, 12.18, 12.19, and pages 87, 88, 90, 91, 93, 94, 95,
96, 99, 108, 183, 188, 192, Architectural Survey

Université de Lyon 3, France **(JL)**
figures 2.8, 2.9

Jean-Michel Wilmotte, *Street Furniture Design for Beirut
Central District*
figures 9.18, 9.19, 9.20, 9.21

Private collections

Aga Khan Trust for Culture
figures 3.1, 3.2, 3.3

Alain Danger
figures 5.34, 5.35

Constantinos A. Doxiadis
figure 3.4

Adib Farès, now Solidere collection
figures 5.19, 5.33 and pages 62-63, 72-73

Publications

**Jean-Lucien Bonillo, René Borruey, Jean-Denis Espinas et
Antoine Picon**, Marseille Ville et Port, Marseille: Editions
Parenthèses, 1991
figure 1.3

G & M
figure 4.1

HR
figure 2.10

MD
figures 5.43a, 5.43b Copyrighted maps and drawings

MFD
figure 5.9

USJ
figure 5.8

Copyrighted maps and drawings

Romain Delahalle
figures 2.6a, 2.6b, 2.7

Pitlenko, *Annuaire d'Architecture de Syrie et du Liban*, 1934
figures 5.25 and page 123 middle left and bottom

Secrétariat Général du Port de Beyrouth
figure 5.16